ZEN

AT

WAR

BRIAN
DAIZEN
VICTORIA

ZEN AT WAR

Second Edition

ROWMAN & LITTLEFIELD PUBLISHERS, INC.
Lanham • Boulder • New York • Toronto • Oxford

ROWMAN & LITTLEFIELD PUBLISHERS, INC.

Published in the United States of America
by Rowman & Littlefield Publishers, Inc.
A wholly owned subsidiary of The Rowman & Littlefield Publishing Group, Inc.
4501 Forbes Boulevard, Suite 200, Lanham, Maryland 20706
www.rowmanlittlefield.com

P.O. Box 317, Oxford OX2 9RU, UK

Cover image: Zen monks at Eiheiji, one of the two head monasteries of the Sōtō Zen sect, undergoing mandatory military training shortly after the passage of the National Mobilization Law in March 1938.

British Library Cataloguing in Publication Information Available

Library of Congress Cataloging-in-Publication Data

Victoria, Brian Daizen, 1939–
    Zen at war / Brian Daizen Victoria.—2nd ed.
        p.   cm.
    Includes bibliographical references and index.
    ISBN-13: 978-0-7425-3927-3 (cl. : alk. paper)
    ISBN-10: 0-7425-3927-X (cl. : alk. paper)
    ISBN-13: 978-0-7425-3926-6 (pbk. : alk. paper)
    ISBN-10: 0-7425-3926-1 (pbk. : alk. paper)
    1. Zen Buddhism—Japan—History. 2. Buddhism—Japan—History—
1868–1945. 3. War—Religious aspects—Zen Buddhism. 4. Buddhism and state—
Japan.   5. World War, 1939–1945—Religious aspects—Zen Buddhism.

BQ9262.9.J3 V54   2006
294.3'927095209034—dc22

                                                  2006043949

Printed in the United States of America

⊚™The paper used in this publication meets the minimum requirements of
American National Standard for Information Sciences—Permanence of
Paper for Printed Library Materials, ANSI/NISO Z39.48-1992.

*Dedicated to the victims of
religious-inspired fanaticism everywhere*

Under conditions of tyranny it is far easier to act than to think.

—Hannah Arendt

Philosophy may safely be left with intellectual minds. Zen wants to act, and the most effective act, once the mind is made up, is to go on without looking backward. In this respect, Zen is indeed the religion of the samurai warrior.

—D. T. Suzuki, *Zen and Japanese Culture*

Positive thinkers and public relations officers for the faiths would repudiate this notion or evade the fact. They want religion to be nothing but *godspel,* good news. Apologists for the faiths usually minimize the distress that can come with religion or that religion can produce. You will not read about the destructive element in religious impulses in the advertisements for the church of your choice. Yet if the pursuit of truth is still to be cherished as a foundational theme in the academy, one must note the feature of religion that keeps it on the front page and on prime time—it kills.

—Martin Marty, University of Chicago

CONTENTS

PREFACE TO THE SECOND EDITION

On the occasion of the publication of the second edition of *Zen at War*, I would like to share with readers some of the positive developments that have occurred since the book's initial release in 1997. I refer, first of all, to European interest in the book as reflected in the publication of German, French, Italian, and Polish editions. Clearly there is broad interest in the West regarding Zen's relationship to Japanese militarism.

Equally if not more significant was the publication in 2001 of a Japanese edition titled *Zen to Sensō (Zen at War)*. This edition contributed to the fact that two major branches of the Rinzai Zen sect, that is, Myōshinji and Tenryūji, admitted and apologized for the first time for their past support of Japanese militarism. In that sense, the book you are about to read is not simply a book about religious history but also one that has *made history*.

Specifically, on September 27, 2001, the Myōshinji General Assembly, meeting in Kyoto, issued a proclamation containing the following passage:

> As we reflect on the recent events [of September 11, 2001,] in the U.S.A., we recognize that in the past our country engaged in hostilities, calling it a "holy war," and inflicting great pain and damage to various countries. Even though it was national policy at the time, it is truly regrettable that our sect, in the midst of wartime passions, was unable to maintain a resolute anti-war stance and ended up cooperating with the war effort. In light of this we wish to confess our past transgressions and critically reflect on our conduct [*mazu kono kako no ayamachi ni taisuru zange to hansei no ue ni tatte*].

A follow-up statement by branch administrators on October 19, 2001, said:

> It was the publication of the book *Zen to Sensō* [i.e., the Japanese edition of *Zen at War*], etc. that provided the opportunity for us to address the issue of our war responsibility. It is truly a matter of regret that our sect has for so long been unable to seriously grapple with this issue. Still, due to the General Assembly's adoption of its recent "Proclamation," we have been able to take the first step in addressing this issue. This is a very significant development.

Myōshinji is the largest branch of the Rinzai Zen sect, with more than 3,400 affiliated temples and 1.6 million adherents. The smaller Tenryūji branch issued a similar statement earlier in 2001, again citing this book as a catalyst. Kubota Jiun, current head of the Sanbō-kyōdan, also apologized in the spring of 2001 for the wartime "errant words and actions" of Zen Master Yasutani Haku'un (introduced in chapter 10 of this book and more thoroughly in chapter 5 of *Zen War Stories*).

As for the Sōtō Zen sect, little has changed since its groundbreaking admission of war responsibility in a January 1993 statement of repentance, introduced in chapter 10. Although a handful of Sōtō Zen–related scholars have continued to pursue this issue, notably Hakamaya Noriaki and Matsumoto Shirō of Komazawa University, their research has focused on highly contentious doctrinal issues having little effect on the sect as a whole. Nevertheless, in December 2005 Tanaka Shinkai, abbot of the Sōtō Zen monastery of Hōkyōji in Fukui prefecture, praised *Zen at War* as being like a graphic depiction of the carnage at the scene of a horrendous car accident. "If we hope to prevent its reoccurrence," he stated, "we must not flinch from exploring just how and why this accident occurred." Tanaka went on to pledge that his temple, itself founded by a Chinese monk in the 13th century, would henceforth hold unprecedented memorial services for the victims of Japanese militarism.

This edition contains a new chapter titled "Was It Buddhism?" which places Zen's collaboration with Japanese militarism in the context of the 2,500-year-long relationship of Buddhism to the state and war. This additional chapter addresses the plaintive cry of one incredulous reader on the Internet who asked, "What the hell went wrong?"

Yet, if it can be said that something "went wrong" in prewar and wartime Zen, it is important to realize that it will take more than apologies, no matter how heartfelt, to make it "right" again. The fact is that Zen leaders who supported Japanese militarism did so on the grounds that Japanese aggression expressed the very essence of the Buddha Dharma and even enlightenment itself. Thus, until and unless their assumptions are closely examined and challenged, there is no guarantee that Zen's future, whether in the East or West, will not once again include support for the mass destruction of human life that is modern warfare.

Regrettably, many Western Zen leaders continue to either evade or rationalize the connection of their own Dharma lineage to Japan's past aggression. For example, in the fall 1999 issue of the Buddhist magazine *tricycle,* one well-known U.S. Zen master, Bernie Glassman, had the following to say about Yasutani Haku'un's wartime militarist and anti-Semitic pronouncements:

> So if your definition of enlightenment is that there's no anti-Semitism in the state of enlightenment. If your definition of enlightenment is that there's no nationalism, or militarism, or bigotry in the state of enlightenment, you better change your definition of enlightenment. For the state of enlightenment is *maha,* the circle with no inside and no outside, not even a circle, just the pulsating of life everywhere.

In response to this assertion, David Brazier, English Buddhist and author of *The New Buddhism* (2002) wrote:

> Glassman is willing to say that if your definition of enlightenment does not allow for anti-Semitism within enlightenment then your definition is not big enough. For Glassman, himself Jewish, to say such a thing is, in one sense, big-hearted. I acknowledge Glassman's big heart. Nonetheless, I assert that he is wrong. My definition of enlightenment does not have room for anti-Semitism. I do not think that the Buddha's definition of enlightenment had room for anything similar either. The Buddha had compassion for bigots, but he did not think they were enlightened.

Expanding on this theme, Brazier went on to assert that the non-dualism of Glassman's "circle with no inside and no outside" is in fact not even Buddhist in origin. "The Non-Dual . . . is essentially a Taoist rather than a Buddhist idea," he wrote.

Needless to say, it is beyond the scope of either this book, or its more recent companion, *Zen War Stories* (2003), to resolve the claims and counterclaims raised above. Nevertheless, it can be readily observed that their resolution goes straight to heart of the nature of enlightenment itself. As such, this and the related issues contained in this book deal with the very essence of the Buddhist faith. Sooner or later, every serious Buddhist practitioner must attempt to resolve them, if only for him- or herself.

Finally, as I did in the first edition, let me close by acknowledging that this book, together with its companion volume, *Zen War Stories*, represents no more than the first steps in coming to an understanding of the relationship between (Zen) Buddhism and warfare. Nevertheless, in a world where religious-supported, if not religious-inspired, violence remains all too prevalent, even first steps are to be valued, for they at least begin to address the scourge that resides in *all* of the world's major faiths—that there can be, under certain circumstances, something "sacred" or "holy" about war. And further, they address the belief that the duty of religious practitioners is to answer the call to war of their nation's leaders, no matter how destructive the ensuing acts of war may be.

In the aftermath of the terrorist attacks of September 11, Islam now appears to be the main if not sole source of religious fanaticism. It is important to recognize, however, that religion-inspired brutality knows no sectarian label. In 1906, for example, General Leonard Wood sent the following cable to President Teddy Roosevelt celebrating his victory over Filipino Muslims still resisting American colonial control: "The enemy numbered six hundred—including women and children—and we abolished them utterly, leaving not even a baby alive to cry for its dead mother. This is incomparably the greatest victory that was ever achieved by the *Christian* soldiers of the United States [italics mine]." In reply, Roosevelt praised the general's "brilliant feat of arms" and the excellent way he had "upheld the honor of the American flag" (quoted in *Mark Twain's Religion* by William E. Phipps, p. 208).

As much as the adherents of the world's faiths may wish to deny it, when it comes to the relationship of religion to violence, it is, as Hemingway has so poignantly stated, a question of "ask not for the whom the bell tolls, it tolls for thee."

ACKNOWLEDGMENTS

In addition to those I gratefully acknowledged in the first edition, the many persons who contributed in innumerable ways to the writing of this book and without whom this book would not be what it is, I would also like to thank here both Susan McEachern and Mark Selden, my editors at Rowman & Littlefield, for their encouragement and assistance in the preparation of this second edition. And having said this, let me end by thanking you, my reader, for investing both your precious time and money in this book. I very much look forward to hearing your reactions and critiques, for over the years readers have been among my very best teachers.

PREFACE

I n the spring of 1970 I was called into the room of Zen Master Niwa Rempō
(1905–93), then the chief abbot of Eiheiji Betsuin temple in Tokyo. He
informed me that since I was a Sōtō Zen priest and a graduate student in
Buddhist Studies at Sōtō Zen sect–affiliated Komazawa University, it was
not appropriate for me to be active in the anti-Vietnam war movement in
Japan. While he acknowledged that my protests were both nonviolent and
legal, he stated that "Zen priests don't get involved in politics." And then
he added, "If you fail to heed my words, you will be deprived of your
priestly status."

Although I did not stop my antiwar activities, I was not ousted from
this sect. In fact, I went on to become a fully ordained priest, which I
remain to this day. This was very much due to the understanding and protection extended to me by my late master, the Venerable Yokoi Kakudō, a
professor of Buddhist Studies at Komazawa as well as a Sōtō Zen master.
Niwa Rempō went on to become the seventy-seventh chief abbot of Eiheiji,
one of the Sōtō Zen sect's two head monasteries. We never met again.

This became one of the defining events in my life, the catalyst for a
twenty-five-year search for the answers to the questions what is and what
should be the relationship of the Zen Buddhist priest to society and its
members, to the state, to warfare, and to politics and social activism. In
looking for the answers to these questions I came across the writings of
Professor Ichikawa Hakugen, a Rinzai Zen sect-affiliated priest and scholar then teaching at Hanazono University in Kyoto. Reading the work of a
man who had gone from staunch supporter to severe critic of Japanese
militarism, I felt as if I had fallen down the proverbial rabbit hole to join
Alice in her adventures through Wonderland.

The ideas and people I encountered in this subterranean realm of Buddhism were the exact inverse of those on the surface. Down below, warfare and killing were described as manifestations of Buddhist compassion. The "selflessness" of Zen meant absolute and unquestioning submission to the will and dictates of the emperor. And the purpose of religion was to preserve the state and punish any country or person who dared interfere with its right of self-aggrandizement.

Disturbing as such sentiments were, I was even more disturbed to learn who was making them. Ichikawa quoted at length, for example, from D. T. Suzuki's writings on war. With his oft-pictured gentle and sagacious appearance of later years, Suzuki is revered among many in the West as a true man of Zen. Yet he wrote that "religion should, first of all, seek to preserve the existence of the state," followed by the assertion that the Chinese were "unruly heathens" whom Japan should punish "in the name of religion." Zen master Harada Sōgaku, highly praised in the English writings of Philip Kapleau, Maezumi Taizan, and others, was also quoted by Hakugen. In 1939 he wrote: "[If ordered to] march: tramp, tramp, or shoot: bang, bang. This is the manifestation of the highest Wisdom [of Enlightenment]. The unity of Zen and war of which I speak extends to the farthest reaches of the holy war [now under way]."

Ichikawa demonstrated that statements such as these had been made over and over again by both lay and clerical Zen leaders during the war years and before. I could not help wondering how it had all come about, especially in light of Rempō's adamant assertion that "Zen priests don't get involved in politics." Did the wartime deaths of millions upon millions of Japanese and non-Japanese alike have nothing to do with politics? Could the prowar statements made by Suzuki, Harada, and many other Zen leaders be fairly described as "nonpolitical"?

This book represents a first attempt to grapple with these complex and difficult questions. Its focus is on the history of institutional Buddhism, particularly Zen, in one country, Japan, during the period from 1868 to 1945. I chose this period not because I see it as representative of the historical relationship between Zen Buddhism and warfare, but, on the contrary, precisely because it is not. In this I have been deeply influenced by a passage from William James's *The Varieties of Religious Experience*: "We learn more about a thing when we view it under a microscope, as it were, or in its most exaggerated form. This is as true of religious phenomena as of any other kind of fact. The only cases likely to be profitable enough to repay our attention will therefore be cases where the religious spirit is unmistakable and extreme."[1]

There can be no question that the relationships which existed between Zen Buddhism and warfare, between Zen Buddhism and the state, were in their most exaggerated form during the period in question. Likewise, for better or worse, the religious spirit was unmistakable and extreme. It is precisely for these reasons, then, that this period can serve as a useful prism through which to examine the broader issues, which remain constant even when the circumstances encompassing them are extreme. In fact, it is possible to argue that the real value of the social ethics of any religion, Buddhism included, ought to be their application to those extreme situations in which secular ethical systems are apt to lose their authority. What test of faith or awareness is there for the fair-weather believer?

Although I focus on the years from 1868 to 1945, looking at this period in isolation from its historical antecedents suggests that a phenomenon such as Zen's endorsement of Japanese militarism can be explained solely by the events of the Meiji period and thereafter. Indeed, some present-day observers have adopted this viewpoint and maintain that this phenomenon was no more than a momentary aberration of modern Japanese Zen or its leaders. More informed commentators such as Ichikawa Hakugen, however, make it clear that the unity of Zen and the sword has deep roots in Zen Buddhist doctrine and history. Regrettably, space limitations preclude me from introducing more than a small fraction of this larger history in the present study.

In an attempt to show at least some of the complexity of the Zen Buddhist response to Japan's military actions, I have included sections on Zen Buddhist war resisters as well as collaborators. On whichever side of the fence these Buddhists placed themselves, their motivations were far more complex than can be presented in a single volume. Nor, of course, can their lives and accomplishments be evaluated solely on the basis of their positions regarding the relationship of Zen to the state and warfare. A holistic evaluation of these leaders, however, is not the subject of this book.

Specialized Buddhist and Japanese terminology has been used only to a limited degree, when it seemed important for understanding. Japanese names are written in the traditional Japanese way, family name first and personal name last. I have not used such titles as "Reverend" or "Venerable" in referring to Buddhist priests; when the priestly status of a figure is relevant, I have mentioned it in the text. After first mention, priests are referred to by their religious rather than family name—for example, Sawaki Kōdō is referred to as Kōdō after first mention.

Notes referring to material found on the same or immediately adjoining pages of a single source have sometimes been telescoped together. In such cases, the last numerical citation in a paragraph refers to all preceding quotations lacking a citation. Complete source citations are provided in the Bibliography.

Macrons have been used to indicate long vowels, with the exception of words such as Tokyo and Bushido, which are already familiar to English readers. The few Sanskrit terms found in the text are all relatively well known, and diacritical marks have been dropped.

Finally, I wish to gratefully acknowledge the many persons who have contributed in innumerable ways to the writing of this book. I refer first of all to the late Ichikawa Hakugen, professor emeritus of Hanazono University. Not only did his pioneering research in Japanese Buddhist war responsibility contribute immeasurably to my own, but his character and personality remain for me a model of the socially engaged scholar-priest. In addition, professors Thomas Dean of Temple University, the late Ishikawa Rikizan of Komazawa University, and Kobayashi Enshō of Hanazono University were ever ready to provide advice and counsel as the book progressed. I am particularly indebted to Professor Jeffrey Shore, also at Hanazono University, for patiently and thoughtfully reading the entire manuscript. As a fellow practitioner and student of Zen, Professor Shore's critical comments significantly enhanced the quality of this work. I would also like to thank Jeffrey Hunter, my editor at Weatherhill, for his patience and professional assistance throughout the long process of seeing this book into print.

At the final stage in the writing of this book I was fortunate to have been a visiting scholar during 1996–97 at the International Research Institute for Zen Buddhism located at Hanazono University in Kyoto. I am grateful to the institute's current director, Nishimura Eshin, and the institute's previous director, Yanagida Seizan, for making this precious opportunity available to me. Not only was the institute's excellent library an extremely valuable resource, but the tireless efforts of the institute's librarian, Ms. Usami Sachiko, made my work immeasurably easier. Dr. Urs App, a professor at the institute, was most helpful during the process of compiling the book's photographic and graphic materials.

I cannot stress too strongly that this book represents no more than the first step in understanding the relationship of Buddhism and Zen to the state and to warfare. However, as the famous Chinese maxim indicates, "A journey of ten thousand leagues begins with the first step."

PART I

THE MEIJI RESTORATION

OF 1868

AND BUDDHISM

CHAPTER ONE:

THE ATTEMPTED SUPPRESSION OF BUDDHISM

Buddhism has a history of approximately 1,500 years in Japan, having first been introduced from Korea in the middle of the sixth century. By the Tokugawa period (1600–1868) Buddhism had, outwardly at least, reached the pinnacle of its power, functioning as a *de facto* state religion. Each and every household in the country was required to affiliate itself with a nearby Buddhist temple. The result was an explosive growth in the number of temples, from only 13,037 temples during the Kamakura period (1185–1333) to 469,934 during the Tokugawa.[1]

There were, however, a number of hidden costs associated with Buddhism's establishment as a state religion. First of all, mandatory temple affiliation effectively turned a large part of the Buddhist clergy into little more than government functionaries. Concurrently, membership in a particular sect often became a matter of political obligation rather than religious conviction. These developments are hardly surprising, since the catalyst for according Buddhism a privileged position in the first place was the Tokugawa regime's determination to expel Christianity, thereby reducing the danger to Japan of being colonized by one of the Western powers. Equally important, the regime wished to insure that indigenous religious institutions, like all other institutions in society, were firmly under its control.

The government exerted control over institutional Buddhism through such policies as dividing the powerful Shin (True Pure Land) sect into two branches, popularly known as the Nishi (West) Honganji and Higashi (East) Honganji after their respective head temples. The Tokugawa regime further made sure that every temple in the land, no matter how humble, was made subservient to a higher-grade temple in pyramidal fashion, with an all-powerful central temple (*honzan*) controlling each sect from the top. While sectarian differences were tolerated, the central temple of each sect was made responsible, and held accountable, for the actions of all of its subordinates, both lay and clerical.

A second and perhaps higher cost that institutional Buddhism paid for government support was what Robert Bellah described as the "general lethargy and uncreativeness of Buddhism in the Tokugawa period."[2] Anesaki Masaharu was even less flattering when he wrote: "The majority of the Buddhist clergy were obedient servants of the Government, and in the long period of peace they gradually became lazy, or else effeminate intriguers."[3]

There were, of course, some clergy, living in richly endowed temples, who turned their energy to learning. There were also reformers and innovators who attempted with some success to revitalize their respective sects.[4] Yet many if not most of the clergy took advantage of their prerogatives as agents of the government to suppress or economically exploit their parishioners. Joseph Kitagawa notes that "the moral and spiritual bankruptcy of established Buddhism inevitably brought criticism and rebellion from within and without."[5] It was all but inevitable that institutional Buddhism would face a day of reckoning.

GOVERNMENT MEASURES DIRECTED TOWARD BUDDHISM

On January 3, 1868, the young Emperor Meiji issued a proclamation announcing that he was resuming the reins of government, although in fact only very limited power had actually been restored to the throne. Nevertheless, a scant three months later, on April 6, 1868, the emperor promulgated the Charter Oath, a document consisting of five articles that clearly expressed the antifeudal aspirations of the new government. The Charter Oath states:

(1) Councils widely convoked shall be established, and all affairs of State decided by public discussion.
(2) All measures, governmental and social, shall be conducted by the united efforts of the governing and the governed.
(3) The unity of the imperial and the feudal governments shall be achieved; all the people, even the meanest, shall be given full opportunities for their aspirations and activities.

(4) All absurd usages of the old regime shall be abolished and all measures conducted in conformity with the righteous way of heaven and earth.

(5) Knowledge shall be sought from all over the world, and thus shall be promoted the imperial polity.[6]

Though the Charter Oath was seemingly innocuous, Article 4 was a harbinger of the impending storm Buddhism would face. What, exactly, were the "absurd usages of the old regime" that were to be "abolished"?

The answer was not long in coming. Only a few days later the first of the "Separation Edicts" (Shimbutsu Hanzen Rei), designed to separate Buddhism from Shinto, were issued by a newly established government bureau known as the Office of Rites (Jingi Kyoku). This first edict stated that all Buddhist clerics were to be removed from Shinto shrines throughout the nation. Henceforth, only *bona fide* Shinto priests were to be allowed to carry out administrative duties related to shrines.

In a second edict, issued less than two weeks after the first, the use of Buddhist names for Shinto deities *(kami)* was prohibited. Not only that, Buddhist statuary could no longer be used to represent Shinto deities, or, for that matter, even be present in a shrine compound. Whatever the authors' original intent may have been, these edicts were often interpreted at the local and regional levels as meaning that anything having to do with Buddhism could and should be destroyed.

In his excellent book on this period, *Of Heretics and Martyrs in Meiji Japan*, James Ketelaar points out that these separation edicts "necessarily included as an integral part of their formulation a direct attack on Buddhism."[7] This is because, first of all, nearly every member of the Office of Rites was an active proponent of National Learning (Kokugaku). This Shinto-dominated school of thought taught that while both the Japanese nation and throne were of divine origin, this origin had been obscured and sullied by foreign accretions and influences, especially those from China. Adherents of this school believed one of the first and most important jobs of the new government was to cleanse the nation of these foreign elements, Buddhism first and foremost.

Just how effective this "cleansing" was can be seen from statistics: over forty thousand temples were closed throughout the nation, countless temple artifacts were destroyed, and thousands of priests were forcibly laicized.[8] Once again, however, the interpretation and enforcement of the Separation Edicts was, in general, left up to the regional authorities. Hence, those areas where there was the greatest support for National Learning among local and regional officialdom were also those areas where the greatest destruction occurred.

In the former Satsuma domain (present-day Kagoshima, southern Miyazaki, and Okinawa prefectures), whose leadership had played a leading role in the Restoration movement, Buddhism had almost completely disappeared by the end of 1869. Approximately 4,500 Buddhist temples and halls were eliminated.[9] The priests housed in these temples were returned to lay life, and those between the ages of eighteen and forty-five were immediately drafted into the newly formed imperial army. Those over forty-five were sent to become teachers in domain schools, while those under eighteen were sent back to their families.

INSTITUTIONAL BUDDHISM'S RESPONSE

In the face of these very real threats to its continued existence, it did not take some elements of institutional Buddhism long to initiate a series of countermeasures. One of the first of these was undertaken primarily by the Higashi Honganji and Nishi Honganji branches of the Shin sect. On the surface, at least, it was a rather surprising measure: the sect lent substantial amounts of money to the then cash-starved Meiji government. In effect, these two branches hoped to bribe the government into ameliorating its policies.

The same two branches also took the lead in the summer of 1868 in forming the Alliance of United [Buddhist] Sects for Ethical Standards (Shoshū Dōtoku Kaimei). This was an unprecedented action for institutional Buddhism, since under the previous Tokugawa regime all intrasectarian Buddhist organizations had been banned. The new organization pledged itself, first of all, to work for the unity of Law of the Sovereign and Law of the Buddha. Second, it called for Christianity to be not only denounced, but expelled from Japan.

Buddhist leaders were quick to realize that their best hope of reviving their faith was to align themselves with the increasingly nationalistic sentiment of the times. They concluded that one way of demonstrating their usefulness to Japan's new nationalistic leaders was to support an anti-Christian campaign, which came to be known as "refuting evil [Christianity] and exalting righteousness" (haja kenshō).

As early as September 17, 1868, the new Ministry of State responded to these "positive actions" on the part of Buddhist leaders by sending a private communique directly to the Higashi Honganji and Nishi Honganji branches of the Shin sect. This letter contained a condemnation of those members of the imperial court who wrongfully, and in contradiction to Emperor Meiji's will, were persecuting Buddhism. The letter further notes that in so doing, these "foul-mouthed rebels . . . antagonize the general populace."[10]

Just how antagonized the general populace had become is shown by the strong protest actions that arose in opposition to the repressive, anti-Buddhist measures of local authorities. These protests started in the Toyama region in late 1870 and were followed by two riots in Mikawa (present Aichi Prefecture) and Ise (present Mie Prefecture) in 1871. In each of the following two years there were also two major protests in widely scattered parts of the country.

The 1873 peasant protests in three counties of Echizen (present Fukui Prefecture) were so large that they had to be put down by government troops. It can be argued that it was the government's fear of these protests that finally forced it to pay serious attention to the plight of Buddhists. The government reached the conclusion that the wholesale supression of Buddhism was neither possible nor safe. A solution had to be found.

RESOLUTION OF THE CONFLICT

The First Attempt   The first major change in the Meiji government's policy toward Buddhism came in early 1872. It was at this time that the Ministry of Rites was transformed into the Ministry of Doctrine (Kyōbushō). The new ministry was given administrative responsibility for such things as the building and closing of both Shinto shrines and Buddhist temples, and the approval of all priestly ranks and privileges. By far its most important function, however, was to propagate the "Great Teaching" (Daikyō) that had been developed the previous year. The three pillars of this teaching were as follows: (1) the principles of reverence for the national deities and of patriotism shall be observed; (2) the heavenly reason and the way of humanity shall be promulgated; and (3) the throne shall be revered and the authorities obeyed.[11] Charged with promulgating these principles, the Ministry of Doctrine created the position of Doctrinal Instructor (Kyōdōshoku). These instructors were to operate through a nation-wide network of Teaching Academies (Kyōin) which would be established in both Buddhist temples and Shinto shrines. The significance to Buddhism of this development is that for the first time Buddhist priests were given permission to serve in this state-sponsored position, together, of course, with Shinto priests and scholars of National Learning.

By establishing the position of Doctrinal Instructor, the state was creating a *de facto* state priesthood. Anyone uncertified by the state was barred from lecturing in public, performing ceremonial duties, and residing in either shrines or temples. Nevertheless, Buddhists saw this as a way to escape from their ongoing oppression and eagerly took advantage of this new opportunity.

How successful they were can be seen from the fact that eventually more than 81,000 of a total of some 103,000 officially recognized Doctrinal Instructors were Buddhist priests. Of this number, Shin sect–affiliated priests numbered nearly 25,000 and were the largest single group.[12] But Buddhists paid a heavy price for their inclusion into the new state religion, for it was clearly Shinto inspired and controlled. All Doctrinal Instructors were expected to wear Shinto robes, recite Shinto prayers, and perform Shinto rituals. Further, although the Ministry of Doctrine selected the famous Pure Land sect temple of Zōjōji in Tokyo as the "Great Teaching Academy," the administrative center for the national doctrine system, the ministry demanded that the temple be extensively renovated for its new role.

Zōjōji's renovation included replacing the statute of Amida Buddha on the main altar with four Shinto deities and building a Shinto gate at the entrance to the temple. The Buddhist leadership was so anxious to support this new scheme that they even arranged to have their subordinate temples pay the renovation costs. Yet, despite this seemingly cooperative beginning, conflict inevitably arose between Buddhist and Shinto elements within the national doctrine system.

As the anti-Buddhist movement began to subside, the Buddhist leaders sought to free themselves from Shinto domination. An additional cause of friction was an announcement made on April 25, 1872, by the Ministry of State. This announcement, known as Order Number 133, stated that Buddhist priests could, if they wished, eat meat, get married, grow their hair long, and wear ordinary clothing. Although this decision neither prohibited nor commanded anything, it was seen by many Buddhist leaders as yet another attack on their religion. In their minds, Order Number 133 represented an extension of the earlier separation of Shinto and Buddhism. It represented the separation of Buddhism from the state itself.

The strong Buddhist opposition to this measure included numerous sectarian protest meetings and petitions criticizing the ministry's decision, at least one of which was signed by over two hundred Buddhist priests. Some angry priests even went directly to the ministry's offices to express their opposition. The irony of these actions is that Order Number 133 was a directive that had been taken at the request of a Buddhist, the influential Sōtō Zen sect priest Ōtori Sessō (1814–1904).

Ōtori was in a unique position to make his views known since, at the time the new Ministry of Doctrine was created, he had been asked to serve as a representative of Buddhist clerics (though he was required to return to lay life for the duration of his government service). Ōtori's overall goal was the ending of the government's anti-Buddhist policies, and like his Buddhist contemporaries he believed that the best way of achieving this goal was to demonstrate Buddhism's usefulness to the state, specifically through the promulgation of the Great Teaching.

Ōtori recognized that a large number of Buddhist priests were already married, in spite of regulations prohibiting it. This made them, at least technically, lawbreakers, and left them in no position to work for the government as Doctrinal Instructors or to effectively fight Christianity. In his mind, lifting the ban against marriage, eating meat, and wearing long hair would make it possible for the Buddhist clergy to more effectively render their services to the nation. Despite the protests, Ōtori was successful in this reform effort, and the new law remained.

In light of their defeat, Buddhist leaders realized that they had to free themselves not only from Shinto control but government control as well. Once again the Shin sect played a major role. Leaders of this sect, particularly Shimaji Mokurai (1838–1911), were at the forefront of the movement for change. Mokurai was particularly well suited to the challenge, not least because he had led troops in support of the Imperial Restoration movement.

As early as 1872, Shimaji wrote an essay critical of the three principles of the Great Teaching. His basic position was that there was a fundamental difference between government *(sei)* and religion *(kyō)*, and he called for the separation of the two *(seikyō bunri)*. While it took some years for Shimaji and those who agreed with him to make a discernible impact on the Ministry of Doctrine, eventually, at the beginning of 1875, the government gave the two Shin branches permission to leave the Great Doctrine movement, and shortly afterward the entire institution of the Great Doctrine was abolished. A new solution had to be found.

The Second Attempt   The Buddhists were not the only religious group to benefit from changing government policy. In 1871 a diplomatic mission sent to the West, headed by Senior Minister Iwakura Tomomi (1825–83), had recommended that if Japan were to successfully revise what it regarded as unequal treaties with the Western powers, it would have to adopt a policy of religious freedom.

The Western powers were, of course, most concerned about the ongoing prohibition of Christianity in Japan. As a result, in 1873 the government reluctantly agreed to abolish this prohibition, a decision which led to a rapid increase in the numbers of both Western Christian missions and missionaries entering the country. Even as they continued their own struggle to free themselves from government control, many Buddhist leaders took this occasion to renew and deepen their earlier attacks on Christianity. In so doing, they allied themselves with Shinto, Confucian, and other nationalist leaders.

Shintoists, too, were undergoing changes at this time. Shinto's strongest supporters, the proponents of National Learning, had demonstrated to Meiji political leaders that they were "too religious to rule."[13] This, in turn, led to a reduction in their political power as evidenced by the 1872 changes in the government's religious policy toward Buddhism. Yet key members of the government were still dedicated to the proposition that one way or another the emperor system, as an immanental theocracy with roots in the ancient state, should be used to legitimatize the new government. The question was, in the face of earlier failures, how could this be accomplished?

Part of the answer came in 1882 when the government divided Shinto into two parts, one part consisting of cultic, emperor-related practices and the other of so-called religious practices. While the religious side of Shinto, or Sect Shinto (Kyōha Shintō), received nothing from the government, the cultic side of Shinto, which came to be known as State Shinto (Kokka Shintō), received both financial subsidies and various other political privileges.

The government maintained that this policy was justified because cultic practices relating to the emperor were patriotic in nature, not religious. Even today there are Japanese Buddhist scholars who continue to support this position. Professor Shibata Dōken of Sōtō Zen sect–affiliated Komazawa University, for example, maintains that "given the fact that Japan is a country consisting of a unitary people, with shared customs and mores, the assertion that [State] Shinto was not a religion can be sanctioned, at least to some degree."[14] Other contemporary scholars of that era, however, held a differing view. Joseph Kitagawa, for example, maintained that "'State Shinto' was essentially a newly concocted religion of ethnocentric nationalism."[15] Helen Hardacre provides a more detailed description:

State Shinto [was] a systemic phenomenon that encompassed government support of and regulation of shrines, the emperor's sacerdotal roles, state creation and sponsorship of Shinto rites, construction of Shinto shrines in Japan and in overseas colonies, education for schoolchildren in Shinto mythology plus their compulsory participation in Shinto rituals, and persecution of other religious groups on the grounds of their exhibiting disrespect for some aspect of authorized mythology.[16]

It is clear that the creation of State Shinto served as a mechanism to facilitate the government's recognition, or at least toleration, of a certain degree of ideological plurality within Japanese society. With a powerful non-religious legitimization of the new order in hand, the leaders of the Meiji government could now address the question of religious freedom, something which was implicit in the call by Shimaji and others for the separation of government and religion.

The final, formal resolution of the religious question appeared in the Meiji Constitution of 1889. Chapter Two, Article Twenty-Eight read as follows: "Japanese subjects shall, within limits not prejudicial to peace and order, and not antagonistic to their duties as subjects, enjoy freedom of religious belief."[17] It appeared that within limits Buddhism, Christianity, and other religions would now be free of government interference or suppression. Appearances proved to be deceiving.

CHAPTER TWO:

EARLY BUDDHIST SOCIAL FERMENT

I n reality the Meiji government had granted the Japanese people only a nominal guarantee of religious freedom. State Shinto, the government's artificial construct, was purposely designed as a cult of national morality and patriotism, to which followers of all religions must subscribe. The Meiji government's policy was, in fact, "nothing but an ingenious and dangerous attempt at superimposing 'immanental theocracy' on the constitutional guarantees of religious freedom."[1]

There were still many influential people both within and without the government who remained highly suspicious of, if not directly opposed to, religion in any form. Representative of these was Professor Inoue Tetsujirō (1855–1944) of Tokyo University. In his opinion, religion was inherently "prejudicial to peace and order," and furthermore those who practiced it could not escape being "antagonistic to their duties as subjects."[2] Inoue's opinions are significant in that the Meiji government looked to him for the philosophical groundwork of its 1890 Imperial Rescript on Education (Kyōiku Chokugo). This key document proclaimed loyalty to the throne and filial piety to be the cardinal virtues to which all imperial subjects should adhere.

It was under these circumstances that Japanese Buddhists, with their newly won yet limited religious freedom, attempted to develop what came to be known by the late 1880s as New Buddhism (Shin Bukkyō). New Buddhism was designed to answer the anti-Buddhist critique of the early and middle years of the Meiji period. Its first priority was to show that priests and temples could make a valuable contribution to the nation's social and economic life. Second, it insisted that although "foreign-born," Buddhism could still effectively promote loyalty to the throne, patriotism, and national unity. Last, the New Buddhism made the case that its basic doctrines were fully compatible with the Western science and technology then being so rapidly introduced into the country.

Some commentators such as Notto Thelle have compared the New Buddhist movement with the sixteenth-century Protestant Reformation of Christianity.3 To the extent that this analogy is valid, however, it must be noted that many of the activists in this movement were moderate reformers loyal to their respective sects. There were others, however, whose radical views would eventually lead them to break with traditional institutional Buddhism.4

Buddhist Responses to the West

The early Meiji period critique of Christianity, which continued on through the end of the era, may be considered one of institutional Buddhism's first responses to the West. It was, however, certainly not the only response. For example, Shimaji Mokurai, mentioned in the previous chapter, visited the West in 1872, a journey which included a pilgrimage to the holy sites of Christianity in Jerusalem. Shimaji went on to visit the sacred sites of Buddhism in India, the first instance of a Japanese Buddhist visiting the original home of his religion.5

What drew priests like Mokurai to the West was a general desire to better understand what had by then become one of Meiji society's principal goals, namely "cultural enlightenment" (bummei kaika). At the same time, these pioneering priests also had more mundane aims, one of which was to find tools for the critique of Christianity in Japan.6

In the fall of the same year, the Higashi Honganji branch, anxious not to fall behind its rival, also sent a contingent of priests to Europe. One of these priests was Nanjō Bun'yū (1849–1927), who became a pioneer in the study of Buddhism in accord with Western academic methodology. In 1876 he went to Oxford to study Sanskrit under the famed Orientalist Friedrich Max Müller (1823–1900). Bun'yū subsequently published a number of scholarly works on Buddhism, including the 1883 *Catalogue of the Chinese Translations of the Buddhist Tripitaka*.

As increasing numbers of Japanese Buddhists pursued their study of Buddhism in the West, they encountered an odd form of religious discrimination. This was the result of the fact that the early generation of European Orientalist scholars often took the view that only early or primitive

Buddhism represented the religion in its pristine form. Accordingly, they identified the Buddhism of the Pali canon found in the countries of South and Southeast Asia as "true" or "pure" Buddhism. The Mahayana Buddhism of East Asia, based on the Sanskrit canon, was regarded not only as a later development but one which was degenerate, syncretic, and corrupt.[7]

Faced with this situation, it is not surprising that a major thrust of Japanese Buddhist scholars was to recast the way in which the Mahayana school had been defined in the West.[8] One example of this effort is the work of Daisetz T. Suzuki (1870–1966). Although he would later become best known for his writings on Zen, one of his first major works in English, published in 1908, was entitled *Outlines of Mahayana Buddhism*. Robert Sharf characterized this work as:

> A rambling and highly idealized introduction to Mahayana doctrine—a curious blend of scholarship and apologetics. . . . Suzuki insists that Buddhism is not a dogmatic creed but rather a "mysticism" that responds to the deepest yearnings in man and yet remains in full accord with the findings of modern science.[9]

The majority of Suzuki's earliest scholarly activities, in both the English and Japanese languages, was dedicated to the promotion of Mahayana Buddhism. In fact, Suzuki's first scholarly effort was the translation into English of Shaku Sōen's (1859–1919) address to the World Parliament of Religions, convened as part of the 1893 World Fair in Chicago, Illinois. Sōen, abbot and head of the Engakuji branch of the Rinzai Zen sect, was very much a New Buddhist in that he had determinedly set out to acquire a modern Western education following completion of his traditional Zen training.

Sōen was one of eight representatives of Japanese Buddhism attending the parliament. Three of these eight were, like himself, Buddhist priests affiliated with various sects, while the others were interpreters and laymen. Sōen's paper was entitled "The Law of Cause and Effect as Taught by the Buddha" and was read to the audience by the parliament's chairman, the Reverend John H. Barrows.

The parliament had great consequences, setting in motion a chain of events that was destined to significantly alter the religious consciousness of the Western world.[10] This was not due so much to the content of the papers presented as it was to the simple fact that such an event was taking place at all. As Thelle has written: "The parliament became a magnificent demonstration of the power of religion and of harmony between different faiths. For the first time in history representatives of all the major religions were gathered under the same roof in peaceful conference."[11]

While the conference appeared to be a model of interreligious cooperation and mutual respect, it is also true that there existed, just beneath the surface, a profound discord between the Western, generally Christian, and the Eastern, Buddhist and Hindu delegates.[12] Yatsubuchi Banryū (1848– 1926), a Shin priest and delegate from Kumamoto, went so far as to state that in light of this underlying tension, the Buddhist delegates saw themselves engaged in a "peaceful war." In this war, Buddhism would emerge, at least in his eyes, "having won the greatest victories and the greatest honor."[13]

Given the strong Christian bent of the conference as a whole, Banryū's assertion may seem somewhat exaggerated, if not self-serving. Nevertheless, the Japanese delegates were convinced that Mahayana Buddhism was exactly what the West needed. In their eyes, Westerners were saturated with material comforts but were sadly lacking in the life of the spirit. The "formless form" of Mahayana Buddhism as found in Japan was, therefore, the perfect antidote.

The Japanese delegates sought to recast Japan's version of Mahayana Buddhism as a true world religion, if not *the* true world religion. This redefinition of their faith gave Japanese Buddhists a mission both at home and abroad, and they willingly shouldered a kind of "Japanese spiritual burden," which included a duty to actively share their faith with the benighted peoples of the world. In 1899, Anesaki Masaharu (1873–1949), one of the most noted Buddhist scholars of that period, expressed this burden as follows: "Our Nation [Japan] is the only true Buddhist nation of all the nations in the world. It is thus upon the shoulders of this nation that the responsibility for the unification of Eastern and Western thought and the continued advancement of the East falls."[14]

BUDDHIST RESPONSES TO DOMESTIC CRITICS

The Buddhist delegates to the World Parliament of Religions returned to Japan as conquering heroes. They were invited to give talks throughout Japan on the material progress they had seen in the West and their own progress in promulgating the teaching of the Buddha to receptive Western audiences.[15] An observer of the time, Ōhara Kakichi, applauded their efforts by stating that it was now possible for "Buddhism in Japan in the Far East to turn the wheel of the Dharma in America in the Far West."[16]

What had particularly impressed domestic observers was the alleged ability of the Japanese delegates to not only hold their own against the far greater number of Christian participants, but to express the nationalistic aspirations of the Japanese people in the process. Hirai Kinzō (d. 1916), a lay Buddhist and the delegation's only fluent English speaker, provided the best example of what was possible in this regard.

Hirai's paper had been entitled "The Real Position of Japan Toward Christianity." It began with a defense of the Tokugawa Shogunate's banning of Christianity in the seventeenth century as a legitimate response to the possibility of the colonization of Japan by Western nations in the name of Christianity. He went on to point out that once again in the Meiji period, Christian nations threatened his country through their imposition of un-equal treaties that unilaterally guaranteed those nations the right of extraterritoriality. In concluding, he invoked America's founding fathers and the preamble to the United States Declaration of Independence in defense of his call for true equality among nations.

Hirai had succeeded in driving home his point as few foreign delegates were able to do, thanks to the fact that he had "out-Christianized" the Christians and "out-Americanized" the Americans.[17] The fact that the predominantly American audience had cheered Hirai at the conclusion of his speech was used as further evidence in Japan of just how effective Buddhists could be in advancing the nation's interests abroad.

Based on their success in America, the Buddhist delegates, especially Yatsubuchi Banryū, eagerly called for increased missionary work as they traveled and spoke throughout the country. Yatsubuchi emphasized the importance of both foreign language and secular education for aspiring missionaries, in addition to rigorous spiritual training. He advocated that such missionaries should first work among Japanese immigrants to other nations, but he also saw other uses for them. Foreshadowing the future, he suggested that they could provide spiritual training for the Japanese military. "'Flashing like a sword and glittering like a flower' . . . the imperial army and navy can, like the faithful Muslims who defeated the Russians in the Crimea, or the soldiers of the Honganji who held back the armies of Nobunaga, face all trials and tribulations with confidence and strength."[18]

Yatsubuchi and his colleagues were not the first to call for Buddhist missionary work. Even in the darkest days of the repression of Buddhism in the early Meiji period, the Shin sect had actively participated in the Meiji government's effort to colonize the northern island of Hokkaido, an area that was then only nominally under Japanese control. The Higashi Honganji branch initially dispatched over one hundred priests to this northern outpost and spent over thirty-three thousand *ryō* (about one hundred ten pounds of gold in 1871) in constructing roads. Hokkaido was seen as an opportunity to prove that Buddhism could make a valuable contribution to the state, even if this meant that Buddhists would themselves become colonizers in the process.

Furthermore, based on the success of this internal missionary work, the Higashi Honganji branch sent a group of priests headed by Ogurusu Kōchō to establish a temple in Shanghai, China, in June 1876. Yet another group, headed by Okumura Enshin, was sent to Korea in September of the following year. As in the case of Hokkaido, these missionary activities were carried on in close collaboration with the government, for even in the Meiji period Japan was determined to advance onto the Asian continent. In fact, after the Sino-Japanese War of 1894–95 these missionary efforts became so closely associated with Japan's continental policies that after each war Japan fought, Buddhist missionary efforts expanded accordingly.[19]

Ogurusu was not simply interested in missionary work abroad. In 1877 he wrote: "Priests of this sect should use aid to the poor as a method of propagating the faith."[20] In common with many of his contemporaries, Ogurusu understood that the New Buddhism had to become active in charitable work. This interest came as a result of the threat the Buddhists recognized from primarily Protestant-based charities. While Buddhist leaders typically pointed out what they considered to be the shallowness of Christian doctrines, they were forced to recognize the remarkable effectiveness of Christian philanthropy as a means of recruiting converts.[21]

Shaku Sōen was also active in this debate, urging Buddhists to overcome the practical superiority of Christianity by "establishing schools for the poor, charity hospitals, and reformatories; organizing work among soldiers and criminals; correcting the corruptions of society; and engaging in active work in every department of life."[22] Yet another advocate of this position was Inoue Enryō (1858–1919), a Shin-sect priest, Buddhist scholar, and reformer. Like Sōen, Enryō hoped to outdo the Christians by copying their educational institutions, hospitals, and reformatories.[23]

Yet, for all their desire to emulate Christian social work, the New Buddhists did not change their overall negative attitude toward Christianity. Enryō in particular was one of the most articulate of the anti-Christian Buddhists. Typically, Enryō would criticize the irrationality of Christianity as contrasted with the rationality of Buddhism. He based his arguments on a simple comparison drawn between the theism of Christianity and the nontheism of Buddhism. Inoue maintained that the latter position was in harmony with Western philosophy and science. The fact that Christianity was the religion of the strong Western nations and seemingly inseparable from their political structures and ambitions were further causes of his antagonism.[24]

In January 1889, Inoue joined with other Meiji Buddhist leaders, including Shimaji Mokurai and the prominent Buddhist layman Ōuchi Seiran (1845–1918), to form a new popular Buddhist organization, the United Movement for Revering the Emperor and Worshiping the Buddha (Sonnō Hōbutsu Daidōdan). The organization's prospectus described its purpose as follows:

> The goal of this organization is to preserve the prosperity of the imperial household and increase the power of Buddhism. The result will be the perfection of the well-being of the great empire of Japan. . . . The time-honored spiritual foundation of our empire is the imperial household and Buddhism. The independence and stability of our empire cannot be maintained if so much as the slightest injury is inflicted upon it. How can true patriots not be inspired and aroused to defend against such injury?[25]

The founders of this new organization wished to exclude Christians from all positions of power in society, especially those connected with politics. Toward this end they worked to induce some 130,000 Buddhist priests throughout the country to become politically active and ensure the election of Buddhist candidates. Some members, especially those living in regions where the Shin sect was strong, went so far as to violently disrupt religious services in local Christian churches.[26]

The establishment of the United Movement for Revering the Emperor and Worshiping the Buddha represented the organizational birth of a Buddhist form of Japanese nationalism that was exclusionist and aggressively anti-Christian in character. The press, however, severely condemned the disruptive and sometimes violent tactics of its regional supporters, which often led to police intervention, and, realizing that violence had become a political liabilty, the group soon gave up such tactics. Just as they were being abandoned, however, a new form of violence arose, on a far, far grander scale: Japan's leaders had decided to go to war.

Sino-Japanese War (1894–95)   The Sino-Japanese War formally began in August 1894. In discussing the war, Ienaga Saburo, a noted historian of modern Japan, wrote: "Government leaders . . . started the quest for glory by fighting China for hegemony in Korea. Domination of Korea became a national goal shared by successive administrations and the public at large."[27] The public at large, of course, included Japan's Buddhist leaders. Not surprisingly, these leaders collaborated very closely with the ethnocentric nationalism that was by then so prevalent in society. For example, by this time Inoue Enryō had become a spokesman for the "imperial way" *(kōdō)*. In a work published in 1893 entitled "Treatise on Loyalty and Filial Piety" *(Chūkō Katsu Ron)*, he wrote that due to the existence of the imperial household, Japan, its land, and its people were, like the emperor himself, all "sacred and holy."[28]

Enryō went on to assert that in Japan, unlike China or the West, loyalty to the sovereign and filial piety were one and the same. This was because all Japanese were offspring of the imperial family. The imperial family was the "head family" of all Japanese, making the emperor and his subjects all part of "one large family."[29] This led Enryō to conclude:

> From ancient times, sacrificing one's physical existence for the sake of the emperor and the country was akin to discarding worn-out sandals. . . . It is this unique feature of our people which has caused the radiance of our national polity and produced the supreme beauty of our national customs.[30]

In 1894 Enryō also published an article on the "philosophy of war" which, echoing the preceding sentiments, was strongly militaristic in temper.[31]

The Nishi Honganji branch of the Shin sect was one of the first to comment on the war. As early as July 31, 1894, the sect's headquarters issued a statement that read in part:

> Since the occurrence of the recent emergency in Korea, the head of our branch has been deeply concerned about the situation, acting on the truth of repaying one's debt to the country through absolute loyalty to it. This is in accordance with the sect's teaching that the law of the sovereign is paramount. . . .Believing deeply in the saving power of Amida Buddha's vow, and certain of rebirth in

his western paradise, we will remain calm no matter what emergency we may encounter, for there is nothing to fear. . . . We must value loyalty [to the sovereign] and filial piety, work diligently, and, confronted with this emergency, share in the trials and tribulations of the nation.³²

In 1895, the Jōdo (Pure Land) sect established the Assembly to Repay One's Debt to the Nation (Hōkoku Gikai). Its purpose was defined as follows: "The purpose of this assembly shall be, in accordance with the power of religion, to benefit both those in the military and their families, to conduct memorial services on behalf of fallen patriots, and to provide relief for their families and relatives."³³

While there was almost no peace movement among Buddhists, there was no lack of Buddhist leaders who justified the war. One line of reasoning they adopted was based on Japanese Buddhism's supposed preeminent position within all of Asian Buddhism. An editorial entitled "Buddhists During Wartime" appeared in the August 8, 1894 issue of the newspaper *Nōnin Shimpō*. It asserted that Japanese Buddhists had a duty to "awaken" Chinese and Korean Buddhists from their indifference to the war, an indifference which allegedly stemmed from the pessimistic nature of the Buddhism in those two countries.

Only a few days later, in the August 16–18 issue of the same newspaper, Mori Naoki expanded on this theme in an article entitled "The Relationship of Japanese Buddhists to the Crisis in China and Korea." He claimed that both Indian and Thai Buddhists were indifferent to the development of their own countries, once again because of the pessimistic nature of the Buddhism found there. Mori then went on to advocate that Japanese Buddhists consider the battlefield as an arena for propagation of the faith, holding high the banner of "benevolence and fidelity."

Coupled with the above was the viewpoint represented in an editorial, entitled "Buddhism and War," appearing in the July 25, 1894 issue of the newspaper *Mitsugon Kyōhō*. This editorial began by acknowledging that the destruction of all weapons of war was the Buddhist ideal. It then went on to assert, however, that when a war was fought for a "just cause," it was entirely appropriate for Buddhists to support it.

Another proponent of this point of view was Shaku Unshō (1827–1909), a Shingon-sect priest and pioneer of Meiji-period Buddhist charitable activities. In an article entitled "A Discussion on the Compassionate Buddhist Prohibition Against Killing," which appeared in the preceding newspaper on January 25, 1885, he stated that there were two types of war: a "just war" and a "lawless war." While Buddhists should oppose the second type of war, they should support, as in this case, a just war because such a war prevents humanity from falling into misery.

In a short but none the less prophetic reference to a Zen connection to the war, the Buddhist reformer Katō Totsudō (1870–1949) wrote the following in the February 1895 issue of *Taiyō* magazine:

> The Zen that philosophers and poets are well acquainted with has [due to the war] also become familiar to military men. Even though the principle of transcending life and death is the basis of all Buddhist schools, Zen has a quality that is most welcomed by soldiers, for it possesses a special kind of vigor. [34]

Despite all the preceding declarations of Buddhist war support, it was actually Japanese Christians who took the lead in such practical activities as providing medical help for wounded soldiers and relief for families who had become poverty stricken as a result of the war. The patriotic fervor of the Christians naturally had a favorable effect on public opinion, and even Buddhists reluctantly expressed admiration for their strenuous efforts. On the other hand, because of their own slow and rather passive response, Buddhist leaders were themselves criticized for their lack of patriotic spirit.[35]

The fervent patriotism of Japanese Christians became the catalyst for not only a new and positive relationship with the state but with institutional Buddhism as well. Specifically, Christian patriotism brought a new climate which promoted, on the one hand, Buddhist-Christian cooperation, while emphasizing Christianity's spiritual solidarity with the East. The end result was that both religions succeeded, in varying degrees, in entrenching themselves in the same citadel of nationalism.[36]

In light of the Christian emphasis on love and the Buddhist emphasis on compassion, it is highly ironic that it was war-generated patriotism and the resulting death and destruction that provided the initial stimulus for a reconciliation between these two religions, long bitter foes.

Russo-Japanese War (1904–5) Japan's victory over China brought with it not only increased power over affairs on the Korean peninsula, but the island of Taiwan, torn from China, became its first overseas colony. Not all of Japan's territorial ambitions were met, however, due to the so-called Tripartite Intervention of 1895. Three Western powers, led by Russia with the support of France and Germany, forced Japan to give up its newly won control of the Liaotung Peninsula in what would have been its first colony on the Asian mainland.

Japan regarded this intervention as a national humiliation and was more determined than ever to develop its military machine. For example, it added six new divisions to the regular army in 1896, thereby doubling its first-line strength. In addition, in 1898, it organized both cavalry and artillery as independent brigades, while at the same time establishing factories for the domestic production of modern armaments. By 1903 Japan could also claim to have a modern navy with some seventy-six major war vessels, including four battleships, sixteen cruisers, and twenty-three destroyers. The Triple Intervention became the pretext for the further development of Japan's military might despite the heavy tax burden it placed on the general populace.

In this atmosphere, the need for continued support of the military was also recognized by Buddhist leaders. In 1898, for example, Higashi Kan'ichi edited a book entitled *Proselytizing the Military (Gunjin Fukyō)*. The purpose of this work was to advocate Buddhism's usefulness in imparting courage to soldiers on the battlefield.

Just how seriously institutional Buddhist leaders took their responsibility in this regard is attested to by Ōtani Kōzui (1876–1948), chief abbot of the Nishi Honganji branch of the Shin sect. He was commended by the emperor for the important role he played in keeping up morale during the Russo-Japanese War. Before examining that war more closely, however, it is important to note that the short period of peace which lasted from 1896 to 1903 was also a time for Buddhist scholars to turn their attention to the theoretical side of the relationship between Buddhism, the state, and war. Interestingly, it was the twenty-six-year-old Buddhist scholar and student of Zen, D. T. Suzuki, who took the lead in this effort. In November 1896, just one month before having his initial enlightenment experience *(kenshō)*, he published a book entitled *A Treatise on the New [Meaning of] Religion (Shin Shukyō Ron)*.

In his book, Suzuki covered a wide variety of topics, examining everything from the meaning of religious faith to the relationship between religion and science. He did, however, devote an entire chapter to "The Relationship of Religion and the State." If only because Suzuki's views in this area are so little known in the West, it is instructive to take a careful look at his comments. Much more important, however, the views that Suzuki expressed then parallel the rationale that institutional Buddhism's leaders would subsequently give for their support of Japan's war efforts up through the end of the Pacific War. For that reason alone, they deserve very close attention.

Suzuki began his discussion on the relationship of religion and the state with this statement:

> At first glance it might be thought that religion and the state are in serious conflict with one another. For example, the state is built upon differentiation [or discrimination] while religion takes the position that everything is equal. Religion takes as its final goal the realization of a universal ideal while the ultimate goal of the state is to preserve itself. . . .[37]

From this beginning, Suzuki went on to assert that the preceding entities only appear to be in conflict with one another. For example, he claimed that "equality without differentiation is 'evil equality,' while differentiation without equality is 'evil differentiation.'" From this and other examples he concluded that "religion and the state must necessarily support each other if they are to achieve wholeness." Further, "religion should, first of all, seek to preserve the existence of the state, abiding by its history and the feelings of its people."[38]

There are scholars who seek to explain away statements such as the above as being somehow unrepresentative of Suzuki's thought. Prominent among these is Professor Kirita Kiyohide (b. 1941) of Kyoto's Rinzai Zen sect–affiliated Hanazono University. He recently wrote a monograph entitled "D. T. Suzuki and the State," which was included in the book *Rude Awakenings.*

On the one hand, Kirita admits being disturbed by Suzuki's statement quoted above, for it "seems to lead to an acceptance of state supremacy."[39] Kirita further criticizes other statements made by Suzuki in the same chapter. About these Kirita says: "His [Suzuki's] rather 'Zen-like' approach to religion and his abstract notion of the way nations operate seem far too unrealistic."[40] The statements Kirita referred to, as quoted in his monograph, are as follows:

> The interests of religion and the state do not conflict but rather aid and support each other in a quest for wholeness. . . . The problem is easily resolved if one thinks of religion as an entity with the state as its body, and of the state as something developing with religion as

its spirit. In other words, religion and the state form a unity; if every action and movement of the state takes on a religious character and if every word and action of religion takes on a state character, then whatever is done for the sake of the state is done for religion, and whatever is done for the sake of religion is done for the state.[41]

In spite of these limited criticisms of Suzuki's thought, however, Kirita concludes that "from his youth and throughout his life Suzuki never regarded the state as absolute and never placed the state above the individual."[42] A few pages later he adds: "[Suzuki] was not a nationalist or national supremacist."[43]

Leaving aside for the moment whether Kirita is correct in his conclusions, the question remains why he chose to avoid any discussion of the three paragraphs which immediately follow his last quotation from Suzuki's work. These three paragraphs are critical to an understanding of Suzuki's thought on this subject:

> If we look at this [unified relationship between religion and the state] from the point of view of international morality, we see that the purpose of maintaining soldiers and encouraging the military arts is not to conquer other countries or deprive them of their rights or freedom. Rather they are done only to preserve the existence of one's country and prevent it from being encroached upon by unruly heathens. The construction of big warships and casting of giant cannon are not to trample on the wealth and profit of others for personal gain. Rather, they are done only to prevent the history of one's country from being disturbed by injustice and outrageousness. Conducting commerce and working to increase production are not for the purpose of building up material wealth in order to subdue other nations. Rather, they are done only in order to develop more and more human knowledge and bring about the perfection of morality.
>
> Therefore, if a lawless country comes and obstructs our commerce, or tramples on our rights, this is something that would truly interrupt the progress of all humanity. In the name of religion our country could not submit to this. Thus, we would have no choice but to take up arms, not for the purpose of slaying the enemy, nor for the purpose of pillaging cities, let alone for the purpose of acquiring wealth. Instead, we would simply punish the

people of the country representing injustice in order that justice might prevail. How is it possible that we could seek anything for ourselves? In any event, this is what is called religious conduct. As long as the state takes care not to lose this moral sense, one can anticipate the step by step advancement of humanity and the fulfilment of universal ideals.

The morality of the individual toward the state is similar to this. That is to say, in peacetime one works diligently, day and night, seeking to promote the advancement of [such endeavors as] agriculture, manufacturing, commerce, art and science, and technology. In so doing, one must not forget that the purpose of these many endeavours is the advancement of all humanity. This is what is called "peacetime religion." However, at the time of the commencement of hostilities with a foreign country, then marines fight on the sea and soldiers fight in the fields, swords flashing and cannon smoke belching, moving this way and that. In so doing, our soldiers regard their own lives as being as light as goose feathers while their devotion to duty is as heavy as Mount Taishan [in China].[44] Should they fall on the battlefield they have no regrets. This is what is called "religion during a [national] emergency." This religion doesn't necessarily have to be described by [the words] "Buddha" or "God." Rather, if one simply discharges one's duty according to one's position [in society], what action could there be that is not religious in nature? [45]

Kirita's conclusions notwithstanding, Suzuki laid out in the above the fundamental positions that Buddhist leaders would collectively adhere to until Japan's defeat in 1945: (1) Japan has the right to pursue its commercial and trade ambitions as it sees fit; (2) should "unruly heathens" (jama gedō) of any country interfere with that right, they deserve to be punished for interfering with the progress of all humanity; (3) such punishment will be carried out with the full and unconditional support of Japan's religions, for it is undertaken with no other goal in mind than to ensure that justice prevails; (4) soldiers must, without the slightest hesitation or regret, offer up their lives to the state in carrying out such religion-sanctioned punishment; and (5) discharging one's duty to the state on the battlefield is a religious act.

Suzuki, it should be noted, was not necessarily the originator of the preceding ideas, for they can also be found in the writings of Shaku Sōen, Suzuki's Zen master. It was Sōen who demonstrated just how easy it was to put Suzuki's theory into practice. He did this by going to the battlefield as a Buddhist chaplain attached to the First Army Division shortly after the outbreak of the Russo-Japanese War in February 1904. He described his reasons for doing so:

> I wished to have my faith tested by going through the greatest horrors of life, but I also wished to inspire, if I could, our valiant soldiers with the ennobling thoughts of the Buddha, so as to enable them to die on the battlefield with the confidence that the task in which they are engaged is great and noble. I wished to convince them of the truths that this war is not a mere slaughter of their fellow-beings, but that they are combating an evil, and that, at the same time, corporeal annihilation really means a rebirth of [the] soul, not in heaven, indeed, but here among ourselves. I did my best to impress these ideas upon the soldiers' hearts.[46]

While on the battlefield Sōen even found time to compose a number of poems. Representative of these is the following:

> Here, marching on [Mount] Nanshan,
> Storming its topmost crest,
> Have thousands of brave men
> With dragon valor pressed.
> Before the foe my heart
> Is calmed, composure-blessed,
> While belching cannons sing
> A lullaby of rest.[47]

Sōen also promoted the idea of a close relationship between Buddhism and war. He wrote:

> Buddhism provides us with two entrances through which we can reach the citadel of perfect truth. One is the gate of love *(karuna)* and the other the gate of knowledge *(prajna)*. The former leads us to the world of particulars and the latter to realm of the absolute. By knowledge we aspire to reach the summit of spiritual enlightenment; by love we strive to rescue our fellow-creatures from misery and crime. View the vicissitudes of things from the unity and eternity of the religious standpoint, the Dharmadhatu, and every-

thing is one, is on the same plane, and I learn to neglect the worldly distinction made between friend and foe, tragedy and comedy, war and peace, samsara and nirvana, passion *(kleça)* and enlightenment *(bodhi)*. A philosophical calm pervades my soul and I feel the contentment of Nirvana. For there is nothing, as far as I can see, that does not reflect the glory of Buddha. . . . In this world of particulars, the noblest and greatest thing one can achieve is to combat evil and bring it into complete subjection. The moral principle which guided the Buddha throughout his twelve years of preparation and in his forty-eight years of religious wanderings, and which pervades his whole doctrine, however varied it may be when practically applied, is nothing else than the subjugation of evil. . . .

War is an evil and a great one, indeed. But war against evils must be unflinchingly prosecuted till we attain the final aim. In the present hostilities, into which Japan has entered with great reluctance, she pursues no egotistic purpose, but seeks the subjugation of evils hostile to civilization, peace, and enlightenment. She deliberated long before she took up arms, as she was aware of the magnitude and gravity of the undertaking. But the firm conviction of the justice of her cause has endowed her with an indomitable courage, and she is determined to carry the struggle to the bitter end.

Here is the price we must pay for our ideals—a price paid in streams of blood and by the sacrifice of many thousands of living bodies. However determined may be our resolution to crush evils, our hearts tremble at the sight of this appalling scene. . . . Were it not for the consolation that these sacrifices are not brought for an egotistic purpose, but are an inevitable step toward the final realization of enlightenment, how could I, poor mortal, bear these experiences of a hell let loose on earth?[48]

The significance of the individual soldier in this "hell let loose on earth" became, as might be expected, a recurrent theme in Buddhist discussions on warfare from this time onwards. About this Sōen had the following to say:

There is but one great spirit and we individuals are its temporal manifestations. We are eternal when we do the will of the great spirit; we are doomed when we protest against it in our egotism and ignorance. We obey, and we live. We defy, and we are thrown into the fire that quencheth not. Our bodily existences are like the sheaths of the bamboo sprout. For the growth of the plant it is necessary to cast one sheath after another. It is not that the body-sheath is negligible, but that the spirit-plant is more essential and its wholesome growth of paramount importance. Let us, therefore, not absolutely cling to the bodily existence, but when necessary, sacrifice it for a better thing. For this is the way in which the spirituality of our being asserts itself.

This being the case, war is not necessarily horrible, provided that it is fought for a just and honorable cause, that it is fought for the maintenance and realization of noble ideals, that it is fought for the upholding of humanity and civilization. Many material human bodies may be destroyed, many humane hearts be broken, but from a broader point of view these sacrifices are so many ph[o]enixes consumed in the sacred fire of spirituality, which will arise from the smouldering ashes reanimated, ennobled, and glorified. . . . We Buddhists are not believers in fiction, superstition, or mythology. We are followers of truth and fact. And what we actually see around us is that the departed spirits are abiding right among ourselves, for we have the most convincing testimony of the fact in our inmost consciousness which deceives not. They descend upon us, they dwell within us; for are we not being moved by their courage, earnestness, self-sacrifice, and love of country? Do we not feel supernaturally inspired and strengthened in our resolution to follow them and to complete the work they have so auspiciously started. . . ?

I am by no means trying to cover the horrors and evils of war, for war is certainly hellish. Let us avoid it as much as possible. Let us settle all our international difficulties in a more civilized manner. But if it is unavoidable, let us go into it with heart and soul, with the firm conviction that our spiritual descendants will carry out and accomplish what we have failed personally to achieve. . . . Mere lamentation not only bears no fruit, it is a product of egotism, and has to be shunned by every enlightened mind and heart.[49]

We must bear in mind, as we evaluate Sōen's words, that they represent the thought of a fully enlightened Zen master recognized by the Rinzai Zen tradition. Sōen had completed his Rinzai-style Zen training, based on the meditative use of koan, at the unusually early age of twenty-four. He had received Dharma transmission in the form of *inka shōmei* (seal of approval), signifying his complete enlightenment, from his master, Imakita Kōsen (1816–92).[50] (Incidentally, the clear echo of Suzuki's thinking in Sōen's words can be traced to the facts that Suzuki was not only the latter's disciple but also the translator of the above passages.)

One passage of Sōen's writing that Suzuki did not translate comes from a somewhat surprising source, the great Russian writer Leo Tolstoi. Because of his own pacifist views, Tolstoi had hoped to enlist the aid of a noted Japanese Buddhist leader to join with him in condemning the war between the two nations. He therefore asked Sōen to join him in this effort, only to receive the following reply:

> Even though the Buddha forbade the taking of life, he also taught that until all sentient beings are united together through the exercise of infinite compassion, there will never be peace. Therefore, as a means of bringing into harmony those things which are incompatible, killing and war are necessary.[51]

Sōen was not, of course, the only Buddhist priest to go to the battlefield. All of the major Buddhist sects assigned chaplains to the military, and by the 1930s they were found attached to every regiment. In addition, the sects provided medics to accompany the troops abroad. Similarly, Sōen was not the only Buddhist leader to justify the war from a purported Buddhist viewpoint. Inoue Enryō, the noted Meiji-period Buddhist scholar-priest, had this to say shortly before the formal outbreak of hostilities:

> Buddhism is a teaching of compassion, a teaching for living human beings. Therefore, fighting on behalf of living human beings is in accord with the spirit of compassion. In the event hostilities break out between Japan and Russia, it is only natural that Buddhists should fight willingly, for what is this if not repaying the debt of gratitude we owe the Buddha?
>
> It goes without saying that this is a war to protect the state and sustain our fellow countrymen. Beyond that, however, it is the conduct of a bodhisattva seeking to save untold millions of living souls throughout China and Korea from the jaws of death. Therefore Russia is not only the enemy of our country, it is also the enemy of the Buddha.

In Russia state and religion are one, and there is no religious freedom. Thus, religion is used as a chain in order to unify the [Russian] people. Therefore, when they [the Russian people] see Orientals, they are told that the latter are the bitter enemies of their religion. It is for this reason that on the one hand this is a war of politics and on the other hand it is a war of religion. . . . If theirs is the army of God, then ours is the army of the Buddha. It is in this way that Russia is not only the enemy of our country but of the Buddha as well.

The peoples of China and Korea are also Orientals, the same "Mongolian" race as ourselves. Thus, these golden-[hued] peoples are our brothers and sisters, for we are one family. Our religions, too, have been one from the beginning. Therefore, putting Russians to death in order to save our family members is not only our duty as citizens, but as fellow Buddhists. . . .

The reason that Buddhism is still in existence in our country today is due to the protection offered by the emperors down through the ages, starting with Prince Shōtoku. Buddhism would not exist [in Japan] without the devotion of the imperial family. When looked at from this viewpoint, it is only natural for Buddhists to fight to the death in order to repay the debt of gratitude they owe to the Buddha and the emperor.[52]

By the end of the Russo-Japanese War in September 1905, the foundation had been laid for institutional Buddhism's basic attitudes toward Japan's military activities. In addition to Suzuki's five underlying principles identified above, we may add the following three points: (1) Japan's wars are not only just but are, in fact, expressions of Buddhist compassion; (2) fighting to the death in Japan's wars is an opportunity to repay the debt of gratitude owed to both the Buddha and the emperor; (3) the Japanese army is composed (or, at least, ought to be composed) of tens of thousands of bodhisattvas, ever ready to make the ultimate sacrifice. Their goal is not only the defense of their country but the rescue of fellow members of the "Mongolian race" from the hands of Western, white, and Christian imperialists.

In the following chapters we will see that these themes were repeated again and again in increasingly jingoistic language and shriller pitch. The Buddhist scholars and priests who voiced these ideas were engaged in yet another attempt to unite religion and politics (seikyō itchi). In so doing, however, they became tools of the government and, together with their Shinto counterparts, glorified the regime while serving its ends.[53]

Faith on the Battlefield The actual fighting that took place on the battlefields of the Russo-Japanese War laid the foundation of one of the more salient features of Japanese Buddhism in the following years: the close connection alleged to exist between a soldier's Buddhist faith and his prowess on the battlefield. In his war reminiscences, General Hayashi Senjūrō (1876–1943), then a deputy brigade commander, wrote:

> I was in the Ninth Division from Kanazawa. This is a very religious area where faith in the Shin sect is especially strong although we officers in this division were initially unaware of the effectiveness of the Buddhist faith.
>
> At the time of the Russo-Japanese War, the Ninth Division formed the center of General Nogi's lines as we advanced on Port Arthur. During the initial attack the division was almost totally destroyed, losing some four out of six thousand soldiers. Furthermore, due to the enemy's fierce bombardment, we were unable to rescue the hundreds of casualities left on the battlefield for some seven days. Many of these casualities were severely wounded and in great pain, but not a single one cried out for help. Instead, they recited the name of Amida Buddha in chorus, even as they died. I was deeply moved by the power of the Buddhist faith as revealed in these soldiers' actions.
>
> Even though the Ninth suffered more casualties than any other division, there were none who complained or bemoaned the circumstances they found themselves in. Thus did I come to realize just how superb their frame of mind was. When people possessing religious faith stand at the verge of death, they are truly great.[54]

The noted Shin sect scholar-priest Ōsuga Shūdō (1876–1962) explained why strong faith in Buddhism should make the kind of difference on the battlefield that Hayashi observed. In a book published on April 20, 1905 entitled *A General Survey of Evangelization during Wartime (Senji Dendō Taikan)*, he suggested:

> Reciting the name of Amida Buddha makes it possible to march onto the battlefield firm in the belief that death will bring rebirth in paradise. Being prepared for death, one can fight strenuously, knowing that it is a just fight, a fight employing the compassionate mind of the Buddha, the fight of a loyal subject. Truly, what could

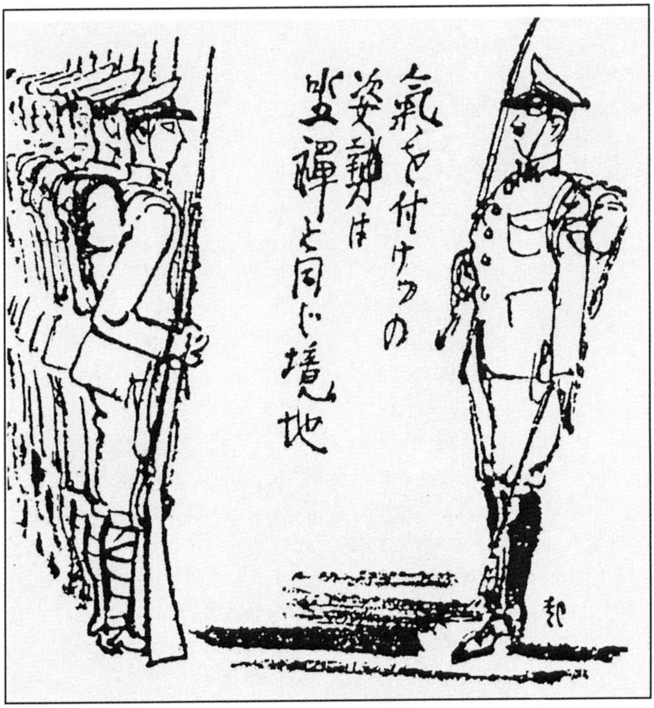
氣を付けの
姿勢は
坐禅と同じ境地

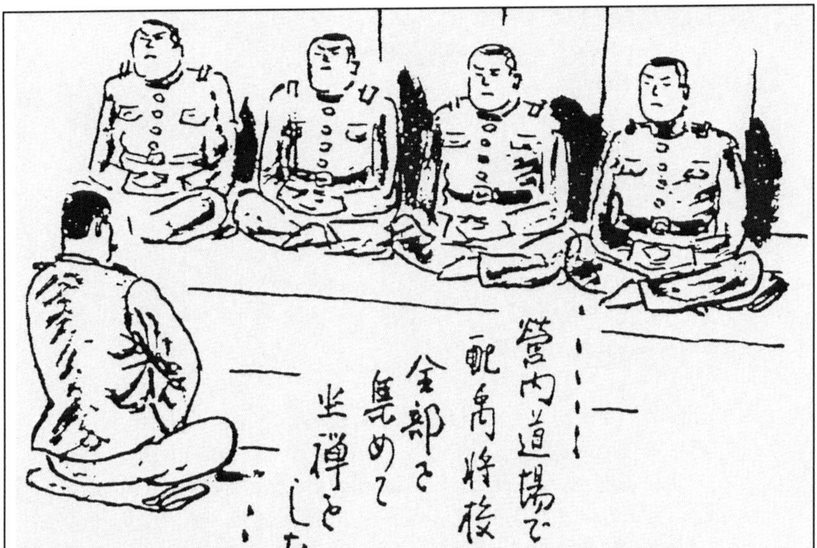
營内道場で
配属将校
全部を
集めて
坐禅をした

Each of these cartoons, appearing as illustrations for a discussion published in the March 1937 issue of the nonsectarian Buddhist magazine Daihōrin, *illustrates a point made by one of the participants.* (FACING PAGE, ABOVE) *The caption reads: "The posture of standing at attention is the same state as that of Zen meditation."* (FACING PAGE, BELOW) *The caption reads: "All of the assigned officers were assembled in the barracks martial arts training hall and did Zen meditation."* (ABOVE) *The caption reads: "The Great Empire of Japan" (on the tree) and "The Religious Spirit" (on the water pouring from the bucket). Note the imperial chrysanthemum crest shining in the upper part of the tree.*

Admiral Tōgō Heihachirō, hero of the naval battle in the Tsushima Straits during the Russo-Japanese War, is shown here on the bridge of his flagship Mikasa. He is known to have believed he was protected during this battle by Bodhisattva Avalokiteshvara, shown standing behind him at the helm.

be more fortunate than knowing that, should you die, a welcome awaits in the Pure Land [of Amida Buddha]?[55]

The Shin sect was by no means alone in attempting to rouse the martial prowess of Japan's soldiers. The Zen sect, too, sought to play a role, a role which can first be observed in the reminiscences of Sawaki Kōdō (1880–1965), one of Japan's best-known modern Sōtō Zen masters and scholars. For many Western Zen practitioners, Kōdō is familiar as the founder of a lay Zen training center at Antaiji, located in Kyoto. In a book entitled *Recollections of Sawaki Kōdō (Sawaki Kōdō Kikigaki)*, Kōdō first talked of the hardships he endured as a draftee in the military just prior to the Russo-Japanese War. With the war's outbreak, however, Kōdō went to the battlefield, where:

> My comrades and I gorged ourselves on killing people. Especially at the battle of Baolisi temple, I chased our enemies into a hole where I was able to pick them off very efficiently. Because of this, my company commander requested that I be given a letter of commendation, but it wasn't issued.[56]

Kōdō records the following conversation among his comrades, describing what they thought about his accomplishment:

> "Who the hell is that guy?"
> "He's only a Zen priest."
> "I see. Just what you'd expect from a Zen priest. A man with guts."[57]

In this simple conversation we find what is perhaps the first modern reference to the effectiveness of Zen training on the battlefield. Although Kōdō himself never fought again, he continued to support the unity of Zen and war. For example, in 1942 he wrote an article entitled "On the True Meaning of the Zen Precepts" for the Buddhist magazine *Daihōrin*. It contained the following passage:

> The Lotus Sutra states that "the Three Worlds [of desire, form, and formlessness] are my existence and all sentient beings therein are my children." From this point of view, everything, including friend and foe, are my children. Superior officers are my existence as are their subordinates. The same can be said of both Japan and the

world. Given this, it is just to punish those who disturb the public order. Whether one kills or does not kill, the precept forbidding killing [is preserved]. It is the precept forbidding killing that wields the sword. It is this precept that throws the bomb. It is for this reason that you must seek to study and practice this precept.[58]

The idea that Kōdō advanced here, that killing and bomb-throwing are done independently of the individual's will, was to become a popular position advocated by Zen adherents, including D. T. Suzuki. If these violent acts are performed independently of the human will, there can of course be no individual choice or responsibility in the matter. It may well be said that in this instance Zen truly "transcends reason."

Another shining example of Zen prowess on the battlefield in the Russo-Japanese was General Nogi Maresuke (1849–1912), commander of the Third Army and one of the war's greatest heroes. Nogi had previously received instruction and undergone koan training with the noted Rinzai Zen master Nantembō (1839–1925). Describing himself and his mission, Nantembō stated, "I am the only one in today's Japan who possesses the true transmission of the Buddhas and Patriarchs. Zen that only looks like Zen must be smashed."[59]

Nantembō has been described as "a staunch nationalist and partisan to the Japanese military."[60] In his personal reminiscences, Nantembō recalled his first meeting with Nogi in October 1887. At that time Nogi asked him one of the fundamental questions of Buddhism, namely, "How should one face the question of life and death?" Nantembō replied, "Apart from loyalty and duty, there is no life and death!"[61] Nogi was so impressed with this answer that he went on to train for some ten years under this master.

Nogi had been first introduced to Nantembō by a second famous lay disciple and Russo-Japanese war hero, General Kodama Gentarō (1852–1906). The relationship between these two is illustrated by an exchange prompted by a question from Kodama: "How should a military man handle Zen?" Nantembō replied by asking the general how he would handle three thousand soldiers if they were in front of him right at that moment. Kodama protested that he did not have any soldiers in front of him, but Nantembō criticized him, saying "This should be obvious to you. . . . You fake soldier!" "How would *you* do it then?" Kodama asked in exasperation. Nantembō thereupon threw Kodama to the ground, jumped on his back, and, slapping his buttocks with a stick, shouted "Troops, forward march!"[62]

As this and similar episodes reveal, Nantembō's training methods consisted of rough-and-tumble encounters with the master followed by intensive periods of meditation. Nantembō wrote that during the time that General Nogi trained under him, he had never shown signs of either laxness or discouragement in spite of the severity with which he was treated. As a result, Nantembō claimed, Nogi was at last able to "richly acquire the essence," or enlightenment.[63] Sōtō Zen master Iida Tōin (1863–1937) confirmed Nogi's spiritual attainment when he bestowed upon the general the highest praise possible: the achievement of "Great Enlightenment" *(daigo)*.[64]

"I have no doubt," said Nantembō, "that Nogi's great accomplishments during the Sino-Japanese and Russo-Japanese wars were the result of the hard training he underwent. The ancient [Zen] patriarchs taught that extreme hardship brings forth the brilliance [of enlightenment]. In the case of General [Nogi] this was certainly the case. . . . All Zen practitioners should be like him. . . . A truly serious and fine military man."[65] Nogi was so fine, in fact, that Nantembō designated him as one of his Dharma successors. Nantembō explained to Nogi that the essence of Zen was contained in the single word *jiki* (direct). Though one word, *jiki* had three interrelated yet distinct meanings: (1) moving forward without hesitation, (2) direct transmission from mind-to-mind, and (3) *Yamato damashii* (the spirit of Japan).[66] There was, furthermore, "no bodhisattva practice superior to the compassionate taking of life."[67]

Nantembō was only one of a long line of Zen masters who would identify Zen with *Yamato damashii*, a concept believed to have derived from Japan's traditional warrior code, or Bushido. While much remains to be said about the relationship between Bushido, *Yamato damashii*, and Zen, it is important to take note that not all Meiji Buddhists were supporters of Japan's new religious nationalism.

CHAPTER THREE:

UCHIYAMA GUDŌ: RADICAL SŌTŌ ZEN PRIEST

B y the time of the Russo-Japanese War it is fair to say that the clerical and scholarly leaders of Japan's traditional Buddhist sects were firm supporters of the government's policies, especially its war policies. But this does not mean that there was no Buddhist resistance to the government. There were, in fact, a few Buddhist priests who not only opposed what they believed to be their government's increasingly repressive and imperialistic policies but actually sacrificed their lives in the process of doing so.

This chapter will focus on one such group of "radical" Buddhists. Because they were quite small in number, it might be argued that this attention is unwarranted, but few as they were, they had a significant impact on the Buddhist leaders of their time, especially as those leaders continued to formulate their individual and collective responses to Japan's military expansion abroad and political repression at home.

RADICAL BUDDHIST PRIESTS AND THE HIGH TREASON INCIDENT

It is the High Treason Incident (Taigyaku Jiken) of 1910 that first brought to light the existence of politically radical Buddhist priests. Twenty-six people were arrested for their alleged participation in a conspiracy to kill one or more members of the imperial family. Four of those arrested were Buddhist priests: Shin sect priest Takagi Kemmyō (1864–1914), a second Shin priest, Sasaki Dōgen; a Rinzai Zen sect priest, Mineo Setsudō (1885–1919); and Sōtō Zen sect priest Uchiyama Gudō (1874–1911). All of the defendants were convicted and twenty-four were condemned to death, though later twelve had their sentences commuted to life imprisonment. Uchiyama Gudō was the only priest to be executed. The remaining three Buddhist priests were among those with commuted sentences, though they also all eventually died in prison, Takagi Kemmyō at his own hand.

As the execution of Gudō indicates, the authorities clearly considered him to be the worst of the four priests. This is not surprising, for of all the priests Gudō was the most actively involved in the movement that the Meiji government found so reprehensible. Gudō also left behind the most written material substantiating his beliefs. This said, even Gudō's writings contain little that directly addresses the relationship he saw between the Law of the Buddha and his own social activism. This is not surprising, since neither he nor the other three priests claimed to be Buddhist scholars or possess special expertise in either Buddhist doctrine or social, political, or economic theory. They might best be described as social activists who, based on their Buddhist faith, were attempting to alleviate the mental and physical suffering they saw around them, especially in Japan's impoverished rural areas.

The Japanese government attempted to turn all of the accused in the High Treason Incident into nonpersons, even before their convictions. The court proceedings were conducted behind closed doors, and no press coverage was allowed, because, the government argued, would be "prejudicial to peace and order, or to the maintenance of public morality."[1] Gudō's temple of Rinsenji was raided and all his writings and correspondence removed as evidence, never to surface again. Only a few statues of Buddha Shakyamuni that Gudō had carved and presented to his parishioners were left behind. Even his death did not satisfy the authorities. They would not allow his name to appear on his gravemarker at Rinsenji. In fact, when one of his parishioners subsequently dared to leave some flowers on his grave, the police instituted a search throughout the village of Ōhiradai, located in the mountainous Hakone district of Kanagawa Prefecture, to find the offender.

UCHIYAMA'S LIFE

Early Life Uchiyama was born on May 17, 1874, in the village of Ojiya in Niigata Prefecture. His childhood name was Keikichi, and he was the oldest of four children. Gudō's father, Naokichi, made his living as a woodworker and carver, specializing in Buddhist statues, family altars, and associated implements. As a child, Gudō learned this trade from his father, and, as noted above, later carved Buddhist statues that he presented to his parishioners at Rinsenji. Even today these simple yet serene nine-inch images of Buddha Shakyamuni are highly valued among the villagers.

Gudō was an able student, earning an award for academic excellence from the prefectural governor. Equally important, he was introduced at an early age to the thinking of a mid-seventeenth-century social reformer by the name of Sakura Sōgorō. Discussions of such issues as the need for land reform to eliminate rural poverty and the enfranchisement of women were an integral part of his childhood education.

Gudō lost his father at the age of sixteen. In his book *Buddhists Who Sought Change (Henkaku o Motometa Bukkyōsha)*, Inagaki Masami identifies this early death as a significant factor in Gudō's later decision to enter the Buddhist priesthood.[2] On April 12, 1897, Gudō underwent ordination in the Sōtō Zen sect as a disciple of Sakazume Kōjū, abbot of Hōzōji temple.

Over the following seven years, Gudō studed Buddhism academically and trained as a Zen novice in a number of Sōtō Zen temples, chief among them the monastery of Kaizōji in Kanagawa Prefecture. On October 10, 1901, Gudō became the Dharma successor of Miyagi Jitsumyō, abbot of Rinsenji. Three years later, on February 9, 1904, Gudō succeeded his master as Rinsenji's abbot, thus bringing to an end his formal Zen training.

The temple Gudō succeeded to was exceedingly humble. For one thing, it had no more than forty impoverished families to provide financial support. Aside from a small thatched-roof main hall, its chief assets were two trees, one a persimmon and the other a chestnut, located on the temple grounds. Village tradition states that every autumn Gudō would invite the villagers to the temple to divide the harvest from these trees equally among themselves.

In his discussions with village youth, Gudō once again directed his attention to the problem of rural poverty. He identified the root of the problem as being an unjust economic system, one in which a few individuals owned the bulk of the land and the majority of the rural population was reduced to tenancy. Gudō became an outspoken advocate of land reform, something that would eventually come to pass, but not until many years later, after Japan's defeat in the Pacific War.

What is significant about Gudō's advocacy of land reform is that he based his position on his understanding of Buddhism. In discussing this period of his life in the minutes of his later pretrial hearing, Gudō stated:

> The year was 1904.... When I reflected on the way in which priests of my sect had undergone religious training in China in former times, I realized how beautiful it had been. Here were two or three

hundred persons who, living in one place at one time, shared a communal lifestyle in which they wore the same clothing and ate the same food. I held to the ideal that if this could be applied to one village, one county, or one country, what an extremely good system would be created.[3]

The traditional Buddhist organizational structure, the Sangha, with its communal lifestyle and lack of personal property, was the model from which Gudō drew his inspiration for social reform.

It was also in 1904 that Gudō had his first significant contact with a much broader, secular social reform movement, anarcho-socialism. Gudō appears to have first come into contact with this movement as a reader of a newly established newspaper, the *Heimin Shimbun* or "The Commoner's News." By the early months of 1904 this newspaper had established itself as Tokyo's leading advocate of the socialist cause, and Gudō later expressed its impact on him: "When I began reading the *Heimin Shimbun* at that time [1904], I realized that its principles were identical with my own and therefore I became an anarcho-socialist."[4]

Gudō was not content, however, to be a mere reader of this newspaper. In its January 17, 1904 edition, he wrote:

> As a propagator of Buddhism I teach that "all sentient beings have the Buddha nature" and that "within the Dharma there is equality, with neither superior nor inferior." Furthermore, I teach that "all sentient beings are my children." Having taken these golden words as the basis of my faith, I discovered that they are in complete agreement with the principles of socialism. It was thus that I became a believer in socialism.[5]

The phrase, "all sentient beings have the Buddha-nature" is one of the central themes of the Lotus Sutra, as is the phrase, "all sentient beings are my children." The phrase, "within the Dharma there is equality, with neither superior or inferior" comes from the Diamond Sutra. Regrettably, this brief statement is the only surviving example of Gudō's understanding of the social implications of the Law of the Buddha.

Even this brief statement, however, puts Gudō in direct opposition to Meiji Buddhist leaders such as Shimaji Mokurai. In his 1879 essay entitled "Differentiation [Is] Equality" *(Sabetsu Byōdō)*, Shimaji maintained that distinctions in social standing and wealth were as permanent as differences in age, sex, and language. Socialism, in his view, was flawed because it emphasized only social and economic equality. That is to say, socialists failed to understand the basic Buddhist teaching that "differentiation is identical with equality" *(sabetsu soku byōdō)*. Or phrased somewhat more philosophically, socialists confused the temporal world of form *(yūkei)* with the transcendent world of formlessness *(mukei)*, failing to recognize the underlying unity of the two. It was Shimaji's position that would gain acceptance within institutional Buddhism.

Village Priest and Social Activist Of the eighty-two persons who eventually expressed their allegiance to socialism in the pages of the *Heimin Shimbun,* only Gudō and one other, Kōtoku Shūsui, were later directly implicated in the High Treason Incident. This suggests that Gudō, like Kōtoku, was a leading figure in the nascent socialist movement, but that was not the case. Gudō's relative physical isolation in the Hakone mountains limited the role that he was able to play. He might best be described as a rural social activist or reformer who, in his own mind at least, based his thought and actions on his Buddhist faith.

Ironically, it was Gudō's relative physical isolation that eventually thrust him into the historical limelight. The Japanese government and police devoted ever-increasing efforts to suppressing the growing socialist movement with its pacifist platform. This suppression took the form of repeated bannings of politically offensive issues of the *Heimin Shimbun;* arresting, fining, and ultimately jailing the newspaper's editors; and forcefully breaking up socialist meetings and rallies. With two of its editors (including Kōtoku Shūsui) on their way to jail for alleged violations of the press laws, the *Heimin Shimbun* printed its last issue on January 25, 1905. When the newspaper closed down, the socialist antiwar movement within Japan virtually came to an end, thereby enabling the government to prosecute its war with Czarist Russia free of domestic opposition.

In September 1905 the war with Russia ended with a Japanese victory. The victory was, however, a costly one, both in terms of the government's expenditures on armaments and the high number of military casualties. When it became general knowledge that the peace terms did not include a war indemnity, riots broke out in Tokyo and martial law was immediately imposed. In this atmosphere of significant social unrest, the government pursued its suppression of socialism even more relentlessly than before. On February 22, 1907, the Socialist Party was banned and socialists were harassed, beaten, and jailed. By 1908, unable to hold public meetings or publish either newspapers or magazines, what was left of the socialist movement went underground. Prohibited from advocating socialism openly, some members of the movement came to believe that the only way they could succeed was to take some form of "direct action" against the imperial house itself.

It was these circumstances which prompted Gudō to visit Tokyo in September 1908. He not only met with Kōtoku Shūsui but purchased the necessary equipment to set up a secret press within his own temple. The printing equipment itself was hidden in the storage area located underneath and to the rear of the Buddha altar in the Main Hall. Gudō used this press to turn out popular socialist tracts and pamphlets, and he also wrote and published his own materials, including his best-known work, *In Commemoration of Imprisonment: Anarcho-Communism-Revolution (Nyūgoku Kinen-Museifu Kyōsan-Kakumei).*

That work is interesting for a number of reasons. It contains a pointed critique of the then prevalent understanding of the Buddhist doctrine of karma. After beginning with a lament for the poverty of tenant farmers, Gudō writes:

> Is this [your poverty] the result, as Buddhists maintain, of the retribution due you because of your evil deeds in the past? Listen, friends, if, having now entered the twentieth century, you were to be deceived by superstitions like this, you would still be [no better than] oxen or horses. Would this please you?[6]

Gudō clearly understood that the Buddhist doctrine of karma was being interpreted as providing the justification for social and economic inequality. That is to say, if tenant farmers were impoverished, they had no one to blame but themselves and their own past actions. Shaku Sōen was typical of the Buddhist leaders who advocated this interpretation: "We are born in the world of variety; some are poor and unfortunate, others are wealthy and happy. This state of variety will be repeated again and again in our future lives. But to whom shall we complain of our misery? To none but ourselves!"[7] Gudō was also critical of certain aspects of Buddhist practice. For example, on May 30, 1904, he wrote a letter of protest to the abbot of Jōsenji, Orihashi Daikō. In this letter he requested that the Sōtō sect cleanse itself of the practice of selling temple abbotships to the highest bidder. When Daikō refused to endorse his position, Gudō expressed his determination to push for this reform on his own.

The real significance of *In Commemoration of Imprisonment* lay not in its critique of certain aspects of Buddhist doctrine, but rather in its blistering rejection of the heart and soul of the Meiji political system, the emperor system. It was, in fact, this rejection of Japan's imperial system that, more than any other factor, led to Gudō's subsequent arrest, imprisonment, and execution. He wrote:

> There are three leeches who suck the people's blood: the emperor, the rich, and the big landowners. . . . The big boss of the present government, the emperor, is not the son of the gods as your primary school teachers and others would have you believe. The ancestors of the present emperor came forth from one corner of Kyushu, killing and robbing people as they went. They then destroyed their fellow thieves, Nagasune-hiko and others. . . . It should be readily obvious that the emperor is not a god if you but think about it for a moment.
>
> When it is said that [the imperial dynasty] has continued for 2,500 years, it may seem as if [the present emperor] is divine, but down through the ages the emperors have been tormented by foreign opponents and, domestically, treated as puppets by their own vassals. . . . Although these are well-known facts, university professors and their students, weaklings that they are, refuse to either say or write anything about it. Instead, they attempt to deceive both others and themselves, knowing all along the whole thing is a pack of lies.[8]

Imprisonment Gudō printed between one and two thousand copies of the tract containing the foregoing passages and mailed them to former readers of the *Heimin Shimbun* in small lots wrapped in plain paper. Its radical content, especially its scathing denial of the emperor system, so frightened some recipients that they immediately burned all the copies they received. Others, however, were so excited by its contents that they rushed out onto to the streets to distribute the tract to passersby. It was not long, predictably, before copies fell into the hands of the police. This in turn sparked an immediate nationwide search for the tract's author and the place and means of its production.

On May 24, 1909, Gudō was arrested on his way back to Rinsenji after having finished a month of Zen training at Eiheiji, one of the Sōtō sect's two chief monasteries. He was initially charged with violations of the press and publications laws and, at first, believed he would simply be fined and released. Upon searching Rinsenji, however, the police claimed to have discovered a cache of explosive materials including twelve sticks of dynamite, four packages of explosive gelatin, and a supply of fuses.

One contemporary commentator, Kashiwagi Ryūhō, claims, though without presenting any proof, that the charges relating to the possession of explosive materials were false. In an article entitled "Martyr Uchiyama Gudō" he states: "The dynamite had been stored at his temple in conjunction with the construction of the Hakone mountain railroad. It had nothing to do with Gudō."9 Nevertheless, Gudō was convicted of both charges and initially sentenced to twelve years' imprisonment. On appeal, his sentence was reduced to seven years.

On July 6, 1909, even before his conviction, officials of the Sōtō Zen sect moved to deprive Gudō of his abbotship at Rinsenji. Once he had been convicted, they quickly moved on to yet more serious action. On June 21, 1910, Gudō was deprived of his status as a Sōtō Zen priest, though he continued to regard himself as one until the end of his life.

Toward a Second Trial On May 25, 1910, two socialists, Miyashita Takichi and Niimura Tadao, were arrested in Nagano Prefecture after police searched their quarters and found chemicals used to make explosives. In the minds of the police this was concrete evidence of the existence of a wider conspiracy against the imperial house. This in turn led to Kōtoku Shūsui's arrest a week later, and the investigation and interrogation of hundreds of men and women in the following months. By this time Gudō had already been in prison for a full year, yet this did not prevent him from becoming a suspect once again.

At the conclusion of its investigation, charges were brought against twenty-six persons, including Gudō and one woman, Kanno Sugako. If convicted under Article 73, "Crimes Against the Throne," of the new criminal code, all of them could face the death penalty. Under Article 73 prosecutors had only to show that the defendants "intended" to bring harm to members of the imperial house, not that they had acted on this intent in any concrete way. Ideas, not facts, were on trial.

The trial commenced in Tokyo on December 10, 1910. Kanno Sugako not only admitted in court that she had been involved in the alleged conspiracy but indicated how many others had been involved as well. Upon being asked by the presiding judge, Tsuru Jōichirō, if she wished to make a final statement, Kanno responded:

From the outset I knew that our plan would not succeed if we let a lot of people in on it. Only four of us were involved in the plan. It is a crime that involves only the four of us. But this court, as well as the preliminary interrogators, treated it as a plan that involved a large number of people. That is a complete misunderstanding of the case. Because of this misunderstanding a large number of people have been made to suffer. You are aware of this. . . .

If these people are killed for something that they knew nothing about, not only will it be a grave tragedy for the persons concerned, but their relatives and friends will feel bitterness toward the government. Because we hatched this plan, a large number of innocent people may be executed.[10]

In her diary entry for January 21, 1911, Kanno identified the other persons involved in the plot as Kōtoku, Miyashita, Niimura, and Furukawa Rikisaku.[11]

Kanno's plea on behalf of the other defendants fell on deaf ears. As for Gudō, Chief Prosecutor Hiranuma Kiichirō went on to identify his earlier writing, with its uncompromising denial of the emperor system, as "the most heinous book ever written since the beginning of Japanese history."[12] He also mentioned a second tract which Gudō had printed, entitled *A Handbook for Imperial Soldiers (Teikoku Gunjin Zayū no Mei)*. Here Gudō had gone so far as to call on conscripts to desert their encampments *en masse*. In addition, Gudō had, as already noted, repeatedly and forcefully advocated both land reform in the countryside and democratic rights for all citizens.

Many years later an alternative view of Gudō's role in the alleged conspiracy came from a somewhat surprising source, namely the administrative headquarters of the Sōtō Zen sect. In the July 1993 issue of *Sōtō Shūhō*, the administrative organ for this sect, an announcement was made that as of April 13, 1993, Uchiyama Gudō's status as a Sōtō priest had been restored. The announcement went on to say, "[Gudō's] original expulsion was a mistake caused by the sect's having swallowed the government's repressive policies."[13]

The explanation as to what caused this turnabout in the sect's attitude toward Gudō was contained in a subsequent article that appeared in the September 1993 issue of the same periodical. Written by the sect's new "Bureau for the Protection and Advocacy of Human Rights," the highlights of the article are as follows:

When viewed by today's standards of respect for human rights, Uchiyama Gudō's writings contain elements that should be regarded as farsighted. We have much to learn from them, for today his writings are respected by people in various walks of life, beginning with the mass media. In our sect, the restoration of Uchiyama Gudō's reputation is something that will both bring solace to his spirit and contribute to the establishment within this sect of a method of dealing with questions concerning human rights. . . .

We now recognize that Gudō was a victim of the national policy of that day. . . . The dynamite found in his temple had been placed there for safekeeping by a railroad company laying track through the Hakone mountains and had nothing to do with him. . . . The sect's [original] actions strongly aligned the sect with an establishment dominated by the emperor system. They were not designed to protect the unique Buddhist character of the sect's priests. . . . On this occasion of the restoration of Uchiyama Gudō's reputation, we must reflect on the way in which our sect has ingratiated itself with both the political powers of the day and a state under the suzerainty of the emperor.[14]

While the Sōtō sect's statement clearly views Gudō as a victim of government repression, it presents no new evidence in support of his innocence. It merely repeats Kashiwagi's earlier unsubstantiated claim that the dynamite found at his temple was put there as part of a nearby railway construction project. All in all, the Sōtō sect's statement must be treated with some scepticism, perhaps as more of a reflection of the sect's regret for what it came to recognize (in postwar years) as its slavish subservience to the state.

Because of this lack of evidence, no definitive statement can be made about the guilt or innocence of those on trial in the High Treason Incident. As noted earlier, much critical evidence was destroyed by the government as it sought to make the accused into "nonpersons." When in 1975 the descendents of one of those originally convicted in the case petitioned for a retrial, the Ministry of Justice stated clearly for the first time that the trial's transcripts no longer existed. Even if the transcripts had existed, it is doubtful that they would have provided definitive evidence, given that everyone directly connected with the trial was by then dead. Historian Fred Notehelfer admits at the end of his study of the case that "an element of mystery . . . continues to surround the trial."[15] It probably always will.

There was never any doubt at the time, however, that the defendants would be found guilty. The only uncertainty was how severe their penalties would be. On January 18, 1911, little more than a month after the trial began, the court rendered its verdict. All defendants were found guilty, and twenty-four of them, Gudō and the three other Buddhist priests included, were condemned to death. One day later, on January 19th, an imperial rescript was issued which commuted the sentences of twelve of the condemned to life imprisonment. Three of the Buddhist priests—Takagi Kemmyō, Sasaki Dōgen, and Mineo Setsudō—were spared the hangman's noose, though all would die in prison.

Toward Execution   Mikiso Hane has suggested why the government was so determined to convict all of the defendants:

> The authorities (under Prime Minister Katsura Tarō, who had been directed by the *genrō* [elder statesman] Yamagata Aritomo to come down hard on the leftists) rounded up everybody who had the slightest connection with Kōtoku and charged them with complicity in the plot.[16]

Yamagata was particularly concerned by the fact that the court testimony of nearly all the defendants revealed a loss of faith in the divinity of the emperor. For Yamagata, this loss of respect for the core of the state represented a serious threat to the future of the nation. Those holding this view had to be eliminated by any means necessary.

Acting with unaccustomed haste, the government executed Gudō and ten of his alleged co-conspirators inside the Ichigaya Prison compound on the morning of January 24, 1911, less than a week after their conviction. Kanno Sugako was executed the following day. Gudō was the fifth to die on the twenty-fourth, and Yoshida Kyūichi records that as he climbed the scaffold stairs, "he gave not the slightest hint of emotional distress. Rather he appeared serene, even cheerful—so much so that the attending prison chaplain bowed as he passed."[17]

The next day, when Gudō's younger brother, Seiji, came to collect his body, he demanded that the coffin be opened. Looking at Gudō's peaceful countenance, Seiji said, "Oh, older brother, you passed away without suffering. . . . What a superb face you have in death!"[18]

CHAPTER FOUR:

INSTITUTIONAL BUDDHISM'S REJECTION OF PROGRESSIVE SOCIAL ACTION

Only four Buddhist priests were involved in the High Treason Incident, yet the incident did have a significant impact on the leadership of Japan's traditional Buddhist sects—first and foremost on the leadership of the Sōtō Zen sect. It was in fact in the reaction of the Buddhist sectarian leadership that we see the most enduring influence of this incident on the subsequent relationship between institutional Buddhism and the state.

THE SŌTŌ ZEN SECT REACTION

Although Gudō had earlier been ousted from the Sōtō Zen priesthood, the administrative head of the sect, Morita Goyū (1834–1915), on the day preceding Gudō's execution, felt obliged to issue a statement abjectly apologizing for not having adequately controlled the likes of Gudō. In part, Morita said:

> I am profoundly dumbstruck that there could have been someone like Uchiyama Gudō in this sect, a sect whose basic principle has been, since its founding, to respect the emperor and protect the state. I therefore apologize most profusely and profoundly and pledge that I will guide and educate the priests of this sect to devote all of their energies to their proper duties and thereby actively practice being of service to society.[1]

In addition to this apology, the Sōtō sect hierarchy also issued a number of directives to all affiliated temples and educational institutions. Typical of these was the directive of February 15, 1911, which, after condemning Gudō yet again, advised sect adherents to "exercise vigilance over both themselves and others . . . in order to expiate this most serious crime in the sect's last one thousand years."[2]

RINZAI ZEN SECT REACTION

In almost identical language, the leadership of the various branches of the Rinzai Zen sect issued similar apologies and directives. In the case of the Myōshinji branch of the Rinzai Zen sect, the administrative head, Toyoda Dokutan (1840–1917) had this to say:

> The essence of the Rinzai sect since its founding in this country has been to protect the nation through the spread of Zen. It is for this reason that in front of the central Buddha image in our sect's temples we have reverently placed a memorial tablet inscribed with the words "May the current emperor live for ten thousand years," thereby making our temples training centers for pacifying and preserving our country. . . .
>
> We make certain that adherents of our sect always keep in mind love of country and absolute loyalty [to the emperor], . . . that they don't ignore the doctrine of karma or fall into the trap of believing in the heretical idea of "evil equality" [as advocated by socialists, et al.].[3]

In Dokutan's condemnation of "evil equality" *(aku byōdō)* can be heard an echo of Shimaji's earlier critique of socialists for their failure to understand the identity of differentiation and equality, and their confusion of the worlds of form and formlessness. The bifurcation of form and formlessness had by then become the dominant theoretical position of Buddhist thought. As such, it served to legitimate Buddhism's involvement in war while providing ammunition for attacking Western expansionist policies in Asia. It further provided justification for institutional Buddhism's assistance to Japan's own expansionist programs.[4]

The Shin sect's leadership, for its part, was no less appalled by the actions of one its own, Takagi Kemmyō. Two administrative leaders of the Higashi Honganji branch of the Shin sect, Ōtani Eiryō and Kuwakado Shidō, issued an admonition to all subordinate temples on January 20, 1911. It stated in part:

> Last year [1910] there were those who, having adopted socialist extremism, hatched an extraordinary plot. Those who did so both violated a basic principle of this sect, which teaches the coexistence of relative and ultimate truth, and cast aside the Buddhist doctrine of causality. This is not the way in which priests of this sect should act. . . . Nevertheless, there is such a priest [Takagi Kemmyō] in this sect. . . .
>
> Adherents of this sect should quickly rectify their thinking in accordance with this sect's teaching that the Law of the Sovereign is paramount and relations between men should be based on benevolence. . . . They must be taught, in accordance with this sect's teaching of the coexistence of relative and ultimate truth, just how deep is the gratitude they owe to both heaven and their country. . . . Especially those in this sect in supervisory roles must pay special attention to what the priests and laity under their supervision are doing. . . . You must eliminate misconceptions, being ever vigilant.[5]

Even though there were no priests of the Nishi Honganji branch directly involved in the trial, the leadership of that sect, in the person of Ōtani Sonyū, felt compelled to issue its own statement. It began by noting that society was being "infected by dangerous thoughts" and went on to point out that "those who mistakenly involved themselves in such lawless speech and actions are not simply enemies of the state but of the [Shin] sect as well."

As justification for his position, Sonyū pointed out that Japan was a "flawless state" to which all sect adherents should selflessly devote themselves. In particular, "as teachers, sect priests should observe tendencies in social thought in order to promote national stability and maintain social order." In so doing, they would insure that "the splendor of our sect will be exalted."[6] Neither Sonyū nor the other Shin leaders, it would appear, ever considered the possibility that the Law of the Sovereign might conflict with the Law of the Buddha, let alone what they would do if it ever did.

SCHOLARLY REACTION

In March 1912, a book entitled *Essays on Reverence for the Emperor and Patriotism (Sonnō Aikoku Ron)* was published. The nineteen essays contained in this work were written by fifteen leading scholars, one government official, and three intellectuals, including the New Buddhist leader, Ōuchi Seiran. Other well-known Buddhist scholar-priests among the contributors were Inoue Enryō, Nanjō Bun'yū, and Murakami Senshō (1851–1929), a noted Buddhist historian.

The book's connection to the High Treason Incident was made clear in its preface. The incident was referred to as "marking the greatest disgrace of the Meiji period."[7] The book's editor, Akiyama Goan, wrote that as a result of the disturbance this incident caused, he had decided to ask the leading thinkers of his day to clarify the true nature of reverence for the emperor and patriotism "in order to exterminate vermin and provide the material to fill up ant holes."[8]

The titles of the various essays provide a good indication of the book's content. Tokyo University Professor Inoue Tetsujirō wrote on "The Noble Cause of the Founding of the State," while Murakami Senshō contributed an essay entitled "Loyalty [to the Emperor] and Filial Piety in Buddhism." Ōuchi Seiran's essay was entitled "On Revering the Emperor and Repaying [One's Debt of Gratitude to] the Buddha." Seiran used his essay to renew the attack on Christianity, writing:

> Christianity and our imperial house can never coexist, for it is impossible to truly revere the imperial house while believing in Christianity. . . . Christianity not only turns its back on the righteous Buddhist teaching of cause and effect, but it is a heretical teaching that tears apart the establishment of our imperial house and destroys the foundation of our country. . . . Therefore we must all join together to prevent this heretical teaching from spreading throughout our land.[9]

Inoue Enryō entitled his essay "A Treatise on the National Polity, Loyalty [to the Emperor], and Filial Piety." In it he presented the following syllogism:

The land of our nation is sacred, and since our nation developed on this sacred land, it should also be called sacred.... Our imperial house is sacred, and since all of the subjects in this land are its off-spring, children of the gods and grandchildren of the emperor, therefore they are sacred. ... Our loyalty [to the emperor] and patriotism are sacred ... whereas in the West such things are private matters and therefore lifeless. Why? Because the people and the king [in Western countries] don't become one family ... since society is based on individuals who only think of themselves.[10]

In the above comments it is not difficult to see that the Buddhist essayists were determined to demonstrate that they were as completely dedicated to the emperor and the state as the most patriotic of secular Japanese. In this effort they were eminently successful. With the state's assistance, vermin such as Uchiyama Gudō had indeed been exterminated. Their role was to fill up the remaining ant holes.

GOVERNMENT REACTION

The Japanese government was just as concerned as Buddhist leaders and scholars that religious figures would never again oppose its policies. With this goal in mind, it sponsored the Conference of the Three Religions (Sankyō Kaidō), which opened on February 25, 1912. This conference was attended by seventy-one representatives from Buddhism, Shinto, and Christianity as well as numerous sponsoring government ministers and officials. The government's unprecedented inclusion of Christian representatives revealed that the patriotic fervor of the new creed, as demonstrated during both the Sino-Japanese and Russo-Japanese wars, had at last been officially recognized.

The conference occupied itself with passing a number of resolutions calling for change, including support of the imperial way *(kōdō)* and promotion of national morality. Conference participants also advocated cooperation between politics, religion, and education to ensure national prosperity. Notto Thelle makes the connection between the High Treason Incident and this conference very clear, when, after describing the conference agenda, he states: "The plot to assassinate the Emperor in 1910 made a great impact upon the political situation.... There is no doubt that the government policy toward religions and its support of religious cooperation was stimulated by apprehensions about socialism and other "dangerous thoughts."[11]

The government was, without question, successful in its efforts. As a result of this conference, many influential leaders in the Buddhist and Christian establishments cooperated with each other not only to strengthen the state but to foster patriotic spirit, national unity, and moral strength in a time they perceived as fraught with danger.[12]

Although the practical results of this cooperation will be discussed in the following chapters, through the end of the Pacific War no major Buddhist or Christian leader ever again publicly spoke out in any organized way against government policies, either civilian or military, domestic or foreign. To conclude that this one conference brought about the subservience of religion to the state would be an exaggeration. This tendency in Japanese Buddhism can be clearly seen throughout the Meiji period, with roots reaching even further back. On the other hand, the conference was the last nail in the coffin of any semblance of Buddhist independence from state policies, especially those relating to questions of war and peace. This blind and total obedience to the government on the part of Japan's religious leaders, Buddhist and non-Buddhist alike, was destined to become the most enduring religious legacy of not just the High Treason Incident but of the entire Meiji period, which came to an end in 1912.

PART II

JAPANESE MILITARISM
AND BUDDHISM

CHAPTER FIVE:

THE INCORPORATION OF BUDDHISM INTO THE JAPANESE WAR MACHINE (1913–30)

WITHIN JAPAN PROPER

Shaku Sōen, it will be remembered, had said that Japan was fighting the Russo-Japanese war with "no egotistic purpose" in mind. Yet, as the historian W. G. Beaseley pointed out:

> The Russo-Japanese war had set Japan on the road toward aquiring an empire of her own. . . . For the first time in modern history, an Asian country had defeated one of the powers in full-scale war. By doing so, it had secured both real advantages and symbols of prestige: a paramount position in Korea and valuable rights in South Manchuria, to be added to Formosa [Taiwan] and a share in the China trade.[1]

Not content with "a paramount position in Korea," Japan proceeded, in 1910, to force the Korean king to sign a Treaty of Annexation. Korea lost its independence and Japan acquired, at last, a major colony on the Asian mainland. This event marked Japan's transformation into a world power, one which was well on the way toward domination of the entire Far East. Hugh Borton noted that Japan "seemed to have been catapulted onto the world stage by an uncontrollable and compelling urge to become strong, to force its will on any who challenged its position, and to be the leader of Asia."[2]

The question was raised, both within and without Japan, what had enabled Japan to so quickly transform itself into a world power. Though certainly not the only voices within Japan attempting to address this question, Japan's Buddhist leaders, especially those in the Zen tradition, believed they knew the answer. Nukariya Kaiten (1867–1934) was a noted Buddhist scholar-priest, personal friend of D. T. Suzuki, and subsequent president of Sōtō Zen–affiliated Komazawa University. In 1913, while lecturing at Harvard University, he wrote a book in English entitled *Religion of the Samurai: A Study of Zen Philosophy and Discipline in China and Japan.* According to Kaiten, not only were Zen ideas "in harmony with those of the New Buddhists," but "it is Zen that modern Japan, especially after the Russo-Japanese War, has acknowledged as an ideal doctrine for her rising generation."[3]

In a later section of his book, Kaiten described the rationale for the renewed interest in Zen as follows:

> After the Restoration of the Meiji the popularity of Zen began to wane, and for some thirty years remained in inactivity; but since the Russo-Japanese War its revival has taken place. And now it is looked upon as an ideal faith, both for a nation full of hope and energy, and for a person who has to fight his own way in the strife of life. Bushido, or the code of chivalry, should be observed not only by the soldier in the battlefield, but by every citizen in the struggle for existence. If a person be a person and not a beast, then he must be a samurai—brave, generous, upright, faithful, and manly, full of self-respect and self-confidence, and at the same time full of the spirit of self-sacrifice.[4]

When Kaiten looked around for a contemporary who embodied the samurai spirit, he found General Nogi, the Zen-trained hero of the Russo-Japanese War. Nogi's spirit of self-sacrifice was so great that upon the death of Emperor Meiji in 1912, the general (and his wife) had committed ritual suicide in a traditional practice known as *junshi,* or following one's lord in death. The practice of *junshi* had been been identified as an antiquated custom and was forbidden by the Tokugawa Shogunate as early as 1663, and Nogi's suicide did not fail to arouse a certain amount of controversy. Intellectuals in particular hotly debated both its ethics and appropriateness in a modern state. Typical of this controversy was the following newspaper editorial:

> General Nogi's death marked the culmination of Japan's Bushido of old. And while emotionally we express the greatest respect,

rationally we regret we cannot approve. One can only hope that this act will not long blight the future of our national morality. We can appreciate the General's intention; we must not learn from his behavior.[5]

If the public debate over Nogi's death was marked by a certain degree of ambivalence, Kaiten had not slightest doubt as to its true significance:

We can find an incarnation of Bushido in the late General Nogi, the hero of Port Arthur, who, after the sacrifice of his two sons for the country in the Russo-Japanese War, gave up his own and his wife's life for the sake of the deceased Emperor. He died not in vain, as some might think, because his simplicity, uprightness, loyalty, bravery, self-control, and self-sacrifice, all combined in his last act, surely inspire the rising generation with the spirit of the samurai to give birth to hundreds of Nogis.[6]

Kaiten was not the only Buddhist leader to express these thoughts. As early as 1905, Shaku Sōen expressed his own views in this regard during the course of his second visit to the United States:

Fortunately, Japan had just won the war, and that made people everywhere sit up and take note of her. In fact, the whole world was surprised that Japan had defeated Russia. It was impossible to explain Japan's string of military victories in terms of military equipment and logistics. . . . [It] was due to the samurai spirit, the Spirit of Japan, nurtured by the country over the past two thousand years.[7]

Sōen went on to state that this "spirit of Japan," or *Yamato damashii*, had come from "a single spiritual teaching," which he identified as having developed out of an amalgamation of Confucianism, Shinto, and Buddhism. In a meeting with President Theodore Roosevelt during his sojourn in the United States, Sōen described the Buddhist contribution to the spirit of Japan as being centered on the concept of "self-sacrifice":

To sacrifice the self, seen from the inside, is centered around the abandoning of what Buddhism calls the small self, so as to serve the greater cause. . . . I believe that the readiness for self-sacrifice is found in the peoples of all other countries, but never is it so clearly manifest as in the Japanese. This spirit is one of the factors contributing to the Japanese victory in the Russo-Japanese War. There are many other factors, but among the more intangible ones is this readiness to give up one's life.[8]

Sōen was equally clear about what this spirit of self-sacrifice should be directed toward. On the one hand, those imbued with this spirit ought "to work for justice and the common good." On the other hand, they should also "serve the State" and recognize "that it is increasingly important that everyone make an effort to serve the Emperor."[9]

In general it can be said that Sōen's Western lectures on Buddhism had two major purposes. The first was to justify Japan's military and colonial efforts. Second, Sōen wished to demonstrate his interest in the popular intellectual pastime of theories concerning the uniqueness of the Japanese.[10]

Even after his return to Japan in 1906, Sōen continued to develop these themes. This in turn led to yet another invitation to travel abroad, though this time the invitation came from the Japanese-owned South Manchuria Railway Company.[11] Thus, Sōen delivered a series of lectures in 1912 entitled "The Spirit of the Yamato Race" to members of the Japanese colonial administration in both Korea and Manchuria. There was nothing particularly unusual about Sōen's trip, for all of Japan's traditional Buddhist sects were committed to a general policy of "[maintaining] Buddhism's reputation as 'protector of the country.'"[12]

Although Sōen's and Kaiten's views may be considered representative of the era following the Russo-Japanese War, not all Buddhist leaders were in agreement with them. One notable voice of dissent came from Ōtani Sonyū (1886–1939), the administrative head of the Nishi Honganji branch of the Shin sect. His was not simply a dissenting voice but, in his conclusion, a prophetic voice as well:

There was a time when the phrase "for the sake of the state" wielded such a power as to suppress all other considerations, making the people subservient to the despotic will of statesmen, and even the spiritual leaders had meekly to submit to their sometimes arrogant and inflexible orders. This was all right if the state was representative of things that are good, just and humane; but as history tells us, no state has ever proved in the past to be such a symbol. In fact, every one of the states that prospered and disappeared, or that are now prospering, has been anything but symbolic of justice and love and liberty. Hence the history of the world has been the record of constant struggles and untold suffering. But fortunately, since the termination of the recent war, the world seems to be realizing the enormity of the loss and the foolishness of the greed for power. We are now growing more conscious than ever of the imperative necessity of emphasizing the spiritual side of human life and the fact that our lives are so closely interrelated that whatever things good or bad happen to one nation are sure to affect another. The time is come when we have to abandon the narrow conception of the state which puts one nation's welfare, especially material welfare, above that of the friendly neighbors. . . .

Statesmen have been wont to urge us to sacrifice our personal interest for the state, to abandon our individual claims and even affections for upholding the state as the highest expression of human life. This is all right if the state is also the perfect and most rational symbol of all that we, as individuals, can conceive as good and just and lovable. If the state, on the contrary, betrays our thoughts of justice and freedom and countermands the dictates of love and humanity, it has no right to continue its existence. If it does not fall by itself, other states will not suffer its ever menacing existence. To obey blindly whatever is claimed by the state, good or bad, just or unjust, is to enslave oneself and to lose one's moral and spiritual individuality. . . .

I believe in the existence of the state, for I think it necessary to the enhancement of real human welfare. But I cannot subscribe to the ideas stoutly upheld by some people who, taking the state for an absolute form of human life, believe in its power to do anything for its own maintenance, regardless of the consequences either to its own members or to the neighboring states. Inasmuch as no one absolute state can exist by itself and in itself, it requires other states to be its friendly neighbors, for no state can ignore the claims of other states, just as in the case of individuals. If it does this and goes on its own way ignoring its fellow organizations, it is sure to meet a sad fate and lose its own existence before long.[13]

Sonyū wrote the above in 1921, and the recent war to which he referred was World War I (1914–19). In this war Japan was allied with Great Britain, France, and the United States against Germany. Carefully choosing to confront the latter nation only where it was weakest, in its colonial outposts in China and the Pacific, Japan once again emerged victorious, at a relatively low cost to itself in both men and materials. Sonyū's comments notwithstanding, institutional Buddhist leaders could also claim a share in Japan's victory, for they had created the Buddhist Society for the Defense of the Nation (Bukkyō Gokoku Dan) to aid the government's war effort.

In spite of its victory, however, the Buddhist scholar Anesaki Masaharu pointed out:

> The collapse of the great empires, the final outcome of the war and its aftermath, these could not fail to produce profound impressions upon the Japanese. . . . The seriousness of social and moral problems began to demand deep reflections.[14]

If Sonyū's critical comments may be considered one expression of the "deep reflections" taking place within the ranks of Buddhist leaders, they must also be viewed as a minority viewpoint. Even Sonyū himself would later abandon his critical stance when, in 1937, he joined the first cabinet of Prince Konoe Fumimaro as the Minister for Colonial Affairs, a position giving him direct responsibility for running Japan's constantly expanding empire. In addition, he also served as the President of the North China Development Corporation, one of the Japanese government–owned development corporations primarily concerned with the exploitation of recently conquered areas in northern China.

Sonyū's prophetic (though short-lived) critique notwithstanding, it was Buddhist leaders such as Arai Sekizen (1864–1927) whose positions carried the day. Sekizen, administrative head of the Sōtō Zen sect and the chief abbot of Sōjiji, made the following comments in 1925:

> Buddhism does not absolutely oppose war. . . . Peace is man's natural ideal. It is the highest ideal of man. Japan is a lover of peace, so even if she goes into war, it is always a war of peace. . . . In advocating peace and racial equality, we must not forget the state we belong to. Real peace cannot be expected if we forget our state in our love of mankind. . . . If we forget our duty to our country, no matter how we advocate the love of mankind, there will be no real peace.[15]

By the end of the 1920s institutional Buddhism had firmly locked itself into ideological support for Japan's ongoing military efforts, wherever and whenever they might occur.

WITHIN THE "GREATER EAST ASIAN CO-PROSPERITY SPHERE"

Institutional Buddhism's support for the Russo-Japanese War had not been confined to ideological support and providing military chaplains. At home it had expressed itself in everything from the conduct of special sutra-recitation ceremonies believed to ensure victory in battle to such social-welfare activities as providing financial and in-kind assistance to soldiers' families, especially the families of those who had fallen on the battlefield. Numerous Buddhist temples had even become detention centers for Russian prisoners of war.

Paralleling these domestic activities were equally ambitious missionary efforts on the Asian mainland, efforts that did not end with the war's conclusion. If anything, these missionary efforts only increased in the postwar years. The Japanese government itself had recognized the political importance of these efforts as early as the conclusion of the Sino-Japanese War, when Prime Minister Itō Hirobumi (1841–1909) demanded that China allow the establishment of Japanese Buddhist missions in that country.

It will be recalled that the Higashi Honganji branch of the Shin sect established a temple in Shanghai as early as 1876 and a further mission in Korea in 1877. With Japan's expansion onto the Asian continent firmly established as a result of its victories in both the Sino-Japanese and Russo-Japanese Wars, these pioneering efforts of the Shin sect multiplied many times over. By 1918 the Nishi Honganji branch of the Shin sect had a total of thirty-four missions in Korea, while the Higashi Honganji branch had fifty-eight. By 1941 these same two branches had a total of fifty-three and eighty missions in Manchuria respectively.

Nor, of course, were these continental missionary efforts limited to the Shin sect. The Sōtō Zen sect, for example, established its first mission in Korea in 1904, a number which grew to more than twenty-one by 1912 and more than one hundred by war's end. In Manchuria, its evangelization efforts began in 1907 and reached a total of thirty-seven missions by 1940. The year 1907 also marked the founding of the first Nichiren-sect mission in Manchuria. This number grew to more than twenty by war's end. The Jōdo sect established its first temple in China in 1905, while the esoteric

Shingon sect had over three hundred priests stationed in various areas of Manchuria and China proper during the war years.

In 1934 Shimizu Ryūzan (1870–1943), president of Nichiren sect-affiliated Risshō University, explained the underlying purpose of these missions:

> The underlying principle of the spirit of Japan is the enlightenment of the world with truth. Just as our brother Manchurians have come to follow us with affection, so also must we lead all the nations of the world into righteousness and establish heaven on earth, where brotherly love and worldwide peace shall prevail and where all men shall be Buddhist saints. This is the true ideal of the spirit of Japan.[16]

In contrast to this idealistic view, the contemporary Buddhist historian Yoshida Kyūichi points out that for the most part these missionary efforts were simply one part of Japan's colonial administration, the ultimate goal of which was "to propagate the benevolent influence of the emperor."[17]

One way in which this latter goal was put into practice by the Shin sect was the placement of "emperor tablets" *(tempai)* on the altars of its continental missions. These large tablets, located beside the central figure of worship, Amida Buddha, were designed to instill reverence, loyalty, and obedience to the Japanese emperor among the colonized peoples. They were a method of inculcating emperor worship in Buddhist clothing. This method, the sect asserted, would be more palatable to the colonized peoples because of their shared Buddhist faith.

Most of institutional Buddhism's missionary efforts on the continent advanced in tandem with the Japanese military's invasions and occupations. This pattern has been identified as "evangelization following the military" in contrast to the typical Western pattern, in which Christian missionaries first entered a potential colonial territory and endeavored to convince its inhabitants not only to accept their faith but also the Western merchants and military who came later.[18] The missionary efforts of the Shin sect, however, did not follow the model mentioned above. Like Christian missionaries, they actually preceded the Japanese military's advance. This practice emerged as a result of the vision of Meiji-era sect leaders such as Ogurusu Kōchō and Okumura Enshin, who advocated using Buddhism as the basis for forming an anti-Western alliance between Japan, China, and India. D. T. Suzuki also shared this ideology, as demonstrated by an essay on Zen he published in English in 1934, in which he wrote:

If the East is one and there is something that differentiates it from the West, the differentia must be sought in the thought that is embodied in Buddhism. For it is in Buddhist thought and in no other that India, China, and Japan representing the East, could be united as one.... When the East as unity is made to confront the West, Buddhism supplies the bond.[19]

Such ideas provided one of the ideological underpinnings for the subsequent development of the "Greater East Asia Co-Prosperity Sphere" (Dai Tōa Kyōei Ken), Japan's rationalization for its aggression in Asia.

While Ogurusu and Okumura may have been pioneers in linking Buddhism to Japan's imperial plans, they were soon joined, as noted above, by the leaders of all institutional Buddhism. The Buddhist missions were not focused so much on propagating their particular sectarian viewpoints as they were on "social welfare activities." These activities included such things as operating Japanese language schools, preparing parcels of treats for soldiers in the field, and providing technical training for local employees of Japanese companies.

In its broadest sense these social welfare activities may be viewed as one part of what was then widely known as "education to create imperial subjects" (kōminka kyōiku). The missions were also used, when necessary, to provide temporary shelter for Japanese troops. Some of them were also connected with "pacification activities" (sembu kōsaku), an espionage program in which mission priests identified to the military authorities locals suspected of being opposed to Japanese domination. When Buddhist priests were actually conscripted into the military, as they increasingly were, it was common for them to be assigned to units involved in these "pacification" efforts. There were even priests whose espionage activities were so sensitive that all documents identifying them as either priests or soldiers were destroyed.[20]

The Buddhist missions on the continent and the priests who staffed them were representatives of the Great Empire of Japan. It is hardly surprising to learn that with the end of war in 1945 every single one of these missions on the Asian continent, regardless of sect affiliation, collapsed, never to be revived.

CHAPTER SIX:

Buddhist Resistance to Japanese Militarism

Organized Resistance: Shinkō Bukkyō Seinen Dōmei

By the 1920s, Japanese institutional Budhism, as a whole, firmly supported Japan's military and colonial policies. There were, however, still a small number of Buddhists who refused to accept the stance of their sectarian leaders. A group of such freethinkers formed the Youth League for Revitalizing Buddhism (Shinkō Bukkyō Seinen Dōmei). This group was a notable exception to institutional Buddhism's subservience to the state, especially as the League members were also deeply involved in social action. Inagaki Masami (b. 1926) noted that the League was "the only sign that there were still conscientious religionists within Buddhist circles."[1]

Another distinguishing feature of this organization was that, as its name implies, the membership was relatively young, mostly in their twenties and thirties. Furthermore, the leadership was composed predominantly of laymen rather than clerics, which freed it to a certain extent from the control of Buddhism's sectarian hierarchies, while at the same time making it more vulnerable to police harassment.

The League was founded on the afternoon of April 5, 1931, with more than thirty persons in attendance, including four uniformed police observers. The first order of business was the selection of officers. A forty-two-year-old Nichiren sect lay activist, Senō Girō (1889–1961), was elected chairman. Next came the reading of the declaration stating the reasons for the League's creation, remarkable for their sharp contrast with the thinking of institutional Buddhist leaders, and quoted here in their entirety:

This is an age of suffering. Our compatriots are seeking affection, yet have had no choice but to struggle. The masses of people seek bread, but are fed repression. To escape or to fight, today the entire world is moving about in confusion and financial difficulty.

In such an age, what should Buddhists be aware of, what contribution should they be making to society? The majority of Buddhists, intoxicated with an easy peace of mind, don't even think about these questions. Through Buddhism these Buddhists possess the highest principles available for the guidance of human beings, yet what contact do they have with the lives of the masses? Furthermore, these Buddhists claim that "religion transcends class differences and values harmony." However, in reality their role is that of an opiate, and they are therefore cursed by the masses and incite the moral indignation of young Buddhists.

This present situation is something that genuine believers cannot bear. However, when we look to already existing sectarian organizations for reform, we are forced to recognize just how serious their corrupt traditions and degeneration are. Faced with this situation, we have no choice but to resolutely propose a movement to revitalize Buddhism. A revitalized Buddhism must be based on self-reflection. It must deny currently existing Buddhism which has already lost its capacity for confrontation while, at the same time, calling on all Buddhists to return to the Buddha. A revitalized Buddhism must recognize that the suffering in present-day society comes chiefly from the capitalist economic system and must be willing to cooperate in a fundamental reform of this system, working to preserve the well-being of the masses. We must revolutionize bourgeois Buddhism and change it to a Buddhism for the masses. A revitalized Buddhism must intensify its speculation and research in an attempt to clarify Buddhist culture for the new age and bring about world peace.

If it does this, a revitalized Buddhism will have absolutely no reason to fear the anti-religious movement which is popular at the moment. The reason for this is that we believe religion will never disappear so long as human beings seek affection and stand up for what they believe in, given their finite nature that longs for the infinite. The religion we seek is not one centered on a creator God. Aren't there too many contradictions between believing in an all-powerful God and the situation we find ourselves in today?

We believe in a Buddhism that necessarily conforms to the truth, and we revere the Buddha who bore witness to love, equality, and freedom through his practice. Our reverence is based on the inherent requirement of life to seek perfection, something which lies at the heart of human existence.

We are convinced that it is as a result of this requirement that human beings have been able to constantly create unique cultural forms. We are further convinced that something like the anti-religious movement is itself either an expression of a lack of awareness of the nature of human life or a process for getting rid of numerous superstitions which have hidden themselves in [Buddhism's] esoteric sanctuaries, thereby providing good material for the revival of true Buddhism.

Young Buddhists, now is the time for us to arise. Without hesitation we must discard tradition and, joining together as one, return to the Buddha. And then, while personally experiencing the Buddhist spirit of love and equality, let us solemnly move forward to reconstruct capitalism. Is this not the way we should endeavour to construct our ideal Buddhist society?[2]

The preceding declaration was adopted unanimously despite the obvious discomfort of the policemen in attendance. However, when it came time to accept the League's "Statement of Principles," a spirited debate erupted. The three proposed principles were:

(1) We revere Buddha Shakyamuni whose character is unexcelled among human beings. We seek to make possible the construction of a Buddha Land according to the teachings of faith in, and love for, our fellow human beings.

(2) We recognize that all existing sects are corpses which desecrate the spirit of Buddhism. We look forward to the elimination of this type of Buddhism and the promotion of a Buddhism consistent with the new age.

(3) We recognize that the organization of our current capitalist economy is contrary to the spirit of Buddhism and injurious to the well-being of the masses. Reforming this, we look forward to the coming of a new society.[3]

The debate centered on the final words of the third principle. Some members of the audience insisted that the final phrase read "a new *socialist* society." After much debate, accompanied by actual "saber-rattling" from the uniformed police officers in attendance, this proposal was abandoned and the principles were adopted as proposed.

To understand why the League had come into existence at this time, it is important to remember that both Japan and the West were then in the midst of the Great Depression, which had begun in 1929. Given Japan's high dependence on foreign trade, the Great Depression spelled economic disaster. On the domestic front Japan suffered from both high unemployment and increasingly severe labor disputes. Farmers found themselves caught between greatly reduced income and unchanging tax assessments. The end result was a rapid increase in rural debt, with some poor tenant farmers selling their daughters into prostitution, and others banding together to resist high land rents.

Things were no better in Japan's overseas colonies There were student-led demonstrations against Japanese rule in Korea in 1929 and an anti-Japanese aboriginal uprising on Taiwan in 1930. All acts of resistance, both overseas and at home, were brutally suppressed by the Japanese military and police. They also created a growing role for right-wing political figures, in and out of government, and their military allies. In addition, the family-owned financial combines known as *zaibatsu* were ever more successful in imposing their wishes on the government, wishes that frequently conflicted with the interests of ordinary citizens.

Given this social turmoil, it is hardly surprising that at least a few Buddhists at the grassroots level chose the path of resistance to the state. The very real danger of this choice in 1930 may explain why there were relatively few such activists. No one understood this danger better than the League's new chairman, Senō Girō. On January 13, 1931, more than two months before the formal founding of the League, Senō made the following entry in his diary:

> This morning as I sat quietly [in meditation], I felt very cold. My fingertips turned to ice, almost to the point of losing all sensation. However, when I thought that in the course of fighting for justice this was just preparation for being taken off to jail, I was filled with joy.[4]

It would be five years before Senō's premonition came to pass. During that time, the League actively engaged in publishing a newspaper and producing pamphlets promoting its views, holding public meetings to increase its membership, and joining together with allies in other, mostly political, organizations that advocated the reform of capitalism. Between 1931 and 1934, the League published a total of six pamphlets detailing its positions on various issues. Of these six, two were written by Senō and the others by leading League members. Senō wrote the first pamphlet published, which was entitled simply "A Lecture on the Revitalization of Buddhism" *(Shinkō Bukkyō no Teishō)*. In this pamphlet he presented a more detailed rationale for the founding of the League together with the doctrinal basis of its program.

Senō's second pamphlet, published in 1933, was entitled "On the Road to Social Reform and the Revitalization of Buddhism" *(Shakai Henkaku Tojō no Shinkō Bukkyō)*. As its name implies, Senō's focus was on the need for social reform based on a Buddhist understanding. For example, he put forth the proposition that international cooperation, rather than narrow nationalism, was the Buddhist approach to world peace. When nations seek only to promote themselves, he wrote, they inevitably resort to military force to achieve their self-centered goals. Such efforts, Senō maintained, were clearly at odds with the Buddhist doctrine of selflessness *(muga)*.

As Uchiyama Gudō had done before him, Senō maintained that the ideal Buddhist society, the Sangha, was a communal organization, organized according to principles directly opposed to the personal acquisitiveness fostered by a capitalist economic system. Senō saw Buddhist temples as the natural agents for the promotion of such a communal society in Japan. Perhaps because of his high hopes for Buddhist social activism, Senō's harshest criticism was directed at Japanese Buddhism and its leaders. Among other things, Senō accused sectarian leaders of having turned the central object of worship in each of their sects (e.g., Amida Buddha in the Shin sect) into absolute deities who had the power to "save" their believers. According to Senō, early Buddhism was clearly atheistic in orientation, with no place for salvation figures to act as religious opiates.

In addition, Senō accused temple priests of being "sermon thieves" *(sekkyō dorobō)*. They deserved this title, in his opinion, because they took the position that social ills and inequities could all be solved if only people would become more spiritually inclined. Yet these same priests assiduously sought their own material welfare by soliciting large donations from the ruling classes, thus becoming their pawns and supporting the status quo.

For Senō there was little if no hope that Japanese Buddhism would be able to reform itself from within. He made this clear in the final sentences of his pamphlet:

As the saying goes, one should not serve new wine from old wine-skins. Members of the Youth League for Revitalizing Buddhism should advance resolutely. Carry the Buddha on your backs and go out into the streets! Go out into the farm and fishing villages![5]

Of all the slogans put forth by League it was this last one, "carry the Buddha on your backs and go out into the streets," that was destined to become the best known. It clearly combined the League's Buddhist doctrinal foundation with a call to social action.

Unsurprisingly, the temple priests described as "sermon thieves" by Senō were none too happy with either the League's activities or its leftist ideology. Initially, institutional Buddhist leaders tried to ignore the League altogether, but as the number of its supporters grew, this became impossible. Things came to a head in May 1933, at the third national conference of the All-Japan Federation of Buddhist Youth Organizations (Zen Nippon Bukkyō Seinenkai Remmei).

Although this Federation was formed in the same year as the League, it was a much larger organization, composed of more than four hundred fifty separate Buddhist groups. One of these groups was the League, which had the same rights as any of the other member organizations to put proposals up for adoption. Exercising this right, League representatives, including Senō, proposed that the Federation go on record as being opposed to "anti-foreign, militarist, and nationalist ideologies," including those movements which promoted the same.[6]

The response of the conference host, Ōtani University (affiliated with the Higashi Honganji branch of the Shin sect), to this and similar League proposals was to force the conference to find a new meeting site off campus. This did nothing to deter the League representatives, who next put forward a motion condemning Hitler and the Nazi Party for their "all-out violent oppression of the Jewish people," their "burning of cultural properties," and their "repression of liberals and peace activists." These violent acts were identified as both "inhumane" and "anti-Buddhist."[7]

None of these League proposals was adopted, for the Federation was being run behind the scenes by both branches of the Shin sect. On the contrary, the Federation ended up passing a resolution of gratitude to the kingdom of Siam for its political support of Japan's newly created puppet government in Manchuria. Federation officials then went on to demand the League's expulsion from the Federation. They were successful, and the League was expelled in the latter part of June 1933.

The leaders of institutional Buddhism were not alone in activities to repress the League. The police were ever ready to do their part. The League's organ, *Shinkō Bukkyō* (New Buddhism), was first censored as early as the November 1931 issue. Over the next five years, on more than ten occasions the police either forbid the sale of the offending League publication altogether or required certain articles to be deleted prior to distribution. The state's repression, moreover, did not stop with censorship alone. League-sponsored public lectures were frequently terminated by police in the audience starting as early as May 1933. Senō himself was first arrested in September 1934 when he attempted to speak at a rally in support of Tokyo's striking streetcar conductors. Although he was only held overnight, he was beaten by the guard the next morning before his release.

In February 1936, Senō was arrested once again, this time together with another League member, Matsuura Fumio. The police were convinced that the League was either connected to the Communist Party or a Communist organization using Buddhism as a cover. Unable to force admissions of Communist affiliation from either man, the police finally released the two League leaders after having held them without charges for nearly one month.

The police were so disturbed by the League because its members took their organization's motto to heart: they did indeed carry the Buddha out into the street. For example, as early as August 1932, League members began collecting signatures on the street for a petition drawn up by the Japan Farmers Union (Nihon Nōmin Kumiai). The League gathered more than two thousand signatures on this petition, which demanded that the government act to increase the incomes of tenant farmers and other workers so as to alleviate the growing disparity between the upper and lower classes. In addition to its efforts on behalf of farmers, the League also took a strong stance against various government and judicial measures that perpetuated discrimination against Japan's traditional outcaste community, members of which were commonly referred to as *burakumin*. League members also supported the activities of the "Anti-Nazi Fascism Annihilation League" (Han-Nachisu Fassho Funsai Dōmei) and took part in many antiwar labor strikes. Senō himself became an editor of the left-wing *Rōdō Zasshi* (Labor Magazine).

The end of Senō's activism came on December 7, 1936, when he was arrested yet again. This time he was charged with treason, for having allegedly plotted the destruction of both the emperor system and capitalism. At first Senō denied the police accusations, insisting that his goals and those of the League were to reform capitalism, work for world peace, and oppose fascism and militarism. After enduring more than five months of relentless police questioning, however, he finally broke down and confessed that all of the charges against him and the League were true. Not only that, he promised that henceforth he would unconditionally support both the emperor and the nation.

Senō's confession was used by the police as the pretext for the wholesale arrest of more than two hundred members of the League, starting in October 1937. Of those arrested, twenty-nine were eventually prosecuted. Despite his pledge to support the emperor and nation, Senō was sentenced to five years in prison on August 29, 1939. In 1942, however, he was given an early release from prison due to ill health. By that time, of course, all traces of the League had been eradicated. So, too, had all traces of any organized Buddhist resistance to Japan's war efforts.[8]

INDIVIDUAL RESISTANCE

Attempting to document individual Buddhist resistance to Japan's wartime policies is a nearly impossible task. Ienaga Saburō relates an incident that typifies the difficulties:

> Some individuals refused military service because of pacifist convictions. Ishiga Osamu was a member of War Resisters International, a Quaker organization. In 1939 he refused to appear at the one-day inspection callup of reservists and turned himself into the Kempeitai [military police]. While being held by the military police, Ishiga heard of another man, a member of the Buddhist Shinshū sect, who refused to take human life.[9]

Who was this Shin sect believer? What was his fate at the hands of the military police? Were there others like him? How did this person come to hold his views? These questions remain unanswered.

Ono Onyū A somewhat better-documented episode is taken from a yearly police report entitled "The State of Social Movements" (*Shakai Undō no Jōkyō*). The report for 1939 refers to a Jōdo-sect chief priest by the name of Ono Onyū. He is recorded as having had the temerity to put up the following notice on his temple bulletin board: "There never was a good war or a bad peace. A reckless war destroys in one year what man took many years to create. [Benjamin] Franklin."[10] Was Onyū persecuted because of this action? Did he do anything beyond this? Once again, our questions remain unanswered.

Kondō Genkō   There is one report of antiwar statements made by Sōtō Zen master Kondō Genkō (b. 1879), abbot of the monastery of Seiunji. One of the trainees at the monastery, Koyama Kishō, recalls an evening talk given by Genkō in the fall of 1937, not long after the outbreak of full-scale war between Japan and China. Genkō said:

> It is troubling that hostilities have broken out between Japan and China. War is an activity in which people kill each other. Whether it be friend or foe, the killing of people is monstrous. There is nothing more sinful in this world than the killing of people. There are big fools who say things like: "We have to enlarge Japan's territory, turning it into a great empire, and increase the amount of red [for Japan] on the maps of the world." It appears that people who feel this way are gradually increasing in number. As for me, I intensely dislike villainous, inhumane things like this war. It must be stopped immediately.[11]

Apparently Genkō made statements like this on more than one occasion, resulting in a visit and a warning from the police. What happened thereafter is unclear, but in 1941 Genkō unexpectedly gave up his abbotship, returned to his home in Akita Prefecture, and promptly disappeared, never to be seen or heard from again. Did he give up his abbotship voluntarily or due to outside pressure? Was foul play involved in his disappearance? These questions remain unanswered.

Takenaka Shōgan   There is one well-documented case of individual war resistance by a Buddhist priest, Takenaka Shōgan (1866–1945). He was affiliated with the Higashi Honganji branch of the Shin sect and was the abbot of Myōsenji temple in Gifu Prefecture. As with Genkō above, the outbreak of war in China in July 1937 was the catalyst for Shōgan's remarks, remarks which were first directed toward parishioners going off to fight in that war.

On September 15, 1937, Shōgan said the following:

> War is both sinful and, at the same time, the enemy of humanity; it should be stopped. In both northern China and Shanghai, [Japan]

should stop with what it has already occupied. War is never a benefit to a nation; rather, it is a terrible loss. Look at the budget for this war: it's enormous, amounting to some two billion and forty million yen. This, combined with the large numbers of draftees headed for the front, is a serious blow to industry at home. Inasmuch as this money will be used to pointlessly kill and maim both men and animals, it may be called a budget for murder. From this point of view as well, it would be wise for the state to stop this war.[12]

It may argued that there was nothing particularly Buddhist in Shōgan's remarks. A fiscal conservative or a secular humanist might have said the same thing. Yet, despite protests from his parishioners, Shōgan's antiwar statements did not stop. The following month, on October 10th, he addressed a group of six of his fellow priests at a nearby temple.

I don't know what others may think about the recent trouble [in China], but it looks to me like aggression. From a Mahayana point of view, it is improper to needlessly deprive either oneself or others of their lives, incurring enormous costs and loss of life in the process. War is the greatest sin there is. Just how much advantage is there in taking such places as Tianjin or Baoding? It would be better to stop the war in such places.[13]

The connection to Buddhism is somewhat clearer in the above quote, and would turn out to be an important factor when Shōgan was brought to trial in December 1937, charged under the section of the law which forbade "fabrications and wild rumor." Although he was found guilty, because his statements were based on religious rather than political grounds, and because he was already seventy-one years of age, Shōgan escaped imprisonment. He was, however, kept under special police surveillance until the end of the war in 1945, which was also the year he died.

Daiun Gikō Finally, there is a rare though fragmentary report of a Sōtō Zen priest and another soldier in his platoon who resisted the war on the battlefield itself. The priest was Daiun Gikō (b. 1922), abbot of Kokushōji, a small mountain temple outside the town of Sasayamaguchi in Hyogo Prefecture. The report was contained in a speech given by Kōno Taitsū (b. 1930), president of Hanazono University, at Komazawa University in October 1995. Taitsū had first learned of the story the previous year when he chanced to visit a local company and was given a copy of the company's mimeographed newsletter. There, under the title "The Story of a Private," the company's former president, Tsuzuki Mana (b. 1920), recounted the following incident:

On December 10, 1943, I entered the 109th Infantry Regiment as a private. On leaving home my mother had given me a small-sized copy of the Christian Bible and told me to "Walk with God." Another well-wisher had given me a large-sized card on which was written the [Zen] Buddhist phrase: "If you become master of each place where you are, then wherever you stand will be the Truth.". . .

On the tenth day after entering the service, I was sent to China. There I was told that I would undergo bayonet and marksmanship training, using as targets live Chinese prisoners tied to trees and without so much as blindfolds.

I remember it as if it were yesterday. It was a morning in February with pure white snow piled deep on the ground. Forty prisoners were tied to a bunch of trees behind the camp in a long line. About ten feet in front of them, forty of us new recruits, with bayonets attached to our rifles, were lined up waiting for the platoon leader to give the order to attack.

The night before, I had lain awake the whole night thinking about what I was going to do. No matter how I looked at it, I could not bear to murder someone. Even if it were the platoon leader's order, this was one thing I couldn't do. Like everyone else, I also knew just how badly I would be treated if I didn't follow orders. And it wouldn't be only me, for according to Japanese army regulations all the members of my squad would receive the same punishment.

I thought maybe I should feign sickness in order not to have to go to the execution grounds. I also recalled stories about weak-kneed soldiers who occasionally deserted. In the end, however, I came to this conclusion, "I'll go to the execution grounds, but I won't kill anyone."

At last the order to attack was given, but not a single soldier moved forward. The platoon leader's face turned red, and he again yelled out, "ATTACK!" This time five or six soldiers went forward. The shrieks and screams of the prisoners, plus their fresh blood, instantly turned the snowy field into a scene of gruesome carnage.

Crazed by the sight of their blood, the remaining soldiers charged their prey like wild bulls. But I stood still. The platoon leader approached, kicked snow at me and yelled, "TSUZUKI, WHAT ABOUT YOU!" But I still didn't move. His red face got even redder, and he yelled "COWARD!" while at the same time raising his foot and kicking me in the back just as hard as he could. Then he grabbed the rifle from my hand and used the butt to send me flying.

There was one more man who had not followed the platoon leader's order. He had come from Sasayama in Tamba and was a Zen priest by the name of Daiun Gikō. That night the two of us were ordered to put our boots in our mouths and make sniffing noises while crawling around in the snow on all fours.

"This is because you're even worse than dogs!" we were told. But both Gikō and I thought to ourselves, "It's people like yourselves who are really inferior to dogs!" And, at the same time, we were secretly happy that we had gotten off with such unexpectedly light punishment.[14]

No doubt it is a misnomer to call this a story of war resistance; more accurately, it is a story of war-atrocity resistance. There is no suggestion that any of the lives of the forty Chinese prisoners were spared, or that either Tsuzuki or Gikō subsequently refused to carry out their other soldierly duties in China. Both men did return safely to Japan after the war, where Tsuzuki died in 1985 and Gikō in 1987.

In concluding the preceding story, Tsuzuki did provide one further piece of information about Gikō.

Due to this incident, we two "dogs" became very close friends. Gikō was an excellent calligrapher so I asked him if he would write his favorite Zen expression for me. I was very surprised when he presented me with a piece of calligraphy on which was written in printed [Sino-Japanese] style: "[In] every place make [yourself] master."[15]

Although none of the preceding incidents of individual war resistance had any appreciable impact on the prosecution of the war, the potential for such impact was not lost on government leaders. In 1937 General Hayashi Senjūrō, who had by then risen to the post of prime minister, gave voice to the government's fears in an article which appeared in the March issue of the Buddhist magazine *Daihōrin*.

Prime Minister Hayashi recalled how, as a staff officer during the First World War, he had been posted to England, Japan's ally. There he encountered a strong and well-organized pacifist movement which opposed, on religious grounds, the government's call for ever more military recruits. Fortunately, according to Hayashi, the pacifist movement remained small, but he recognized the potential for a serious confrontation between religion and state. In light of this, he said:

> Buddhism and the state's policies must be united. . . . Without this it would be like the situation in England where religion and the state were going their separate ways. This would be troubling. I therefore call on both Buddhists and Shintoists to pay close attention to this issue and strive to become one with the state.[16]

In the event exhortations didn't achieve their desired effect, the government was equally prepared to force compliance with its policies. In the same year the headquarters of the Special High Police (Tokubetsu Kōtō Keisatsu), whose job it was to ferret out disloyal elements, issued the following instructions to its personnel: "The erroneous words of Buddhist priests and missionaries can have a not inconsiderable impact on the masses. In light of this, you must pay special attention to being on the alert for and controlling such statements."[17]

Given that there were then approximately 200,000 priests in some 70,000 temples in Japan, one can only wonder what the effect would have been on Japanese society, including the government, if even a few hundred of those priests had spoken out or, more important, taken action against the war on religious grounds. As Ketelaar has observed: "[Buddhism] was indeed one, if not the only, organization capable of offering effective resistance to state policy."[18] Large-scale resistance, of course, never occurred, but those few Buddhists who did oppose Japan's war policies demonstrated that resistance was possible if one were prepared to pay the price. Each and every Japanese Buddhist did have a choice to make.

CHAPTER SEVEN:

THE EMERGENCE OF IMPERIAL-WAY BUDDHISM

The personal and institutional choices of Japan's Budhist leaders toward their country's expansionist policies had been made long before the 1930s, reaching at least as far back as the Russo-Japanese War. What happened next may be considered the logical extension, if not the logical conclusion, of these previous decisions. The emergence of imperial-way Buddhism (*kōdō Bukkyō*) in the 1930s was not so much a new phenomenon as it was the systematization or codification of previous positions. Stated in Buddhist terms, imperial-way Buddhism represented the total and unequivocal subjugation of the Law of the Buddha to the Law of the Sovereign. In political terms, it meant subjugation of institutional Buddhism to the state and its policies.

BUDDHISM AND THE IMPERIAL STATE

In Japan of the 1930s the state was represented by the person of the emperor. In theory, the government did nothing which did not enjoy his support and consent. Whether or not this was true has long been a subject of scholarly debate. Interesting as that debate is, it is not relevant here. Our concern is how institutional Buddhism's leaders understood the emperor system from a doctrinal standpoint, not the question of the emperor's actual political power.

Saeki Jōin One of the clearest expressions of this understanding is contained in a book entitled *Nation-Protecting Buddhism (Gokoku Bukkyō)*. This book, published by the Ōkura Research Institute for Spiritual Culture

(Ōkura Seishin Kenkyūjo) in January 1938, consists of a number of essays written by institutional Buddhist leaders and scholars. Among the contributors was Saeki Jōin (1867–1952), a Hossō sect priest and chief abbot of Hōryūji, one of Japan's oldest and most famous temples. His essay was entitled, "Japanese Buddhism and the Concept of the National Polity" (Nihon Bukkyō to Kokutai Kannen).[1]

Jōin began his essay with a laudatory description of the many and varied contributions that Japan's emperors had made over the centuries to the development of the nation and society. In particular, Prince Regent Shōtoku (573–621), a major figure in the establishment of Buddhism in Japan, came in for special praise. Prince Shōtoku "should be considered the model for creating a new culture in today's Shōwa period [1926–89], for without his ideals neither the betterment of society nor its purification can be accomplished."[2]

Building on the idea of Prince Shōtoku as a model for the Japanese society of his day, Jōin went on to quote from the Seventeen Article Constitution that has traditionally been ascribed to Shōtoku. Article Three stated, "If you receive an imperial edict you must revere it, for the ruler is heaven and the people are the earth." From this Jōin concluded: "The emperor, being holy and divine, is inviolable.... The emperor's edicts, being holy and divine, are inviolable ... and they must always be revered.[3] While there doesn't seem to be a connection to Buddhism in the above, Jōin was convinced there was. He wrote:

> As expressed in the Lotus Sutra, the Buddha in his compassion regards [beings in] the three worlds [of desire, form, and formlessness] as members of his family. That is to say, he doesn't think of his family as composed of just his blood relatives, or only the few members of his immediate family, or simply those in his local area.
>
> No, his family includes everyone in the whole world, in the entire universe. For him, everyone in the world is a member of his family. In fact, he does not limit his family members to human beings alone. Even animals and all living things are included. . . . There is nothing that the Tathagata [fully enlightened being] in his great compassion does not wish to save. . . . There is no one who he does not consider to be his child. . . . When this faith in the great compassion and mercy of the Tathagata is applied to the political world, there is not a single member of the Japanese nation who is not a child of the emperor. . . . This expresses in the political realm the ideal of a system centered on the emperor.[4]

Fukuda Gyōei Jōin was not the only contributor to *Nation-Protecting Buddhism* to identify Buddhism with the emperor. A second essay was entitled: "The Tendai Sect of Japan and Pacifying and Preserving the State" *(Nihon Tendai to Chingo Kokka)*. It was written by Fukuda Gyōei (1889–1971), a Tendai priest and former president of Taishō University, one of Japan's oldest Buddhist universities. This university was affiliated in a unique configuration with three separate sects—Jōdo, Shingon, and Tendai.

Gyōei began his essay by noting that it was in Japan where "pure Mahayana [Buddhism]" was to be found.[5] This was so, according to him, because Saichō (767–822), the eighth-century founder of the Tendai sect in Japan, took it as an article of faith that "all Japanese had the disposition of bodhisattvas."[6] As bodhisattvas they were both treasures and benefactors of the nation.

Gyōei was quick to point out that Buddhism in Japan was not simply Indian or Chinese Buddhism transplanted. Rather, the Tendai sect in particular had been established "based on a deep understanding of the Japanese national character . . . as a religion to pacify and preserve the nation."[7] This had all been made possible through the "gracious wish" of successive Japanese emperors.

Shiio Benkyō *Nation-Protecting Buddhism* contained one more seminal essay, which is the most complete exposition of imperial-way Buddhism extant. It was written by Dr. Shiio Benkyō (1876–1971), a Jōdo sect priest who later became president of Taishō University. He entitled his one-hundred thirty-two-page essay simply "Imperial-way Buddhism."

Benkyō began his essay with a discussion of the life and teachings of Buddha Shakyamuni. He then went on to declare that as far as contemporary Buddhism was concerned, the limited amount of Buddhism left in India was a "failure," as was that in China. "On the contrary," he wrote, "it can be said that it is in Japan where it is possible to draw near to a Buddhism like that of the time when Buddha Shakyamuni was alive."[8]

In explaining the purity of Japanese Buddhism, Benkyō also went back to Prince Shōtoku, for whom "building one great Sangha in this land was of the greatest importance."[9] Shōtoku was motivated to do this because he viewed the Sangha as "a great harmonious body."[10] Later founders of Japanese Buddhist sects, including Hōnen (1133–1212), Nichiren (1222–82), and Eisai (1141–1215) were, despite their sectarian differences, united in the belief that the Sangha was "synonymous with the state."[11]

The third section of Benkyō's essay was entitled "The Superior National Character of Japan" *(Takuetsu seru Nihon no Kunigara)*. As the title suggests,

Benkyō continued to develop his theme of the superiority of Japanese Buddhism over that found in other Asian countries.

> Buddhism in India collapsed due to [the nature of] Indian culture. Buddhism in China collapsed because it ran directly contrary to the history and nature of the Chinese state, and was therefore only able to produce a few mountain temples. On the other hand, thanks to the rich cultivation Japanese Buddhism received on Japanese soil, it gradually developed into that which the Buddhist teaching was aiming toward.[12]

Why and how had this all come about? Benkyō's answer was as follows:

> The priceless customs and manners of our country are the fundamental reasons for this occurrence. These customs and manners are to be found throughout the land, but their heart lies with the emperor and the imperial household, through whose efforts they have been guided and fostered.[13]

In the following, fourth section of the essay, Benkyō came at last to a definition of imperial-way Buddhism:

> The reason that Buddhism was able to develop in Japan was completely due to the imperial household, especially to the fact that each of the successive emperors personally believed in and guided Buddhism so that it could accomplish its task. Although it is true that Japanese Buddhism has developed through the power of devotion of illustrious priests and lay persons, the fact that such persons were able to believe and practice their faith was due to the imperial household and emperors who fostered its development through the continual issuance of imperial edicts and their own personal example. This is something that cannot be seen in other countries. It is for this reason it ought to be called imperial-way Buddhism.[14]

For Benkyō the fundamental historical characteristic of Japanese Buddhism was its "nationalism" *(kokkateki)*. Since the emperor was the state, and Buddhism and the state were one, then the emperor and Buddhism were also one. Benkyō described the nature of the imperial household as follows:

Within the imperial household lives the great life of the universe. Within this true life lives true [religious] faith, and within true faith is the power to detect the path of true faith. Those who truly seek righteousness will find righteousness. Within our imperial household can be found the truest of true righteousness which is itself the righteousness of the universe . . . which is the truth-seeking power of the universe. . . . Or said in a different way, if one seeks the location of this enduring imperial power, that is, the location of the spirit of Japan, it is found in the imperial household.[15]

Benkyō went on to explain that it was the imperial edicts which gave expression to true righteousness. The imperial edicts also gave expression to the spirit of Japan. He continued:

Thus, the imperial edicts are the national polity. They are the life of the nation. If issued, these edicts must be revered. . . . In looking at the past we see that imperial edicts from successive emperors taught us the proper way to make offerings of even a single flower [to the Buddha], or offer even one stick of incense, or read the sutras with the correct pronunciation, or worship in the Buddha Hall. The power to select and protect each of the sects, to determine each and every temple observance—all have their roots in imperial edicts. Japanese Buddhism acts on the basis of imperial edicts. This is what distinguishes it from the Buddhism of foreign countries.[16]

Benkyō concluded his essay by describing what the true purpose of imperial-way Buddhism was. He did this by first noting that during the Meiji period there were a number of "august edicts" issued by the emperor. At that time, he noted: "The power of the people to revere these edicts without question was very strong."[17] The problem was that with the passing of Emperor Meiji there had been a gradual decrease in the people's ability to properly revere the edicts of the emperors who followed, especially those of the current emperor, Hirohito. The people had become "very lax" and "careless" in their attitudes.

Imperial-way Buddhism, then, was designed to address these alleged deficiencies in the national character:

The Buddha Dharma is nothing other than modestly doing one's duty while upholding righteousness. This is the meaning of the

Buddha Dharma that successive emperors have taught. Seen in this light, it must be admitted that during the Taishō [1912–26] and Shōwa [1926–89] periods, the people have been careless in their unquestioning reverence of imperial edicts. This means that they have also been careless in their attitude toward the national polity. This is the reason that Japanese Buddhism must rise to the occasion.

When we think about this situation, we recognize that it was truly due to the power of the imperial household that Japanese Buddhism in the past was able to expand. Not only that, I believe that it will only be possible for Buddhism to accomplish its task in the future if we take the lead in obeying the will of the imperial household, thereby guarding and maintaining the prosperity of the imperial Throne evermore. To venerate the Three Treasures [of Buddhism] means to revere imperial edicts without question. This is the attitude we should have as we reflect deeply on the reality before us.[18]

In identifying veneration of the Three Treasures with unquestioning obedience to imperial edicts, Shiio's imperial-way Buddhism represents the most intimate connection of Buddhism and the imperial state conceivable.

Nichiren Sect Imperial-way Buddhism quickly evolved into a broad-based, pan-Buddhist movement. For example, in April 1938, only three months after the publication of *Nation-Protecting Buddhism,* a number of leading clerics in the Nichiren sect formed the "The Association for the Practice of Imperial-Way Buddhism" (Kōdō Bukkyō Gyōdō Kai). The association was led by the administrative head of the sect, Takasa Nichikō and claimed to have more than eighteen hundred members nationwide.[19]

The association's principles asserted that:

Imperial-way Buddhism utilizes the exquisite truth of the Lotus Sutra to reveal the majestic essence of the national polity. Exalting the true spirit of Mahayana Buddhism is a teaching which reverently supports the emperor's work. This is what the great founder of our sect, Saint Nichiren, meant when he referred to the divine unity of Sovereign and Buddha. . . . That is to say, imperial-way Buddhism is the condensed expression of the divine unity of Sovereign and Buddha ... put into contemporary language. For this reason the principle image of adoration in imperial-way Buddhism is not Buddha Shakyamuni who appeared in India, but his majesty, the emperor, whose lineage extends over ten thousand generations.[20]

Shin Sect While it took the Shin sect a little longer to formally join the imperial-way Buddhist movement, it did so as early as June 1942, when the Nishi Honganji branch distributed a pamphlet entitled "A Unitary View of the Debt of Gratitude [Owed to the Emperor]—The Essence of Imperial-Way Buddhism" *(On Ichigen Ron: Kōdō Bukkyō no Shinzui)*. This pamphlet included the following:

> The Shin sect . . . takes the Law of the Sovereign as its basis, teaching to reverently and faithfully follow imperial commands without question. Therefore, should there be any who commit high treason, Amida would also exclude them from salvation. In the Shin sect there can be no teaching that does not advocate submission to the imperial national polity. That is to say, it is because one is anchored in Amida's salvation that it is possible to be a good imperial subject. Without question, it is the Shin sect that is in accord with the imperial national polity.[21]

In March of the following year, the Higashi Honganji branch also chose to participate in this movement. The occasion was the meeting of the branch's Twenty-Fourth General Assembly. The branch's organ, *Shinshū*, trumpeted the following headline about the assembly: "The Imperial Way Shin Sect Establishes the Path for Public Service."

For the Higashi Honganji branch, the term "imperial-way Shin sect" meant the absolute recognition of the power and authority of the emperor. It must be stressed, however, that there was nothing fundamentally new in this development. The contemporary Shin scholar, Daitō Satoshi, recognized this when he wrote:

> During the fifteen years of war [1931–45] the content, the actual activities of the sect, can be said to have been those of the "imperial-way Shin sect." In fact, to be precise, it can be said that the imperial-way Shin sect was only the completion of what had been passed down from the Meiji and Taishō periods.[22]

Daitō's remarks about the Shin sect can be said to apply to institutional Buddhism as a whole, and the activities of the various branches of the Zen sect will be examined in the following chapter. First, however, it is important to ask how institutional Buddhism viewed warfare. No matter how unquestionably one might revere the emperor's edicts, wasn't there a basic conflict between the Buddhist precept prohibiting the taking of life in any form and serving as a soldier in the imperial army or navy?

BUDDHISM AND WAR

Hayashiya and Shimakage It was left to two Zen scholars, both affiliated with the Sōtō Zen sect, to put forth a doctrinal understanding of the relationship between Buddhism and war which was compatible with Japan's national polity, an understanding that enabled institutional Buddhism to directly support Japan's war effort. This was done in a 1937 book written by Komazawa University Professor Hayashiya Tomojirō (1886–1953) with the assistance of Shimakage Chikai (b. 1902). It was entitled simply and appropriately *The Buddhist View of War (Bukkyō no Sensō Kan).*

In the book's preface, Hayashiya lamented the fact that "although recently there has been a great deal of discussion about war in various circles, within Buddhism there has still been but little." He then went on to admit that "Buddhist scriptures contain very little material directly concerning war." Yet, despite this, "I would like to say a little something, basing my views on Buddhist compassion and the need for deliverance from suffering."[23]

On the first page of the text itself, the authors made it clear that the outbreak of full-scale war between Japan and China was the catalyst which had caused them to examine this issue. In particular, they referred to a proclamation of support for Japan's war actions signed by institutional Buddhist leaders from each of the major sects on July 12, 1937. This proclamation, issued by a pan-Buddhist organization known as the Myōwa Kai, read as follows:

> Revering the imperial policy of preserving the Orient, the subjects of imperial Japan bear the humanitarian destiny of one billion people of color. Faced with the outbreak of the incident in northern China, it is a time of deep pain and yet a time to eliminate tyranny. Our imperial government has already issued an earnest appeal aimed at both domestic and foreign audiences. Based on this, the Myōwa Kai, an organization composed of each of the sects

of Buddhism, will work together to resolve this increasingly urgent national emergency. We are prepared to conduct consolation activities on behalf of front-line imperial army troops in the field. Likewise we are willing to cooperate in such other activities as the protection of Japanese nationals [in China]. Furthermore, within the country we are prepared, as part of our self-sacrificial public duty, to work for the spiritual general mobilization of the people. We take this occasion to express the firm resolution of Japanese Buddhists.[24]

The authors note that the preceding statement had a significant effect on Chinese Buddhists, who responded with a number of protest letters. The Myōwa Kai saw no merit to these protests and issued the following statement on July 28, 1937, reaffirming its position. It read in part:

In order to establish eternal peace in East Asia, arousing the great benevolence and compassion of Buddhism, we are sometimes accepting and sometimes forceful. We now have no choice but to exercise the benevolent forcefulness of "killing one in order that many may live" *(issatsu tashō)*. This is something which Mahayana Buddhism approves of only with the greatest of seriousness. . . .
We believe it is time to effect a major change in the course of human history, which has been centered on Caucasians and inequality among humanity. To realize the true happiness of a peaceful humanity and construct a new civilization, it is necessary to redirect the path of world history's advance from this false path to the true path. Rooted in this sublime view of history, the mission and responsibility of Mahayana Buddhists is to bring into being true friendship between Japan and China.[25]

The authors saw in these exchanges an indication of the difference between Chinese and Japanese Buddhists. This difference was described as follows:

In general it can be said that Chinese Buddhists believe that war should absolutely be avoided no matter what the reason. Japanese Buddhists, on the other hand, believe that war conducted for a [good] reason is in accord with the great benevolence and compassion of Buddhism.[26]

The conflict between Japan and China, the authors admitted, was one that had deep historical, even geographic, roots. It also involved the national characters of the two peoples. Fundamentally, however, it was a question of how Buddhism viewed war. The remaining ninety-six pages of their book were devoted to answering this question.

They began by pointing out that Buddhism saw war as being neither inherently good nor bad. This was because according to the Buddhist world view there is nothing, including war, which has its own "self-nature" (jisshō). This lead them to the following conclusion:

> The reason that Buddhism hasn't determined war to be either good or bad is that it doesn't look at the question of war itself but rather to the question of the war's purpose. Thus, if the war has a good purpose it is good, while if it has a bad purpose it is bad. Buddhism doesn't merely approve of wars that are in accord with its values; it vigorously supports such wars to the point of being a war enthusiast.[27]

Having established that war is neither intrinsically good nor evil, the authors went on to develop one of the central themes of their book, that war was a method of accomplishing Buddhist goals. Thus they wrote that "Buddhist war is always war used as a means toward an end. The end is to save sentient beings and guide them properly."[28]

The role of "saving and the guiding" falls to the long-term "protector" of Buddhism in Japan, the emperor. In fact, the authors wrote that the emperor of Japan was actually a "Golden Wheel–Turning Sacred King" (konrin jōō), one of the four manifestations of the ideal Buddhist monarch or cakravartin-raja. "The reason Japanese Buddhism regards the emperor as a Golden Wheel–Turning Sacred King" they wrote, "is because he is the Tathagata [fully enlightened being] of the secular world."[29]

One of the characteristics of a Golden Wheel–Turning Sacred King is that due to a "lack of wisdom of his subjects" he is unable to rule by his virtue alone and must resort to such things as laws, taxes, and, significantly, weapons. The same holds true for his relationships with other countries. When "injustice" and "lawlessness" abound in these countries, he must "grasp the weapons of force."[30]

When the Golden Wheel–Turning Sacred King wields force, however, it is not the force of hatred and anger. Rather, it is the force of compassion, the same force that parents use when, out of love, they strike their children.

That is to say, it is a compassionate act designed to "perfect their children's character and bring them happiness."[31]

The authors did admit that when the Golden Wheel–Turning Sacred King actually employs force it may not appear to be an act of compassion. Nevertheless, because a war conducted by a Golden Wheel–Turning Sacred King is for the purpose of achieving Buddhism's goals, "it can be seen that, from a Buddhist viewpoint, it is working as a force to promote the advancement of society."[32]

Concluding their discussion of the emperor as an ideal Buddhist monarch, the authors argued that Buddhism's protection of life does not mean that life is protected for its own sake. Rather, it is protected merely as one aspect of compassion. Therefore Buddhism does not reject the killing of masses of people that takes place in war, for it sees such warfare as an inevitable part of creating an ever stronger and more sublime compassion.

The theme of war as an act of compassion was a central theme in both *The Buddhist View of War* and the statements of the Myōwa Kai, but it is described in much greater detail in the book. Hayashiya and Shimakage pointed out, first of all, that the critical aspect of a Buddhist-sanctioned war is that "it gives life to the state."[33] While admitting that wars are costly in terms of both money and lives, "the most important question is the clear, steadfast continued existence of the state itself."[34]

When war was necessary to give life to the state, then "the best war possible should be fought without hesitation."[35] In this situation, individual citizens have to recognize that they are "of one body and mind with the state," admitting that "they cannot exist without the state."[36] While it may be true that war destroys individual lives, it is not, the authors claimed, that it offers no good to individuals. This is because Buddhist-sanctioned wars are not aimed solely at the perfection of the state but at the perfection of individuals as well. In fact, "if individuals were perfected, wars would not occur."[37]

The cause of war, the authors asserted, is in the "as yet low levels of wisdom of human beings," and is definitely "not to be found in either the state or the Golden Wheel–Turning King."[38] Thus, when the Golden Wheel–Turning King takes up weapons, he does so for the perfection of the state and the advancement of human beings. It is an expression of his compassion and his desire to save sentient beings. "The reason, then, for fighting a war is not to continue war, but to eliminate war."[39] That is to say, war can be eliminated through the perfection of both the state and the individuals within it.

The fifth subsection of chapter 3 is titled "War Which Also Benefits One's Enemy." It begins with a quotation from a statement made by then Prime Minister Konoe Fumimaro (1891–1945) on the North China Incident of 1937. He had explained that Japan was not an aggressor against China but was "acting cooperatively" with that country. The goal of that cooperation was as follows:

> Japan has no intention of sacrificing China for its own benefit. Rather Japan and China should stand on the basis of mutual equality, mutually helping each other, and thereby contributing to the enhancement of Oriental culture and the prosperity of East Asia. . . . Japan respects the territorial integrity of China and wants nothing more than for people of north China to reflect on their conduct and return to their innate Oriental character just as quickly as possible.[40]

The authors asserted that the prime minister's statements were in full accord with Buddhism. Given this, it was Buddhism's responsibility to ensure that China got "some degree of benefit" out of the war. This concern was in accord with the fact that "Japan was first in the world in understanding the true spirit of Buddhism."[41] As to what benefit China might expect to get out the war with Japan, it would have "its unreasonableness corrected and an opportunity to reflect on its conduct."[42]

Finally, the authors asked how war could be prevented. They responded by stating that the key was understanding the way in which one could be delivered from suffering as taught in the Four Noble Truths of Buddhism. Just as there was suffering at an individual level, so, too, did it exist within society as a whole. The cause of both types of suffering was "defilements" (bonnō), which caused a gap between the ideal and reality. This gap in turn resulted in wrong conduct. Without changing this wrong conduct there was no hope of eliminating suffering.

The problem, of course, was that the situation in China had been caused by that country's failure to understand the Four Noble Truths. Not only that, "[the Chinese] had not the least understanding of the spirit of Buddhism."[43] Consequently, they could not understand that it was "Chinese defilements" which had caused the war. "If only," the authors urged, "they would wake up to this fact, they would realize that in order to eliminate their nation's suffering it is critical that they reform their politics and restore their national strength."[44]

The authors further pointed out that Japan itself had done exactly that. That is to say, its present developed state was due to its having gradually increased its national power "while bearing the almost intolerable insults of the Western countries."[45] Although China should do the same, its people "had no sense of a nation" and "its statesmen only valued greed."[46] In this situation who else was there capable of "saving" China but Japan!

Although the authors did not make the previous statement, it was clearly implied in the last section of their book. The last paragraph of this section (and the book) expresses the essence of their message:

Were the level of wisdom of the world's peoples to increase, the causes of war would disappear and wars cease. However, in an age when the situation is such that it is impossible for humanity to stop wars, there is no choice but to wage compassionate wars which give life to both oneself and one's enemy. Through a compassionate war, the warring nations are able to improve themselves, and war is able to exterminate itself.[47]

In the meantime, of course, Japan would continue and constantly escalate its "war of compassion" against China, all the while enjoying the total backing and full cooperation of institutional Buddhism's leaders. It was, after all, their religious duty as Asia's most advanced Buddhists.

Furukawa Taigo Another book published in 1937 also contained a lengthy discussion of the relationship of Buddhism and war. Entitled *Rapidly Advancing Japan and the New Mahayana Buddhism (Yakushin Nihon to Shin Daijō Bukkyō)*, it was written by Furukawa Taigo, a prolific writer on Buddhist-related topics who had also made numerous appearances on the radio.

In the preface of his book, Furukawa described himself as having been involved in Buddhist educational efforts for more than thirty years, but more recently he had been "occupied with providing spiritual education for the imperial army's officer training program."[48] His goal in doing so, he wrote, "was to modify Buddhism, the greatest leader of the nation's thought, from its passive Indian-style attitude to an aggressive Japanese-style attitude."[49]

Furukawa's book is in many ways an expanded version of *The Buddhist View of War*, though in some respects it is even more extreme. For example, according to Furukawa, Japan was not simply the most advanced Buddhist country in Asia, it was "the only Buddhist country."[50] Furthermore, referring to the North China Incident, he stated that Japan was "presently using the sword in Manchuria to build a second divine country [after Japan], just as it would go on to do in China and India." This meant that it would be possible for Japan, as a divine nation, "to transform the world into a pure Buddha Land as spoken of in Buddhism."[51]

Furukawa made the following appeal to his fellow believers:

> All Buddhists in the country! Resolutely arise and participate in this rarest of holy enterprises. What difference does it make what the League of Nations does? Just who do England and the United States think they are anyway? The arrow has already left the bow. Do not hesitate in the least. A firm will makes even demons run away. The only thing is to push on resolutely.[52]

Furukawa devoted the second chapter of his book to the relationship of Buddhism to war. Although he, too, found Buddhist participation in warfare entirely fit and proper, he did recognize that "early Buddhism" (genshi Bukkyō) had not held that position. According to Furukawa, as society gradually became more complicated and the number of Buddhist believers increased, the need to preserve the Dharma, by force if necessary, was recognized. Furukawa asserted that it had been Buddhists affiliated with the Mahayana, as opposed to the Hinayana school, who had first sanctioned killing in order to preserve the true Dharma. Mahayana Buddhists knew, he claimed, that:

> Strict observance of the precept against killing at any time and at any place was absolutely impossible. Similarly, it was utterly absurd to disavow the use of deadly force under all conditions, for to do so would mean that human society could not be maintained for so much as a day.[53]

Building on the above, Furukawa asserted that Buddhism clearly recognizes a just war. Applying this to the situation at hand, he wrote:

> Looking at the war in Manchuria from the point of view of a believer in Buddhism, it can be approved of as a just war. Anyone discussing this war who is a Japanese would agree. That is to say, no one could fail to see that this is a fight to defend Japan's legitimate rights and interests. . . . Given that our actions toward China

are legitimate, it is not only we who benefit from what we do, but the whole Orient, nay, the whole world. Beyond that, China ought to benefit as well.[54]

In recognizing that early Buddhism was originally pacifist in nature but abandoned this position with the emergence of both a complicated society and the Mahayana school of Buddhism, Furukawa adopted a somewhat different stance than had the authors of *The Buddhist View of War*. Nevertheless, his conclusions were almost indistinguishable from theirs. Their shared assertion that Japan had gone to war "for the benefit of China" has to be the most amazing of all their conclusions.

The Buddhist View of War and *Rapidly Advancing Japan and the New Mahayana Buddhism* were, like the imperial-way Buddhism movement of which they were a part, pan-Buddhist in their orientation. At the same time, the individual sects of Japanese Buddhism continued their sectarian activities in support of Japan's war effort. Each sect employed its sect-sponsored newspapers, magazines, and evangelistic materials to mobilize its adherents behind the war. Two examples will suffice to illuminate these sectarian activities.

In July 1938, following the government-sponsored order for "national spiritual mobilization" *(kokumin seishin sōdōin)*, the Chief Abbot of Eiheiji, Sōtō Zen master Hata Eshō (1862–1944), wrote the following in the introduction to an article which appeared in the Buddhist magazine *Daihōrin*:

Buddha Shakyamuni, during his religious practice in a former life, participated in a just war. Due to the merit he acquired as a result, he was able to appear in this world as a Buddha. Thus, it can be said that a just war is one task of Buddhism. Likewise, achieving the capitulation of the enemy country may also be counted as the religious practice of a Buddhist. . . . I believe the brilliant fruits of battle that have been achieved to date are the result of the power of the people's religious faith [in Buddhism].[55]

In 1942, the Tendai sect issued a ninety-six-page pamphlet entitled "Evangelism Materials" *(Fukyō Shiryō)*. Its preface read in part:

The Greater East Asian War has entered another year. We reverently celebrate the majestic appearance of the invincible imperial military. It is in these circumstances that we hereby publish a second volume of evangelization materials for use as teaching texts by interested parties. . . .

In so doing it is our intention to clarify the principles concerned with the new age and Buddhism which is the essence of the national spirit. We will be very happy if these materials are employed to spread the spirit of dying for one's country in order to protect the state, save the world, and benefit people.[56]

As these and countless other materials from all of Japan's major sects reveal, institutional Buddhism had wedded itself to the state and the emperor system. Institutional Buddhist leaders refused to recognize the possibility of there being so much as the slightest contradiction between the doctrines of their faith and Japan's war effort.

CHAPTER EIGHT:

The Emergence of Imperial-State Zen and Soldier Zen

The involvement of Japan's two major Zen sects, Rinzai and Sōtō, in their country's war effort was not an isolated phenomenon but part of the overall relationship between institutional Buddhism and the Japanese state. It is important to be aware of this because, as Robert Sharf has noted, from the late nineteenth century onward, proponents of Japanese Zen had promoted it not merely as one school of Buddhism but as "the very heart of Asian spirituality, the essence of Japanese culture, and the key to the unique qualities of the Japanese race."[1]

A parallel development during this period was the tendency to explain Japan's string of Asian military victories as stemming from the allegedly ancient code of Bushido, the Way of the Warrior. Zen spokesmen identified Bushido as the very essence of Japaneseness. If both Zen and Bushido comprised the essence of Japanese culture, the question naturally arises as to the relationship between these two seemingly disparate phenomena.

The answer to this question is the key to understanding the eventual emergence of "imperial-state Zen" *(kōkoku Zen)*. A complete investigation of the relationship between Zen and Bushido is both beyond the scope of this book and unnecessary. The important question for our discussion is not the actual historical relationship so much as how Zen adherents from the Meiji period onward perceived and interpreted it. In other words, what did post-Meiji Zen adherents find in the relationship between Zen and Bushido that justified their own fervent support of Japan's war effort?

We have seen that the Meiji-period connection between Zen and martial prowess became pronounced as early as the Russo-Japanese War, thanks to such personages as Rinzai Zen masters Shaku Sōen and Nantembō, as well as the latter's famous student, General Nogi Maresuke. A full explication of the symbiotic relationship alleged to exist between Zen and Bushido comes, however, from a rather surprising source.

Nitobe Inazō That source was a book written in English by Dr. Nitobe Inazō (1862–1933) entitled *Bushido: The Soul of Japan* and published in 1905. The surprising thing about this book is that it was written not by a Buddhist but a Christian, for Dr. Nitobe identified himself as such in the preface. Nevertheless, he stated that he had chosen to act as a "personal defendant" of the creed "I was taught and told in my youthful days, when feudalism was still in force."[2]

In chapter 2, "Sources of Bushido," Nitobe clarified the relationship between Bushido and Zen as follows:

> I may begin with Buddhism. It furnished a sense of calm trust in Fate, a quiet submission to the inevitable, that stoic composure in sight of danger or calamity, that disdain of life and friendliness with death. A foremost teacher of swordsmanship, when he saw his pupil master the utmost of his art, told him, "Beyond this my instruction must give way to Zen teaching."[3]

Nitobe offered little detailed explanation of Zen teaching, but he did write that:

> [Zen's] method is contemplation, and its purport, so far as I understand it, [is] to be convinced of a principle that underlies all phenomena, and, if it can, of the Absolute itself, and thus to put oneself in harmony with this Absolute. Thus defined, the teaching was more than the dogma of a sect, and whoever attains to the perception of the Absolute rises above mundane things and awakes "to a new Heaven and a new Earth."[4]

Although Nitobe's discussion of Zen was limited, he was far more forthcoming in his description of Bushido's role in modern Japan: "Bushido, the maker and product of Old Japan, is still the guiding principle of the transition, and will prove the formative force of the new era."[5] When Nitobe sought proof of Bushido's ongoing influence on modern Japan, he found it in none other than the Sino-Japanese war:

> The physical endurance, fortitude, and bravery that "the little Jap" possesses, were sufficiently proved in the Chino[Sino]-Japanese war. "Is there any nation more loyal and patriotic?" is a question asked by many; and for the proud answer, "There is not," we must thank the Precepts of Knighthood [i.e. Bushido]. . . .
>
> What won the battles on the Yalu, in Corea and Manchuria, were the ghosts of our fathers, guiding our hands and beating our hearts. They are not dead, those ghosts, the spirits of our warlike ancestors. To those who have eyes to see, they are clearly visible.[6]

What, then, of the future? Nitobe devoted the last chapter of his book to that very question. On the one hand, he acknowledged that without feudalism, its mother institution, Bushido had been left an orphan. He then suggested that while Japan's modern military might take it under its wing, "we know that modern warfare can afford little room for its continuous growth."[7] Would Bushido, then, eventually disappear?

It should come as no surprise to learn that Nitobe didn't believe Bushido was slated for extinction. On the contrary, in the concluding paragraph of his book, he saw it as still "bless[ing] mankind" with "odours . . . floating in the air." His book concludes:

> Bushido as an independent code of ethics may vanish, but its power will not perish from the earth; its schools of martial prowess or civic honour may be demolished, but its light and its glory will long survive their ruins. Like its symbolic flower, after it is blown to the four winds, it will still bless mankind with the perfume with which it will enrich life.
>
> Ages after, when its customaries will have been buried and its very name forgotten, its odours will come floating in the air as from a far-off, unseen hill, "the wayside gaze beyond"; —then in the beautiful language of the Quaker poet,
> "The traveller owns the grateful sense
> Of sweetness near, he knows not whence,
> And, pausing, takes with forehead bare
> The benediction of the air."[8]

The proponents of imperial-way Buddhism had been able to put forth the remarkable proposition that the Japanese invasion of China was for that country's benefit. Nitobe's intellectual gymnastics here, tying the code of the Japanese warrior to the poetry of a pacifist Quaker, are no less remarkable.

Nukariya Kaiten Nukariya Kaiten, the Sōtō Zen priest and scholar who wrote *The Religion of the Samurai* while lecturing at Harvard University in 1913, only eight years after Nitobe published *Bushido*, was introduced in chapter 5. In his book he maintained that:

> Bushido . . . should be observed not only by Japan's soldiers on the battlefield, but by every citizen in the struggle for existence. If a person be a person and not a beast, then he must be a samurai—brave, generous, upright, faithful, and manly, full of self-respect and self-confidence, and at the same time full of the spirit of self-sacrifice.[9]

Kaiten may be said to have anticipated the future use of Bushido in two important respects. The first is that in Japan after the Meiji Restoration, every citizen was expected to adopt the code of the warrior, in what may be regarded as preparation for the militarization of Japanese society as a whole. Second, for all the admonitions to be "generous, upright, faithful," and so forth, "the spirit of self-sacrifice" would come over time, especially after 1937, to be proclaimed the essential element of Bushido.

Shaku Sōen Shaku Sōen, too, continued speaking out on what he believed Zen could and should contribute to the nation's advancement. In this context, he joined the discussion of Bushido's modern significance in a book entitled *A Fine Person, A Fine Horse (Kaijin Kaiba)*, published in 1919. The date is significant in that World War I had only just ended. Once again, war had become the pretext for a discussion of Zen's contribution to Japan's military prowess.

In Japan's fight against Germany, Sōen lamented what he saw as the Japanese people's increasing "materialism," "extreme worship of money," and general decadence. In his mind the solution was clear: "the unification of all the people in the nation in the spirit of Bushido." For Sōen, as for Kaiten, the essence of this code was found "in a sacrificial spirit consisting of deep loyalty [to the emperor and the state] coupled with deep filial piety."[10]

Where does Zen fit into the picture? Sōen's answer was as follows:

> The power that comes from Zen training can be called forth to become military power, good government, and the like. In fact, it can be applied to every endeavor. The reason that Bushido has developed so greatly since the Kamakura period is due to Zen, the essence of Buddhism. It was the participation of the Way of Zen which, I believe it can be said, gave to Bushido its great power.[11]

The belief that the power resulting from Zen training could be converted into military power was to become an ever more important part of the Zen contribution to Japan's war effort. In fact, as will be seen in the following section, it was the basic assumption underlying the emergence of imperial-state Zen. This said, it is equally important to understand that for Sōen, the modern role of Bushido, empowered as it was by Zen, was not limited to military action. He emphasized this point yet again when he stated:

> Today, my sixty million compatriots are in the maelstrom of a world war. It can be said that not only military men, but also industrialists, politicians, and the general populace are all equipped with a Bushido-like virile and intrepid spirit. As I look toward to the future economic war, however, I cannot help having some doubts as to whether . . . there will be persons who can accomplish wonderfully marvelous deeds.[12]

For Sōen, then, not only was Bushido valuable for all segments of society, starting with the military, but it was also equally valuable in Japan's coming "economic wars."

Fueoka Seisen The discussion of the relationship between Zen and Bushido was not limited to scholarly works on Zen or the writings of a few nationalistic Zen masters. On the contrary, it was to be found in even the simplest of introductory books on Zen. *A Zen Primer (Zen no Tebiki)*, published in 1927 by Fueoka Seisen, is an example of such a work. Seisen focused on historical incidents in which he found a connection between Zen and Bushido. Seisen began his discussion of these incidents with the following observation:

> Zen was introduced into Japan at the beginning of the Kamakura period, at a time when Bushido had risen to power. The simple and

direct teachings of Zen coincided with the straightforward and res-
olute spirit of samurai discipline. In particular, the Zen teaching on
life and death was strikingly clear and thorough. Because samurai
stood on the edge between life and death, this teaching was very
appropriate for their training. They very quickly came to revere and
have faith in it.[13]

One of the first incidents Seisen introduced was to become probably
the most often cited example of the historical connection between Zen and
the warrior spirit. It is an exchange between a Chinese Zen master known
in Japan as Sogen (Ch. Ziyuan, 1226–86) and his lay disciple, Hōjō Tokimune
(1251–84), Japan's military ruler. Tokimune was faced with a series of Mongolian invasions that extended over nearly two decades. Seisen recorded the
following exchange between Tokimune and Sogen, which supposedly took
place after they had heard the news that the Mongolian invaders were sea-
borne and on their way to attack Japan:

> "The great event has come." said Tokimune.
> "How will you face it?" asked Sogen.
> "*Katsu!*" shouted Tokimune.
> "Truly a lion's child roars like a lion. Rush ahead and never turn
>   back!" replied Sogen.[14]

If this exchange marked the first incident in Japan of the linkage of Zen
training to mental military preparedness, it also marked, in Seisen's view,
"the enhancement of national glory." Martial incidents of this nature revealed that "the spirits of Japan's many heroes have been trained by Zen,"
and that "Zen and the sword were one and the same."[15]

Seisen wanted to make sure his readers understood that the Zen spirit
which infused Bushido was, in fact, very relevant to the Japan of their day:

> Zen enlightenment is not a question of ability, but of power. It is
> not something acquired through experience, but is the power that
> immediately gushes to the surface from one's original nature, from
> one's original form. . . . This power can be utilized by persons in all
> fields, including those in the military, industrialists, government
> ministers, educators, artists, farmers, and others. It underlies all of
> these pursuits.[16]

Everyone in contemporary Japan could utilize the power of Zen, just as everyone could benefit from its "strikingly clear and thorough teaching on life and death."

Following the Manchurian Incident of September 1931 and the establishment of the Japanese puppet state of Manchukuo the following year, Japan entered a period of ever-increasing military activity on the Asian continent, first and foremost in China. Under these circumstances, the need to further strengthen the bonds between Zen, Bushido, and the state became ever more pronounced. One of the first to respond to this need was Sōtō Zen master Iida Tōin.

Iida Tōin　Given Tōin's previously noted praise for General Nogi, it is hardly surprising to find that he devoted an entire chapter of his 1934 book *Random Comments on Zen Practice (Sanzen Manroku)* to what he called "warrior Zen" *(bujin Zen)*. The titles of its subsections give a good sense of what this chapter was about: "Zen and Bushido," "What is the Spirit of Japan?" "The Essence of the Japanese People," and "The Flower of Loyalty." Tōin insisted that the concepts underlying all of these were "unique to Japan" and "beyond the ability of foreigners to understand."

Tōin summarized his argument in the final section of this chapter, which was entitled "The Perfection of Warrior Zen." The highlights of this section are as follows:

> There is truly no end to the numbers of warriors who from ancient times practiced Zen, and it is important to recognize how much power it gave to Bushido. The fact that of late the Zen sect is popular among military men is truly a matter for rejoicing. No matter how much we might practice zazen, if it had no application to today's situation, it would be better not to do it. Are you, at this moment, prepared to die or not? Can you laugh and find eternal peace? Can you face danger without being disturbed? Do you have the great courage required to sacrifice your personal affections for a just cause?
>
> I call on you to wake from your sleep. I call on you to discard your desire for fame and fortune. Without Zen people could not exist. Without people the nation could not exist. Would you put the nation at risk in order to seek fame and fortune for yourself? If you cannot bear to forgo this, what can you bear to forgo? Zen is the general repository for Buddhism. Is not the goal of our practice

to save others before we save ourselves? . . . The nobility of spirit expressed in the willingness to sacrifice one's life seven times over to repay the debt of gratitude owed the sovereign is purer than the purest snow. Is not sincerity the true essence of the Japanese spirit?

Death is not the end of everything. A basic principle of the universe is that energy does not dissipate and matter is preserved. Those [leaders] who have great strength will ensure the survival of the many. We must take this matter to heart.

Warrior Zen requires no more than to become a warrior. In both the present and the future, and beyond, it is sufficient to be a warrior. To be lionhearted, plunging forward and never retreating—this is the perfection of warrior Zen.[17]

Tōin was a disciple and eventual Dharma successor of Harada Daiun Sōgaku (1870–1961), whose own similar views on this topic will be introduced shortly. If it is possible to transmit the light of the Dharma lamp from master to disciple, perhaps it is also possible to transmit darkness.

Daihōrin *Discussion* By the beginning of 1937 the likelihood of all-out war between Japan and China was growing. As war approached, discussions and writings detailing the connections among Zen, Bushido, and the imperial military increased. One particularly salient discussion took place on January 16, 1937. Sponsored by the major nonsectarian Buddhist magazine *Daihōrin*, the discussion numbered among its participants the prime minister (army general Hayashi Senjurō), another army general, and a navy vice-admiral. In addition, there were lesser-ranking military officers and representatives from both leading academic institutions and the business community.

The purpose of the discussion was "to clarify the direction the people's minds should be heading in light of the present situation." This could only be done, the participants agreed, by looking at "the relationship between Buddhism and the people's spirit."[18] Not surprisingly, the ensuing conversation quickly focused on Zen and the contribution it could make to developing the martial spirit of both those within and without the military. The magazine company's president, Ishihara Shummyō, who was also a Sōtō Zen priest, had this to say:

Zen is very particular about the need not to stop one's mind. As soon as flintstone is struck, a spark bursts forth. There is not even the most momentary lapse of time between these two events. If ordered to face right, one simply faces right as quickly as a flash of lightning. This is proof that one's mind has not stopped.

Zen master Takuan taught . . . that in essence Zen and Bushido were one. He further taught that the essence of the Buddha Dharma was a mind which never stopped. Thus, if one's name were called, for example "Uemon," one should simply answer "Yes," and not stop to consider the reason why one's name was called. . . .

I believe that if one is called upon to die, one should not be the least bit agitated. On the contrary, one should be in a realm where something called "oneself" does not intrude even slightly. Such a realm is no different from that derived from the practice of Zen.[19]

If the preceding statement may be considered indicative of the spirit that Zen could contribute to the imperial military, the following statement by army major Ōkubo Kōichi, another military participant in the discussion, demonstrates what it was the military, for its part, sought to find in Zen. He said:

[The soldier] must become one with with his superior. He must actually become his superior. Similarly, he must become the order he receives. That is to say, his self must disappear. In so doing, when he eventually goes onto the battlefield, he will advance when told to advance. . . . On the other hand, should he believe that he is going to die and act accordingly, he will be unable to fight well. What is necessary, then, is that he be able to act freely and without [mental] hindrance.[20]

Furukawa Taigo If the preceding comments provide a basic conceptual link among selfless Zen, Bushido, and the imperial military, it was left to Furukawa Taigo to present a detailed exposition of the doctrinal relationship among these entities. Furukawa, it will be recalled, was the popular commentator on Buddhism who had written the book *Rapidly Advancing Japan and the New Mahayana Buddhism* in 1937. According to Furukawa, Bushido had eight major characteristics: (1) great value placed on fervent loyalty; (2) a high esteem for military prowess; (3) an abundance of the spirit of self-sacrifice; (4) realism; (5) an emphasis on practice based on self-reliance; (6) an esteem for order and proper decorum; (7) respect for truthfulness and strong ambition; and (8) a life of simplicity.[21]

What, then, was the relationship between the above and Zen doctrine? Furukawa noted six points, which I paraphrase below, though there is considerable repetition and overlap among them.

(1) The doctrine of emptiness is the foundation of all Buddhism. It is, furthermore, the fundamental principle of Zen, providing Zen with its practical orientation. For this reason Zen was able to become the driving force behind the self-sacrificing spirit of Bushido, grounded, as the latter is, on the emptiness of self.

(2) The realistic, this-worldly nature of Zen is based on the teaching that our ordinary world of life and death is identical with Nirvana. Zen takes the position that the ordinary world, just as it is, is the ideal world, and it does not seek salvation in the hereafter. This simple, frank, and optimistic spirit of Zen has enabled it to exert a profound influence on the down-to-earth and patriotic spirit of Japan's warriors.

(3) Within the Mahayana branch of Buddhism, the Zen sect alone has faithfully transmitted the thoroughgoing atheism and self-reliance of early Buddhism. Zen abjures reliance on the assistance of Buddhas or gods. Its goal is to see deeply into one's nature and become a Buddha through the single-minded practice of zazen. Zen thus resonated deeply with the independent, self-reliant, and virile spirit of Japan's warriors.

(4) Zen takes a very practical stance based on its teaching of the transmission of enlightenment from master to disciple. This transmission takes place independent of the sutras and cannot be expressed in words. Having discarded complicated doctrines, Zen maintains that the Buddha Dharma is synonymous with one's dignified appearance and that proper decorum is the essence of the faith. This is identical to the silent practicality of Bushido, which rejects theoretical argument and instead urges the accomplishment of one's duty.

(5) In leading a plain and frugal life, Zen practitioners maintain a tradition dating back to Buddha Shakyamuni and his first disciples. This life style appealed to the straightforward and unsophisticated warrior temperament, further promoting the development of these qualities among the warrior class.

(6) Unlike Zen in India and China, Japanese Zen was able to transcend the subjective, individualistic, and passive attitude toward salvation that it inherited and become an active, dynamic force influencing the entire nation. It thereby became the catalyst for warriors to enter into the realm of selflessness. This, in turn, resulted in self-sacrificial conduct on behalf of their sovereign and their country. It was the imperial household that made all of this

possible, for the emperor was the incarnation of the selfless wisdom of the universe. It can therefore be said that Mahayana Buddhism didn't simply spread to Japan but was actually created there.[22]

Furukawa's final point concerning Bushido was that it was wrong to say that the samurai had disappeared at the time of the Meiji Restoration. On the contrary, all Japanese men became samurai at that time. Up to the Restoration, only members of the samurai class were allowed to carry weapons in order to fulfil their duty to protect their sovereign and the country. Now that duty had passed to all enfranchised citizens, and all Japanese men were now samurai, bound to uphold the code of Bushido.

As previously noted, Furukawa wrote the above in 1937, some ten years after Seisen published *A Zen Primer* and immediately preceding the outbreak of full-scale war with China. At that time all Japanese males were subject to military conscription. This was also a period marked by increasing tension between Japan and the United States and Britain, which, if only to protect their own economic interests in China and throughout Asia, were unwilling to ignore Japanese expansionism.

D. T. Suzuki   It was against this backdrop that D. T. Suzuki once again entered the picture. By this time he had written widely in both English and Japanese and established himself as a scholar of Buddhism in general, and Zen in particular. Suzuki had in fact begun to write about Zen in English as early as 1906, when his essay entitled "The Zen Sect of Buddhism" appeared in the *Journal of the Pali Text Society*. From this very first English-language effort, Suzuki sought to make his readers aware of the connection between Zen and Bushido, and the inspiration the combination of these two had provided Japan's victorious soldiers in the Russo-Japanese War:

> The Lebensanschauung of Bushido is no more nor less than that of Zen. The calmness and even joyfulness of heart at the moment of death which is conspicuously observable in the Japanese, the intrepidity which is generally shown by the Japanese soldiers in the face of an overwhelming enemy; and the fairness of play to an opponent, so strongly taught by Bushido—all these come from the spirit of the Zen training, and not from any such blind, fatalistic conception as is sometimes thought to be a trait peculiar to Orientals.[23]

Despite this early effort, Suzuki did not make his best-known statement on the relationship of Zen and Bushido until 1938, when he published a book in English entitled *Zen Buddhism and Its Influence on Japanese Culture*. This work was later revised and republished in 1959 by Princeton University Press as *Zen and Japanese Culture*. Given the almost universal approval this work has met with over the years in both the United States and Europe, it is somewhat surprising to learn that Suzuki's description of the relationship between Zen and Bushido contained in three of this book's eleven chapters is basically a reiteration and elaboration of everything that had come before.

Suzuki began his description of the relationship between Zen and Bushido in the book's second chapter. He described the "rugged virility" of Japan's warriors versus the "grace and refinement" of Japan's aristocracy. He then stated: "The soldierly quality, with its mysticism and aloofness from worldly affairs, appeals to the will-power. Zen in this respect walks hand in hand with the spirit of Bushido ("Warriors' Way")."[24] On the one hand, Suzuki claimed that "Buddhism . . . in its varied history has never been found engaged in warlike activities." Yet in Japan, Zen had "passively sustained" Japan's warriors both morally and philosophically. They were sustained morally because "Zen is a religion which teaches us not to look backward once the course is decided." Philosophically, they were sustained because "[Zen] treats life and death indifferently."[25]

Suzuki was clearly taken with the idea of Zen as "a religion of the will."[26] Over and over again he returned to this theme. For example: "A good fighter is generally an ascetic or stoic, which means he has an iron will. This, when needed, Zen can supply."[27] Less than a page later, Suzuki went on to say: "Zen is a religion of will-power, and will-power is what is urgently needed by the warriors, though it ought to be enlightened by intuition."[28]

Together with his fascination with the relationship of Zen and will-power, Suzuki is attracted to the relationship between Zen discipline and the warrior:

> Zen discipline is simple, direct, self-reliant, self-denying; its ascetic tendency goes well with the fighting spirit. The fighter is to be always single-minded with one object in view, to fight, looking neither backward nor sideways. To go straight forward in order to crush the enemy is all that is necessary for him.[29]

Although Suzuki first maintained that it was the Zen philosophy of "treat[ing] life and death indifferently" which had sustained Japan's warriors, he then went on to deny that Zen had any philosophy at all. He wrote:

Zen has no special doctrine or philosophy, no set of concepts or intellectual formulas, except that it tries to release one from the bondage of birth and death, by means of certain intuitive modes of understanding peculiar to itself. It is, therefore, extremely flexible in adapting itself to almost any philosophy and moral doctrine as long as its intuitive teaching is not interfered with. It may be found wedded to anarchism or fascism, communism or democracy, atheism or idealism, or any political or economic dogmatism. It is, however, generally animated with a certain revolutionary spirit, and when things come to a deadlock—as they do when we are overloaded with conventionalism, formalism, and other cognate isms — Zen asserts itself and proves to be a destructive force.[30]

Suzuki's statement that Zen could be found wedded to anarchism or communism is a fascinating comment, since Uchiyama Gudō and his fellow Buddhist priests had earlier attempted to accomplish something very much like that. For their efforts, of course, they were condemned by the leaders of the Sōtō and Rinzai Zen sects and the leaders of all other sects of Japanese Buddhism.

Perhaps what Suzuki was really trying to do in the above statement was justify the close relationship which by 1938 already existed between Zen and the Japanese military. Not only did Suzuki identify Zen as a "destructive force," but he also wrote favorably of the modern relationship among Zen, Bushido, and Japan's military actions in China:

There is a document that was very much talked about in connection with the Japanese military operations in China in the 1930s. It is known as the *Hagakure*, which literally means "Hidden under the Leaves," for it is one of the virtues of the samurai not to display himself, not to blow his horn, but to keep himself away from the public eye and be doing good for his fellow beings. To the compilation of this book, which consists of various notes, anecdotes, moral sayings, etc., a Zen monk had his part to contribute. The work started in the middle part of the seventeenth century under Nabeshima Naoshige, the feudal lord of Saga in the island of Kyūshū. The book emphasizes very much the samurai's readiness to give his life away at any moment, for it states that no great work has ever been accomplished without going mad—that is, when expressed in modern terms, without breaking through the ordinary level of consciousness and letting loose the hidden powers lying further below. These powers may be devilish sometimes, but there is no doubt that they are superhuman and work wonders. When the unconscious is tapped, it rises above individual limitations. Death now loses its sting altogether, and this is where the samurai training joins hands with Zen.[31]

As the following conclusion to the above makes clear, Suzuki was also very concerned with the warrior's (and soldier's) use of Zen to "master death":

The problem of death is a great problem with every one of us; it is, however, more pressing for the samurai, for the soldier, whose life is exclusively devoted to fighting, and fighting means death to fighters of either side. . . . It was therefore natural for every sober-minded samurai to approach Zen with the idea of mastering death.[32]

Another belief which Suzuki shared with his contemporaries was that Bushido was neither dead nor limited to imperial soldiers, the modern equivalent of Japan's traditional warriors:

The spirit of the samurai deeply breathing Zen into itself propagated its philosophy even among the masses. The latter, even when they are not particularly trained in the way of the warrior, have imbibed his spirit and are ready to sacrifice their lives for any cause they think worthy. This has repeatedly been proved in the wars Japan has so far had to go through.[33]

Finally, Suzuki could not avoid addressing the fundamental question of how the death and destruction caused by the samurai's sword could be related to Zen and Buddhist compassion. He therefore addressed two chapters (i.e., "Zen and Swordsmanship I" and "Zen and Swordsmanship II") to this very question. He began his discussion by noting what he considered to be the "double office" of the sword:

The sword has thus a double office to perform: to destroy anything that opposes the will of its owner and to sacrifice all the impulses that arise from the instinct of self-preservation. The one relates itself to the spirit of patriotism or sometimes militarism, while the other has a religious connotation of loyalty and self-sacrifice. In the case of the former, very frequently the sword may mean destruction pure and simple, and then it is the symbol of force, sometimes devilish force. It must, therefore, be controlled and consecrated by the second function. Its conscientious owner is always mindful of this truth. For then destruction is turned against the evil spirit. The sword comes to be identified with the annihilation of things that lie in the way of peace, justice, progress, and humanity.[34]

It is instructive to note here that the tenor of the preceding quote is quite similar to Suzuki's thesis in *A Treatise on the New [Meaning of] Religion* previously discussed. There he said:

The purpose of maintaining soldiers and encouraging the military arts is not to conquer other countries or deprive them of their rights or freedom. . . . The construction of big warships and casting of giant cannon is not to trample on the wealth and profit of others for personal gain. Rather, it is done only to prevent the history of one's country from being disturbed by injustice and outrageousness. Conducting commerce and working to increase production is not for the purpose of building up material wealth in order to subdue other nations. Rather, it is done only in order to develop more and more human knowledge and bring about the perfection of morality. Therefore, if there is a lawless country which comes and obstructs our commerce, or tramples on our rights, this is something that would truly interrupt the progress of all humanity. In the name of religion our country could not submit to this. Thus, we would have no choice but to take up arms, not for the purpose of slaying the enemy, nor for the purpose of pillaging cities, let alone for the purpose of acquiring wealth. Instead, we would simply punish the people of the country representing injustice in order that justice might prevail.[35]

Even more closely related to Suzuki's earlier quote are the sentiments of his master, Shaku Sōen. It will be recalled that at the time of the Russo-Japanese War he said: "In the present hostilities, into which Japan has entered with great reluctance, she pursues no egotistic purpose, but seeks the subjugation of evils hostile to civilization, peace, and enlightenment."[36] In any event, Suzuki's mental gymnastics on this issue did not stop with the above comments. He went on to directly address the seeming contradictions among Zen, the sword, and killing:

> The sword is generally associated with killing, and most of us wonder how it can come into connection with Zen, which is a school of Buddhism teaching the gospel of love and mercy. The fact is that the art of swordsmanship distinguishes between the sword that kills and the sword that gives life. The one that is used by a technician cannot go any further than killing, for he never appeals to the sword unless he intends to kill. The case is altogether different with the one who is compelled to lift the sword. For it is really not he but the sword itself that does the killing. He had no desire to do harm to anybody, but the enemy appears and makes himself a victim. It is as though the sword performs automatically its function of justice, which is the function of mercy. . . . When the sword is expected to play this sort of role in human life, it is no more a weapon of self-defense or an instrument of killing, and the swordsman turns into an artist of the first grade, engaged in producing a work of genuine originality.[37]

Previous commentators, it will be recalled, have identified a Buddhist-sanctioned war as an act of compassion. As the above quotation makes clear, Suzuki agreed with this position. He further spoke with apparent approval of the Zen spirit manifested in Japan's military operations in China. Moreover, he clearly approved of a war "identified with the annihilation of things that lie in the way of peace, justice, progress, and humanity." But perhaps his most creative contribution to the discourse of his day was the assertion that the Zen-trained swordsman (and, by extension, the modern soldier) "turns into an artist of the first grade, engaged in producing a work of genuine originality."

Suzuki was, moreover, not simply interested in making his views on the relationship between Zen and the sword known outside of Japan. Less than one month before Pearl Harbor, on November 10, 1941, he joined hands with such military leaders as former army minister and imperial army general Araki Sadao (1877–1966), imperial navy captain Hirose Yutaka, and others to publish a book entitled *The Essence of Bushido (Bushidō no Shinzui)*. In his foreword, the book's editor, Handa Shin, explained the importance of Bushido: "It is Bushido that is truly the driving force behind the development of our nation. In the future, it must be the fundamental power associated with the great undertaking of developing Asia, the importance of which to world history is increasing day by day."[38] Addressing the reason for publishing the book at that time, Handa said that the book's purpose would be accomplished "if our young men and boys find even a little something enticing in it."[39]

The connection of this book to the goals and purposes of the imperial military was unmistakable. The book's very first entry consisted of the *Field Service Combatants' Code (Senjinkun)*, promulgated on January 8, 1941, by the army minister at the time, Tōjō Hideki (1884–1948). The code, which all imperial army soldiers were required to memorize, had clear religious overtones, including such statements as "faith is power" and "duty is sacred."[40] More important, the seventh section, entitled "View of Life and Death," read as if it had come directly from the hands of Suzuki, Shaku Sōen, and others of similar views:

> That which penetrates life and death is the lofty spirit of self-sacrifice for the public good. Transcending life and death, earnestly rush forward to accomplish your duty. Exhausting the power of your body and mind, calmly find joy in living in eternal duty.[41]

In addition, the book's final entry consisted of the 1932 "Essentials of the Imperial Rescript to Soldiers and Sailors" *(Gunjin Chokuyu Yōgi)*, the original version of which had been promulgated by Emperor Meiji in 1882.

Suzuki's personal contribution, entitled simply "Zen and Bushido," consisted of a fourteen-page distillation of his earlier thought. It did not cover any new intellectual ground. Suzuki's favorite themes were present as always, including his oft-repeated assertion that "The spirit of Bushido is truly to abandon this life, neither bragging of one's achievements, nor complaining when one's talents go unrecognized. It is simply a question of rushing forward toward one's ideal."[42] The book's editor pointed out in his introduction to Suzuki's essay that "Dr. Suzuki's writings are said to have strongly influenced the military spirit of Nazi Germany."[43]

In this connection, it is interesting to note the comments made by the Japanese ambassador to Nazi Germany on September 27, 1940. Following the signing of the Tripartite Pact between Japan, Germany, and Italy, a reception was held in Hitler's chancellory in Berlin. In his congratulatory speech Ambassador Kurusu Saburō (1888–1954) said:

> The pillar of the Spirit of Japan is to be found in Bushido. Although Bushido employs the sword, its essence is not to kill people, but rather to use the sword that gives life to people. Using the spirit of this sword, we wish to contribute to world peace.[44]

Whether by design or accident, Suzuki's sentiments as first expressed in 1938 had, two years later, become government policy or, perhaps more accurately, government rationalization.

Seki Seisetsu   *The Promotion of Bushido (Bushidō no Kōyō)* was published in 1942, the year following Japan's attack on Pearl Harbor. It was a series of talks by Seki Seisetsu (1877–1945), a "fully enlightened" Zen master who served both as the head of the Tenryūji branch of the Rinzai Zen sect and as a military chaplain. A second Rinzai priest, Yamada Mumon (1900–1988), edited this work. After the war, Mumon, Seisetsu's disciple, became president of Hanazono University and chief abbot of the university's ecclesiastical sponsor, the Myōshinji branch of the Rinzai Zen sect.

One of the most striking features of Seisetsu's book is its cover, which depicts the Japanese fairy-tale hero Momotarō. Dressed in samurai clothing, Momotarō stands with his sword pinning down two devils, Winston Churchill and Franklin Roosevelt. This representation is clearly a slightly humorous reflection of the wartime epithet, "the devilish Americans and English" *(kichiku beiei).*

Like so many of his predecessors, Seisetsu began his description of Bushido as "being nothing other than the Spirit of Japan." Zen had contributed its "profound and exquisite enlightenment" to Bushido, leading to the latter's "unique moral system." Thus had Bushido become "the precious jewel incorporating the purity of the spiritual culture of the Orient."[45]

In what was by now a familiar litany, Bushido was said to "prize military prowess and view death as so many goose feathers."[46] Samurai "revered their sovereign and honored their ancestors."[47] They also valued loyalty, frugality, simplicity, decorum, and benevolence. All of these values were identical with those of modern soldiers. Not only that, these values applied equally to "the people of this country who are now all soldiers, for I believe that every citizen ought to adhere to the Bushido of the present age."[48]

In his conclusion Seisetsu argued that the unity of Zen, the sword, and Bushido had only one goal: world peace. He wrote:

The true significance of military power is to transcend self-interest, to hope for peace. This is the ultimate goal of the military arts. Whatever the battle may be, that battle is necessarily fought in anticipation of peace. When one learns the art of cutting people down, it is always done with the goal of not having to cut people down. The true spirit of Bushido is to make people obey without drawing one's sword and to win without fighting. In Zen circles this is called the sword which gives life. Those who possess the sword that kills must, on the other hand, necessarily wield the sword which gives life.

From the Zen vantage point, where Manjushri [the bodhisattva of wisdom] has used his sharp sword to sever all ignorance and desire, there exists no enemy in the world. The very best of Bushido is to learn that there is no enemy in the world rather than to learn to conquer the enemy. Attaining this level, Zen and the sword become completely one, just as the Way of Zen and the Way of the Warrior [Bushido] unite. United in this way, they become the sublime leading spirit of society.

At this moment, we are in the sixth year of the sacred war, having arrived at a critical juncture. All of you should obey imperial mandates, being loyal, brave, faithful, frugal, and virile. You should cultivate yourselves more and more both physically and spiritually in order that you don't bring shame on yourselves as imperial soldiers. You should acquire a bold spirit like the warriors of old, truly doing your duty for the development of East Asia and world peace. I cannot help asking this of you.[49]

To the belief that Zen-sanctioned war was both just and compassionate, benefiting even one's enemy, must now be added the belief that it was all being done "for . . . world peace." Like Shaku Sōen (and many others) before him, Seisetsu also carried his message of peace and the unity of Zen and the sword to the battlefield on more than one occasion. One such visit took place in February 1938, when Seisetsu, accompanied by his disciple Yamada Mumon, made a sympathy call on General Terauchi Hisaichi (1879–1946) at his headquarters in northern China. More will be said about the relationship between Seisetsu and Terauchi in chapter 10.

The reader will recall that one of the chief goals of the so-called New Buddhism of the late Meiji period was to prove its loyalty to the throne. This theme was further developed by the noted Buddhist scholar Yabuki Keiki (1879–1939), who wrote in 1934 that Buddhism had the potential "to become a most effective instrument for the state."[50] In 1943 a Western scholar of Japanese religion, D. C. Holtom, emphasized that "Buddhism fosters the qualities of spirit that make for strong soldiers."[51]

If the preceding statements held true for institutional Buddhism as a whole, it should now be clear that they were particularly relevant to the Zen school. Leading Zen figures made unsurpassed efforts to foster loyalty to the emperor and make spiritually strong soldiers. Did anyone notice? That is to say, was the imperial military actually influenced by their words and actions?

A quantitative answer to this question, it must be admitted, is almost certainly beyond the realm of historical research. How would one accurately determine, more than fifty years after the end of the war, either the extent or depth of such influence? This said, it is important to note that the imperial military, the imperial army in particular, was more than merely receptive to the type of Buddhist support described above. It actively solicited that support.

As previously discussed, the military had cooperated with frontline visits by Buddhist priests like Shaku Sōen as early as the Russo-Japanese War. From that war Japanese military leaders such as General Hayashi Senjūrō had come to realize just how critical spirit was in overcoming a better equipped and numerically superior enemy. In his book *The Way of the Heavenly Sword*, Leonard Humphreys explained it as follows:

> The overriding lesson of the [Russo-Japanese] war appeared to be the decisive role of morale or spirit in combat. Japan's centuries-old samurai tradition had strongly emphasized the importance of the intangible qualities of the human spirit *(seishin)* in warfare, and this war served to reestablish their primacy. Since spirit was the universally acclaimed key to Japan's victory, the leadership tended to emphasize the irrational quality *seishin* and rest content with attained levels in the rational elements of war technology and its practical utilization through organization and training. After fifty years of borrowing from the West, the Army, like the people,

was now relieved and proud to find new relevance in the nation's traditional values. . . . The sole key to victory lay in *Yamato-damashii* [Spirit of Japan].[52]

Based on this belief, the army proceeded between 1908 and 1928 to issue a number of changes to its standing orders. Each new military handbook or field manual placed increasing emphasis on developing military spirit, while actively promoting Bushido as the epitome of that spirit.

One example of this was the new infantry field manual issued in 1909, which made the infantry attack with small-arms fire, followed by a bayonet charge, the imperial army's chief tactical doctrine. This placed the burden for attaining victory on the infantry. Technology was thereby relegated to a secondary role, while the development of an irresistible attack spirit became paramount. A critical part of this spirit was absolute and unquestioning obedience to one's superiors, who acted on behalf of the emperor. Through training, this spirit of obedience had to transcend mere habit and become instinctive, unthinking.

In 1928 a revised *The Essential Points of Supreme Command (Tōsui Kōryō)* was issued. The continued emphasis on spirit as superior to material in combat resulted in the deletion in this revision of such words as "surrender," "retreat," and "defense." In addition, the term emperor's army, or *kōgun*, was used officially for the first time. Each infantryman's rifle had the imperial chrysanthemum seal stamped on its barrel and was regarded as a precious, even holy gift from the emperor himself. For this reason, it must never, ever, be allowed to fall into enemy hands.

The year 1928 also marked the debut of a series of books and pamphlets devoted exclusively to developing the military spirit. The first, issued by the Inspectorate General of Military Training, was entitled simply *A Guide to Spiritual Training (Seishin Kyōiku no Sankō)*. This was followed in 1930 by the two-volume *The Moral Character of Military Men (Bujin no Tokusō)*. These works opened a floodgate of both official and unofficial materials written on this topic during the 1930s. Needless to say, Zen-related figures were anxious to have their say.

As we have seen, an earlier popular Buddhist commentator on Bushido, Furukawa Taigo, had identified himself as being engaged "in spiritual training for army officer candidates." This training program was focused chiefly on the officer corps. Cadets were first exposed to it at the military preparatory school level and then further indoctrinated during their eighteen months at the military academy. How effective was this spiritual training? A study by historian Mark Peattie caused him to rate it quite highly. "With the possible exception of the pre-World War I French army," he wrote, "no other army articulated such an extreme code of sacrifice in the attack."[53]

The writings of one military officer, Lieutenant Colonel Sugimoto Gorō (1900–1937), clearly indicate the type of soldier this training produced and are a powerful testimonial to the influence that Bushido, incorporating the alleged unity of Zen and the sword, had on both imperial soldiers and the general public. Lieutenant Colonel Gorō was destined, albeit posthumously, to become widely known and honored as a "god of war" (gunshin).

LIEUTENANT COLONEL SUGIMOTO GORŌ, THE ZEN-MILITARY IDEAL

Born in Hiroshima Prefecture on May 25, 1900, Sugimoto Gorō completed his primary and secondary education in local schools. He joined the imperial army in December 1918 and was selected for officer-candidate school the following year. After graduation in 1921, he was appointed to the rank of second lieutenant and attached to the Eleventh Infantry Regiment. Sugimoto continued his military education and was promoted to first lieutenant in 1924. He saw service in the China Incident of 1928 and was awarded the sum of one hundred yen in 1929 as a gesture of appreciation for his service. In 1931 Sugimoto was promoted to captain and assumed the position of battalion adjutant within the Eleventh Infantry Regiment. Shortly thereafter he went on to become a company commander in the same regiment. In December 1931 Sugimoto was ordered to Tianjin in northern China as part of the military response to the Manchurian Incident. He returned to Japan in July 1932 and was awarded the Distinguished Service Medal for Creating [the Country of] Manchukuo in March 1934. One month later he also received an award of four hundred yen for his participation in that campaign.

Sugimoto was promoted to the rank of major in August 1937 and shortly thereafter dispatched to northern China once again. On September 14, 1937 Sugimoto was mortally wounded in a battle which took place in Shanxi Province. He was posthumously promoted to the rank of lieutenant colonel and awarded several decorations.

Sugimoto was in every sense a good soldier and officer, if not necessarily a particularly distinguished one. The monetary awards and decorations he received, even his final posthumous promotion, were commonplace among the officer corps of a rapidly expanding military. What made him stand out from his peers were his absolute reverence for and loyalty to the emperor, his many years of Zen practice, and his writings, posthumously published under the title *Great Duty (Taigi)*.

The following two passages are representative of his attitude to the emperor. The first of them is taken from the first chapter of his book and was entitled simply "The Emperor":

The emperor is identical to the Great [Sun] Goddess Amaterasu. He is the supreme and only God of the universe, the supreme sovereign of the universe. All of the many components [of a country] including such things as its laws and constitution, its religion, ethics, learning, and art, are expedient means by which to promote unity with the emperor. That is to say, the greatest mission of these components is to promote an awareness of the nonexistence of the self and the absolute nature of the emperor. Because of the nonexistence of the self everything in the universe is a manifestation of the emperor . . . including even the insect chirping in the hedge, or the gentle spring breeze.

Stop such foolishness as respecting Confucius, revering Christ, or believing in Shakyamuni! Believe in the emperor, the embodiment of Supreme Truth, the one God of the universe! Revere the emperor for all eternity! Imperial subjects of Japan should not seek their own personal salvation. Rather, their goal should be the expansion of imperial power. Needless to say, they will find personal salvation within imperial power. Inasmuch as this is true, they must pray for the expansion of imperial power. In front of the emperor their self is empty. Within the unity of the sovereign and the people, the people must not value their self, but value the emperor who embodies their self.

Loyalty to the emperor, which is the highest moral training, should never be done with the expectation of receiving anything in return. Rather, it should be practiced without any thought of reward, for the emperor does not exist for the people, but the people exist for the emperor. . . . The emperor does not exist for the state, but the state exists for the emperor.

This great awareness will clearly manifest itself at the time you discard secular values and recognize that the emperor is the highest, supreme value for all eternity. If, on the other hand, your ultimate goal is eternal happiness for yourself and salvation of your soul, the emperor becomes a means to an end and is no longer the highest being. If there is a difference in the degree of your reverence for the emperor based on your learning, occupation, or social position, then you are a self-centered person. Seeking nothing at all, you should simply completely discard both body and mind, and unite with the emperor.[54]

The second quotation comes from the fifth chapter of his book, "The Imperial Way":

The imperial way is the Great Way that the emperor has graciously bestowed on us to follow. For this reason, it is the Great Way that the multitudes should follow. It is the greatest way in the universe, the true reality of the emperor, the highest righteousness and the purest purity. . . . The imperial way is truly the fundamental principle for the guidance of the world. If the people are themselves righteous and pure, free of contentiousness, then they are one with the emperor; and the unity of the sovereign and his subjects is realized.

Is there anything that can be depended on other than the emperor's way? Is there a secret key to the salvation of humanity other than this? Is there a place of refuge other than this? The emperor should be revered for all eternity. Leading the masses, dash straight ahead on the emperor's way! Even if inundated by raging waves, or seared by a red-hot iron, or beset by all the nations of the world, go straight ahead on the emperor's way without the slightest hesitation! This is the best and shortest route to the manifestation of the divine land [of Japan].

The emperor's way is what has been taught by all the saints of the world. Do not confuse the highest righteousness and the purest purity with mere loyalty to this person or that, for only those who sacrifice themselves for the emperor possess these qualities. This is the true meaning of loyalty and filial piety.[55]

On the surface, these passages seem to be the writings of an extremist, Shinto-inspired, ethnocentric nationalist, and they seem to have little if any connection to either Buddhism in general or Zen in particular. Sugimoto even goes so far as to advocate abandoning belief in Buddha Shakyamuni. While a whole chapter of his book is devoted to a discussion of the imperial way or the emperor's way *(tennōdō)*, there is not the slightest mention of imperial-way Buddhism or imperial-state Zen.

The concept of an imperial way was by no means an invention of institutional Buddhism. From as early as the Meiji period it had been promoted by the state, especially the Department of Education. Joseph Kitagawa described the concept as follows:

> The underlying assumption of the "imperial way" was that the nation is in essence a patriarchal family with the emperor as its head. It was taken for granted that individuals exist for the nation rather than the other way around. Equally important was the assumption that some men are born to rule while others are to be ruled because men are by nature unequal.[56]

Sugimoto was simply repeating the popular conception of this term, though perhaps in a somewhat more extreme form. Imperial-way Buddhism incorporated the same values. What, then, was Sugimoto's contribution? First of all, Sugimoto also had this to say about Buddha Shakyamuni:

> When Shakyamuni sat in meditation beneath the Bodhi tree in order to see into his true nature, he had to fight with an army of innumerable demons. Those who rush forward to save the empire are truly great men as he was, pathfinders who sacrifice themselves for the emperor.[57]

Though Sugimoto had relatively little to say about Buddhism as such, he readily used Buddhist terminology to make his points. For example, he quoted the Nirvana Sutra on the importance of "protecting the true Dharma by grasping swords and other weapons." He then went on to assert that "the highest and only true Dharma in the world exists within the emperor." Likewise, he quoted the same sutra on the need to "keep the [Buddhist] precepts." Combining these ideas, he concluded that "everyone in the world should grasp swords and other weapons to reverently protect the emperor. This is the world's highest observance of the precepts, the highest morality, and the highest religion."[58]

In a later chapter entitled "War," Sugimoto also revealed a Buddhist influence: "The wars of the empire are sacred wars. They are holy wars. They are the [Buddhist] practice *(gyō)* of great compassion *(daijihishin)*. Therefore the imperial military must consist of holy officers and holy soldiers."[59]

As previously noted, the belief that war was an expression of Buddhist compassion had long been an article of faith within institutional Buddhism.

If references to Buddhism in general were relatively limited in Sugimoto's writings, the same cannot be said about his references, both direct and indirect, to Zen. In the introduction to his book he writes, "If you wish to penetrate the true meaning of 'Great Duty,' the first thing you should do is to embrace the teachings of Zen and discard self-attachment."[60] Sugimoto went on to explain why self-attachment should be discarded: "War is moral training for not only the individual but for the entire world. It consists of the extinction of self-seeking and the destruction of self-preservation. It is only those without self-attachment who are able to revere the emperor absolutely."[61]

Sugimoto also found inspiration for his beliefs in the teachings of some of Zen's greatest masters. For example, he wrote about Dōgen, the thirteenth-century founder of the Sōtō Zen sect in Japan, as follows:

Zen Master Dōgen said, "To study the Buddha Dharma is to study the self. To study the self is to forget the self." To forget the self means to discard both body and mind. To discard beyond discarding, to discard until there is nothing left to discard.... This is called reaching the Great Way in which there is no doubt. This is the Great Law of the universe. In this way the great spirit of the highest righteousness and the purest purity manifests itself in the individual. This is the unity of the sovereign and his subjects, the origin of faith in the emperor.[62]

Sugimoto was equally ready to enlist the greatest of the Chinese Zen masters in his cause. About Nanquan Puyuan (748–834) he wrote:

An ancient master [Nanquan] said, "One's ordinary mind is the Way."... In the spring there are hundreds of flowers, and in the fall, the moon. In the summer there are cool breezes, and in the winter, snow. Laying down one's life in order to destroy the rebels is one's ordinary mind. If one does not fall victim to an idle mind, this is truly the practice of Great Duty. It is this that must be called the essence of faith in the emperor.[63]

Sugimoto added that "sacrificing oneself for the emperor is one's ordinary mind," and those who possess this mind are true imperial subjects.[64]

In addition to passages such as those above that show a direct Zen influence, Sugimoto used a number of Zen terms throughout his writing. For example, he devoted an entire chapter to the question of life and death. In the best Zen fashion he explained that "life and death are identical." As to how one comes to this realization, he stated, "It is achieved by abandoning both body and mind, by extinguishing the self."[65]

Though that may sound like orthodox Zen teaching, Sugimoto continued:

> Warriors who sacrifice their lives for the emperor will not die. They will live forever. Truly, they should be called gods and Buddhas for whom there is no life or death. . . . Where there is absolute loyalty there is no life or death. Where there is life and death there is no absolute loyalty. When a person talks of his view of life and death, that person has not yet become pure in heart. He has not yet abandoned body and mind. In pure loyalty there is no life or death. Simply live in pure loyalty![66]

And finally, closely connected with the above sentiments is the statement for which Sugimoto was destined to be best remembered: "If you wish to see me, live in reverence for the emperor! Where there is the spirit of reverence for the emperor, there will I always be."[67]

Some might argue that Sugimoto's interpretation of Buddhism and Zen was no more than one ultranationalist's willful distortion of those traditions, but in fact leading Zen masters of the day readily agreed with Sugimoto in his identification of Zen with both war and the emperor. First and foremost of those Zen masters who supported Sugimoto was Yamazaki Ekijū (1882–1961), chief abbot of the Buttsūji branch of the Rinzai Zen sect and head of the entire sect toward war's end (1945–46).

Sugimoto's Zen Master, Yamazaki Ekijū

In one sense it is hardly surprising to find Ekijū lending his support to Sugimoto; after all, Sugimoto had been his lay disciple. Ekijū's support took the concrete form of a one-hundred-four-page eulogy attached to the end of Sugimoto's book. It began:

> I once said at a lecture I gave, "The faith of the Japanese people is a faith that should be centered on his imperial majesty, the emperor."

At that time Sugimoto said that he was in complete agreement with me. He then went on to add, "I had felt exactly as you do, but I had been unable to find the right words to express it. Present-day religionists raise a fuss about the need for faith, but their faith is mistaken. Buddhists say that one should have faith in the Buddha, or Mahavairocana, or Amida Buddha, but such faith is one that is limited to religion alone. Japanese Buddhism must be centered on the emperor; for if were it not, it would have no place in Japan, it would not be living Buddhism. Buddhism, including Shakyamuni's teachings, must conform to the national polity of Japan."

Sugimoto continued,

> The Buddhist statues that are enshrined in temples should, properly speaking, have the emperor reverently enshrined in the center and such figures as Amida Buddha or Mahavairocana at his sides. It is only the various branches of the Zen sect in Japan who have his majesty enshrined in the center. . . . All of Japanese Buddhism should have His Majesty, the emperor as their central object of worship.[68]

Ekijū then expressed his own feelings of reverence for the emperor:

> For Japanese there is no such thing as sacrifice. Sacrifice means to totally annihilate one's body on behalf of the imperial state. The Japanese people, however, have been one with the emperor from the beginning. In this place of absoluteness there is no sacrifice. In Japan, the relationship between His Majesty and the people is not relative but absolute.[69]

Ekijū's reverence for the emperor was, if anything, even more extreme than Sugimoto's. Attracted to the absoluteness of Ekijū's position, Sugimoto, already an experienced Zen practitioner, went on to train a further nine years under Ekijū. With evident satisfaction in his lay disciple's level of realization, Ekijū quoted a statement Sugimoto had once made:

> The national polity of Japan and Buddhism are identical. In Buddhism, especially the Zen sect, there is repeated reference to the identity of body and mind. In order to realize this identity it is

necessary to undergo training with all one's might and regardless of the sacrifice.

Furthermore, the essence of the unity of body and mind is to be found in egolessness. Japan is a country where the sovereign and the people are identical. When imperial subjects meld themselves into one with the august mind [of the emperor], their original countenance shines forth. The essence of the unity of the sovereign and the people is egolessness. Egolessness and self-extinction are most definitely not separate states. On the contrary, one comes to realize that they are identical.[70]

The egolessness of which Sugimoto spoke is the well-known Zen term of *muga* (no-self). In his book *Zen and Japanese Culture,* Suzuki identified *muga* as being identical with not only *musō* (no-reflection) and *munen* (no-thought), but also *mushin* (no-mind),[71] terms which he described as follows:

> *Mushin (wu-hsin)* or *munen (wu-nien)* is one of the most important ideas in Zen. It corresponds to the state of innocence enjoyed by the first inhabitants of the Garden of Eden, or even to the mind of God when he was about to utter his fiat, "Let there be light." Enō (Hui-neng), the sixth patriarch of Zen, emphasizes *munen* (or *mushin*) as the most essential element in the study of Zen. When it is attained, a man becomes a Zen-man, and . . . also a perfect swordsman.[72]

Was Sugimoto, then, the Zen-man of whom Suzuki wrote? It is clear that Ekijū believed he was:

> As far as the power of his practice of the Way is concerned, I believe he [Sugimoto] reached the point where there was no difference between him and the chief abbot of this or that branch [of Zen]. I think that when a person esteems practice, respects the Way, and thoroughly penetrates the self as he did, he is qualified to be the teacher of other Zen practitioners. That is how accomplished he was. In my opinion his practice was complete.[73]

Ekijū compared Sugimoto to Bodhidharma, the legendary fifth-century founder of the Zen sect in China: "Altogether Sugimoto practiced Zen for nearly twenty years. Bodhidharma practiced [meditation] facing the wall for nine years. Sugimoto's penetrating zazen was as excellent as that. He was thoroughly devoted to his unique imperial-state Zen."[74] This is Ekijū's first mention of imperial-state Zen, and it appears to be a term that Ekijū invented to describe Sugimoto's emperor-centered faith. It is not found in Sugimoto's writings, but according to Ekijū, Sugimoto did once say:

> The Zen that I do is not the Zen of the Zen sect. It is soldier Zen (*gunjin Zen*). The reason that Zen is important for soldiers is that all Japanese, especially soldiers, must live in the spirit of the unity of sovereign and subjects, eliminating their ego and getting rid of their self. It is exactly the awakening to the nothingness (*mu*) of Zen that is the fundamental spirit of the unity of sovereign and subjects. Through my practice of Zen I am able to get rid of my ego. In facilitating the accomplishment of this, Zen becomes, as it is, the true spirit of the imperial military.[75]

Sugimoto went on to explain exactly why it was that the spiritual training provided to the military was focused on the officer class:

> Within the military, officers must use this [Zen] spirit in the training of their troops. In the training of troops mere talk is not enough. If you don't set the example or put it into practice yourself, your training is a lie. . . . What one hasn't seen for oneself cannot be taught to one's troops. As the senior, one must first be pure oneself. Otherwise, one cannot serve the state through extinguishing and discarding the ego.[76]

There is no real difference between what Sugimoto describes as soldier Zen, what Ekijū calls imperial-state Zen, and the descriptions of imperial-way Buddhism we have examined previously. The same spirit of absolute obedience and subservience to the emperor's will runs through them all.

One interesting question remains. What kind of soldier did Sugimoto, with all his Zen training, actually become? Was he in fact Suzuki's perfect swordsman? Ekijū described Sugimoto's military prowess on the battlefield:

> I don't know what degree [of attainment] he had in the way of the sword, but it appears he was quite accomplished. . . . When he went to the battlefield it appears that he used the sword with consum-

mate skill. . . . I believe he demonstrated the action that derives from the unity of Zen and the sword.[77]

Ekijū also recorded the following conversation the two men had shortly before Sugimoto went off to fight in China in 1931:

Sugimoto asked, "Master, what kind of understanding should I have in going over there?"
I answered, "You are strong, and your unit is strong. Thus I think you will not fear a strong enemy. However, in the event you face a [numerically] small enemy, you must not despise them. You should read one part of the Prajnaparamita Hridaya Sutra every day. This will insure good fortune on the battlefield for the imperial military."[78]

This conversation clearly echoes the one seven centuries earlier between Hōjō Tokimune and his Chinese Zen master, Sogen, though this time there is no shout of *"Katsu!"* to demonstrate Sugimoto's level of attainment. Ekijū went on to add that when Sugimoto did eventually return safely from China, he reported, "I died once while I was in Tianjin." About this Ekijū commented, "Through the awareness Sugimoto achieved in becoming one with death, there was, I think, nothing he couldn't achieve."[79]
Ekijū also described Sugimoto's death, based on reports he had received. Sugimoto had been leading his troops into battle when an enemy hand grenade landed behind him and exploded.

A grenade fragment hit him in the left shoulder. He seemed to have fallen down but then got up again. Although he was standing, one could not hear his commands. He was no longer able to issue commands with that husky voice of his. . . . Yet he was still standing, holding his sword in one hand as a prop. Both legs were slightly bent, and he was facing in an easterly direction [toward the imperial palace]. It appeared that he had saluted though his hand was now lowered to about the level of his mouth. The blood flowing from his mouth covered his watch. . . .[80]

In Ekijū's mind, at least, this was his lay disciple's finest moment, when he most clearly displayed the power that was to be gained by those who practiced Zen. Sugimoto had died standing up. As the master explained:

From long ago, the true sign of a Zen priest has been his ability to pass away while doing zazen. Those who were completely and thoroughly enlightened, however, ... could die calmly in a standing position.... This was possible was due to *samadhi* power *[jōriki]*.[81]

Samadhi refers to the concentrated state of mind, the mental "one pointedness," that is achieved through the practice of zazen. Suzuki, Seisen, Furukawa, and others had written of this meditation-derived power, available to Japanese warriors past and present through the practice of Zen. According to Ekijū, Sugimoto's life, and especially his death, were living proof of its effectiveness in battle.

At last Ekijū was ready to complete his eulogy of Sugimoto:

To the last second, Sugimoto was a man whose speech and actions were at one with each other. When he saluted and faced the east, there is no doubt that he also shouted, "May His Majesty, the emperor, live for ten thousand years!" It is for this reason that his was the radiant ending of an imperial soldier. Not only that, but his excellent example should be a model for future generations of someone who lived in Zen....

Although it can be said that his life of thirty-eight years was all too short, for someone who has truly obtained *samadhi* power, long and short are not important. The great, true example of Sugimoto Gorō was that of one who had united with emptiness, embodying total loyalty [to the emperor] and service to the state. I am convinced he is one of those who, should he be reborn seven times over, would reverently work to destroy the enemies of the emperor (written on the 11th of February of the 2,598th year of the imperial reign) [1938].[82]

Although the preceding words mark the end of Sugimoto's book *Great Duty*, they by no means mark the end of the influence that his writings, and those of his Zen master, were to have on the Japanese people, especially its youth. As Ekijū hoped, Sugimoto did indeed become the model of a military figure who had thoroughly imbibed the Zen spirit. The publication of *Great Duty* became the catalyst for a flurry of activity, including both long and short written pieces extolling the virtues of this "god of war."

Members of the Rinzai sect were not the only ones eager to promote Sugimoto's ideology. The Sōtō Zen sect found him equally praiseworthy.

One example of this was an article entitled "The Zen of Clothing and Food," which appeared in the April 1943 issue of *Sanshō*, the official organ of Eiheiji, the Sōtō Zen sect's largest monastery. The article's author, Takizawa Kanyū, wanted to encourage frugality among the Japanese civilian population in anticipation of the decisive battle that he believed was imminent. Looking for a Zen-inspired model of the frugality he advocated, he wrote:

> In the past, there were men like the "god of war," Lieutenant Colonel Sugimoto Gorō. He never complained about [the quality of] his food. No matter how humble it was, he ate it gladly, treating it as a delicacy. Further, he was indifferent to what he wore, wearing tattered, though never soiled, clothing and hats. This is according to Zen master Yamazaki Ekijū's description of the Colonel as contained in the latter's posthumous book, *Great Duty*.[83]

Sugimoto had admirers beyond Zen circles as well, including the support of leading members of the imperial military, especially its officer corps. Two generals contributed works of calligraphy that were published as part of the introduction to *Great Duty*. When one of Sugimoto's fellow lay Zen trainees wrote a second account of his life, army lieutenant colonel Kozuki Yoshio contributed one of the prefaces. This book, entitled *Lieutenant Colonel Sugimoto Goro's Reverence for the Emperor and Zen (Sugimoto Gorō Chūsa no Sonnō to Zen)*, was written by Ōyama Sumita, a government official. Lieutenant Colonel Kozuki's preface concluded with the following words: "For the sake of our imperial nation there is nothing that would make me happier than for this book to result in the birth of a second and third Sugimoto".[84]

Leading government officials lent their strong support to the promotion of Sugimoto's ideas as well. In a second preface to the same book, the vice-minister of the Communications Ministry, Ōwada Teiji, wrote:

> At present, all the people of our nation have risen to the challenge of attaining the goals of this sacred war. At such a time it is indeed felicitous for this invincible country to have obtained this book, which promotes the rebirth of the Lieutenant Colonel's great spirit within the minds of one hundred million citizens. What an unlimited joy it is for East Asia![85]

But Sugimoto's *Great Duty* was destined to have its greatest impact not on Zen masters, generals, or bureaucrats but on the school-age youth of Japan. In his war recollections, Okuno Takeo wrote of the effect that *Great Duty* had on his and his schoolmates' lives:

> By 1943 and 1944, the war situation in the Pacific War had gradually worsened. Middle school students began to read Sugimoto Gorō's *Great Duty* with great enthusiasm. . . . By word of mouth we got the message, "Read *Great Duty*, it's terrific! It teaches what true reverence for the emperor really is!" I was then attending Azabu middle school [in Tokyo].
>
> In 1943 my friends and I took turns reading a single copy of *Great Duty* that we had among us. As a result, we decided to form a student club we called the Bamboo-Mind Society (Chikushin Kai) to put into practice the spirit of *Great Duty*. . . .
>
> We brought in instructors from the outside and held study meetings. The same kind of *Great Duty* study circles sprang up in all the middle schools in Tokyo. We then started to communicate among ourselves. . . . I later learned that in almost all middle schools throughout Japan *Great Duty* had been fervently read and student study societies created.[86]

While it may be argued that these youth were, after all, still students, it should be remembered that 1943 marked the end of deferments for students in universities, technical colleges, and higher schools. In the lower grades, mobilization took place informally through quotas for youth volunteers (boys fifteen to seventeen years of age) and volunteers for Manchuria-Mongolia Development Youth Patriotic Units. Ienaga Saburō has described this development graphically:

> Made responsible for filling the quotas, teachers pressured the children directly by saying, "Any Japanese boy who doesn't get into this 'holy war' will be shamed for life." The teachers would visit a student's home and get his parents' tearful approval. Many boys in their mid-teens became youth pilots and youth tankers, or "volunteered" for service in Manchuria and Mongolia. These rosy-cheeked teenagers were put in special attack units and blew themselves up crashing into enemy ships.[87]

The unity of Zen and the sword advocated by such Zen leaders as Ekijū and Suzuki had come to this: drafting young boys into special attack units to become the infamous *kamikaze* (divine wind) pilots headed on a one-way trip to oblivion. Truly may it be said that their lives were now "as light as goose feathers."

CHAPTER NINE:

OTHER ZEN MASTERS AND SCHOLARS IN THE WAR EFFORT

I t would be comforting, though incorrect, to believe that Ekijū and his "imperial-state Zen" were somehow unique or isolated phenomena within Zen circles during the war years. The truth is that he was merely representative of what other leading Zen masters were saying and doing at this time. For example, there are numerous instances of Zen masters conducting intensive meditation retreats, typically lasting five days, for officers. The retreats would take place in the unit's martial-arts training hall, with the officers using their folded army blankets as makeshift meditation cushions.[1]

If there is anything that distinguished Ekijū from his contemporaries, it was that his lay disciple Sugimoto Gorō came to epitomize what many Zen masters and scholars merely talked about. Yet the importance of this talking by Zen masters should not be underestimated, for, as previously discussed, the government clearly appreciated its importance as a morale booster. Sugimoto described what he believed the appropriate role was of not only Zen but all Buddhist priests:

> Each Buddhist temple should be a training center for developing spiritual discipline within the people. Priests should be the leaders of this training. In so doing they can claim the right to be called men of religion.[2]

Ekijū commended this passage by Sugimoto, commenting that it displayed a "grand attitude."[3] Yet he was far from alone in the Zen world in his acceptance of this role for Zen priests.

Hata Eshō Sōtō Zen master Hata Eshō, Eiheiji's chief abbot, agreed with
Ekijū. He wrote the following in the December 1942 issue of *Sanshō:*

> One full year has elapsed since the outbreak of the Greater East
> Asian War. It is said that the war has entered a stage of protracted
> fighting. In such a stage the need for materials will increase more
> and more. . . . We Zen priests cannot directly produce so much as
> a grain of rice or a sheet of paper. However, in terms of developing
> the spiritual power of the people, there is a way for us, incompe-
> tent though we be, to do our public duty. I believe that we should
> do everything in our power to go in this direction.[4]

If there is any question as to what this leading Sōtō Zen master thought
of Japan's war effort, or Buddhism's relationship to that effort, Eshō clarified his position in the same issue of *Sanshō:*

> On December 8 Buddha Shakyamuni looked at the morning star
> and realized perfect enlightenment while seated under the bodhi
> tree. One year ago, on this very day, through the proclamation of
> the imperial edict to annihilate America and England, our country
> started afresh toward a new East Asia, a great East Asia. This signi-
> fies nothing less than the enlightenment of East Asia. . . . As we now
> welcome the first anniversary of the outbreak of the Greater East
> Asian War, we realize that the future will not be easy. We must
> therefore renew our conviction that nothing else but certain victory
> lies ahead.[5]

Even before Eshō's exhortation, Sōtō Zen leaders had focused their
efforts on developing the spiritual power of the people. Typical of this effort
was an article written on January 1, 1941, by the sect's administrative head,
Ōmori Zenkai (1871–1947). He quoted the very same passage from Zen
Master Dōgen about "forget[ting] the self" that Sugimoto had previously.
Zenkai went on:

> The essence of the practice of an [imperial] subject is to be found
> in the basic principle of the Buddha Way, which is to forget the self.
> It is by giving concrete form to this essence in any and all situa-
> tions, regardless of time or place, that Buddhism is, for the first
> time, able to repay the debt of gratitude it owes the state.[5]

Yamada Reirin   One year later, in 1942, Sōtō Zen master Yamada Reirin (1889–1979) wrote a book entitled *Evening Talks on Zen Studies (Zengaku Yawa)*. In post-war years Reirin became president of Komazawa University and then chief abbot of Eiheiji.

Reirin began his book by pointing out that Emperor Kimmei (539–71) first allowed Buddhism into Japan because he recognized that "it would be of service to him."[7] Reirin then went on to speculate as to whether or not Buddhism was still able to render such service. He wrote:

> Japan has now plunged into the most serious situation it has faced since the beginning of its history. The question is whether or not Buddhism can now be of service to the emperor. In both quantity and quality, it is necessary for Buddhism to provide such excellent service. All Buddhists, regardless of sectarian affiliation, must come forward to do their great duty in support of imperial rule.[8]

Reirin clearly believed he was doing his part in this effort. He devoted an entire chapter to addressing one of the most difficult problems on the wartime home front, the consolation of parents whose sons had fallen in battle. Utilizing the Buddhist-influenced folk belief in Japan concerning the transmigration of souls, Reirin provided the following explanation:

> The true form of the heroic spirits [of the dead] is the good karmic power that has resulted from their loyalty, bravery, and nobility of character. This will never perish. . . . The body and mind produced by this karmic power cannot be other than what has existed up to the present. . . . The loyal, brave, noble, and heroic spirits of those officers and men who have died shouting, "May the emperor live for ten thousand years!" will be reborn right here in this country. It is only natural that this should occur.[9]

Finally, like so many of his predecessors, Reirin pointed out the "virility" Hōjō Tokimune received from his Zen training.[10] Zen made possible the maintenance of an adamantine mind and the welling up of a pure and fiery spirit.[11] If one would but "annihilate the ego," he wrote, then an "absolute and mysterious power and radiance will fill one's body and mind,"[12] together with "an unlimited gratitude to the imperial military" for their "wonderful fruits of battle."[13]

Kurebayashi Kōdō Sōtō Zen scholars of the period were no less supportive of Japan's war effort than were the sect's Zen masters. One of the sect's best-known scholar-priests, a specialist in the thought of Zen master Dōgen (1200–1253), was Dr. Kurebayashi Kōdō (1893–1988). In the postwar years he succeeded Yamada Reirin as president of Komazawa University. At the outbreak of full-scale war with China in 1937, he wrote an article entitled "The [China] Incident and Buddhism."

Kōdō's article, appearing in the October 1937 issue of *Sanshō,* began with the now standard advocacy of the "just-war" theory. "It goes without saying," he said, "that the North China Incident is a war on behalf of justice." Not only that, but "all of Japan's wars since the Sino-Japanese War have been such wars." And, in case there were any doubt, he added, "Should there be further wars in the future, there is no doubt they will also be just."[14]

Aside from giving present and future Japanese governments *carte blanche* to fight whenever and wherever they wished, Kōdō's statement is notable for the rationale he provided to justify his position:

> The reason [Japan's wars are just] is, I dare say, because of the influence of the Buddhist spirit. The spirit of Japan which was nurtured by Buddhism is ceaselessly working towards cooperation among peoples and eternal peace in the Orient. Without the influence of Buddhism, a thoroughgoing, international fraternal spirit would be impossible.[15]

Kōdō went on to assert that Japan's actions in China were the "practice of compassion:"[16]

> Wherever the imperial military advances there is only charity and love. They could never act in the barbarous and cruel way in which the Chinese soldiers act. This can truly be considered to be a great accomplishment of the long period which Buddhism took in nurturing [the Japanese military]. In other words, brutality itself no longer exists in the officers and men of the imperial military who have been schooled in the spirit of Buddhism.[17]

Kōdō concluded the article by reminding his readers that "it was only the Japanese people who embodied the true spirit of Buddhism. . . . "Without a faith in Buddhism," he asserted, "this nation cannot prosper, nor can humanity find happiness."[18] One can only wonder what Kōdō would have said to Ienaga's well-documented assertion that "there were so many atrocities [committed by Japanese troops] that one cannot even begin to list them all."[19]

Hitane Jōzan Kōdō was not, of course, the only Zen scholar to voice his support for Japan's war efforts. Dr. Hitane Jōzan (1873–1954), a scholar-priest at Rinzai Zen sect–affiliated Rinzai Gakuin (the predecessor of Hanazono University), also wrote an article about the same incident. It was entitled, "The Current Incident and the Vow and Practice of a Bodhisattva," and it appeared in the October 1937 issue of *Zenshū*, a monthly periodical jointly supported by all branches of the Rinzai Zen sect.

Jōzan began his article with the assertion that up to this point Japan's modern wars had been a matter of self-defense. "It is impossible," he wrote, "to find any other meaning to either the Sino-Japanese War, the Russo-Japanese War, or the Manchurian Incident [of 1931]."[20] The current fighting, however, was different:

> Speaking from the point of view of the ideal outcome, this is a righteous and moral war of self-sacrifice in which we will rescue China from the dangers of Communist takeover and economic slavery. We will help the Chinese live as true Orientals. It would therefore, I dare say, not be unreasonable to call this a sacred war incorporating the great practice of a bodhisattva.[21]

Fukuba Hōshū It was difficult for some adherents of the Zen school to justify the Japanese invasion of China because violence was being employed against the very country that had been the birthplace of their tradition. How could they reconcile repaying the debt of gratitude they felt they owed the classical Chinese Chan patriarchs with the devastation of their homeland?

A colleague of Hidane Jōzan at Rinzai Gakuin, a Rinzai Zen scholar-priest named Fukuba Hōshū (1895–1943), provided a way out of this quandary in an article entitled "What Is Japanese, What Is Chinese" (*Shinateki to Nihonteki*) published in the November 5, 1939 issue of the journal *Zengaku Kenkyū*. According to Hōshū, the solution was really quite simple. The Chinese Zen masters had never fully realized the true meaning of Zen. That is to say, the Chinese Zen patriarchs' understanding of Zen had been limited by the faulty cultural values of Chinese society, values that the Chinese Zen patriarchs had been unable to overcome. In contrast to this, "the social and historical norms that existed in Japan allowed . . . Zen's true nature to be made manifest."[22]

On the one hand, Hōshū admitted that Chinese society had traditionally valued both loyalty to the sovereign and filial piety to one's parents and family. However, when the two values came into conflict the Chinese "without regret chose filial piety over loyalty."[23] What was even worse was that in times of political and economic unrest, the Chinese blamed the ruler for the nation's troubles and "readily believed that a revolution was justified."[24] This kind of thinking had, according to Hōshū, brought nothing but internal divisions and turmoil to Chinese society, even to the present day.

Japan, on the other hand, was quite different. It was a country where family and state had become one unified, communal entity due to the fact that "the family had been warmly embraced by the state."[25] This, of course, had been made possible because of the existence and benevolence of the imperial house and the contributions made to national morality by such pioneer Zen masters as Eisai, Kokan Shiren (1278–1346), and others. Therefore, "if ever one or the other [loyalty or filial piety] had to be chosen, there is no question that it would be the former. . . for this represents the superiority, the absoluteness of the virtue of loyalty in Japan."[26]

Japanese Zen, then, had both contributed to and benefited from this understanding of loyalty. In concluding his article, Hōshū pointed out that this understanding had facilitated Japanese Zen's recognition that the spread of Zen was identical with *(soku)* the protection of the state. Hōshū's closing statement was "I believe it is through the manifestation of Zen's true nature [in Japan] that we can repay the benevolence of the Chinese patriarchs."[27]

Harada Daiun Sōgaku There is one other lineage or school of Zen Buddhists whose wartime words and actions are worthy of consideration. This lineage, though relatively small in number, has been quite influential in spreading its interpretation of Zen in the West, especially the United States. The founder of this group was Zen Master Harada Daiun Sōgaku (1870–1961). Philip Kapleau, a prominent descendent of this lineage, described this master in *The Three Pillars of Zen*:

> Nominally of the Sōtō sect, he [Daiun] welded together the best of Sōtō and Rinzai and the resulting amalgam was a vibrant Buddhism which has become one of the great teaching lines of Japan today. Probably more than anyone else in his time he revitalized, through his profound spiritual insight, the teachings of Dōgen-

zenji, which had been steadily drained of their vigor through the shallow understanding of priests and scholars of the Sōtō sect in whose hands their exposition had hitherto rested. . . .

Like all masters of high spiritual development, he was the keenest judge of character. He was as quick to expose pretense and sham as he was to detect it. Exceptional students he drove mercilessly, exacting from them the best of which they were capable. From all he demanded as a *sine qua non* sincerity and absolute adherence to his teachings, brooking not the slightest deviation. Casual observers often found him rigid and narrow, but disciples and students who were faithful to his teachings knew him to be wise and compassionate.[28]

Another prominent member of this lineage, Maezumi Hakuyu Taizan (1930–95), founder of the Zen Center of Los Angeles, had this to say about Daiun:

Daiun Harada Roshi was a Zen master of rare breadth and accomplishment in twentieth-century Japan. . . . He became abbot of Hosshinji and during the next forty years, until his death in 1961, made the monastery famous as a rigorous Zen training center, known for its harsh climate, its strict discipline, and its abbot's keen Zen eye.[29]

Daiun was also one of the most committed Zen supporters of Japan's military actions. If, as Kapleau claims, Daiun "revitalized" Zen, he did so by creating something he called "war Zen" *(sensō Zen)* as early as 1915, at the time of Japan's entry into World War I. It was in this year that he published *A Primer on the Practice of Zen (Sanzen no Kaitei)*, of which "War Zen" was the eleventh chapter.

The first subsection of this chapter was entitled "The Entire Universe Is at War." For Daiun there was nothing strange about Japan being at war, for "if you look at all phenomena in the universe you will see that there is nothing which is not at war."[30] In the natural world, for example, plum seeds try to conquer the world for plums, while rice grains try to conquer the world for rice. The human world is the same, with politicians struggling with one another to conquer the political world, and merchants struggling with one another to conquer the business world.

Buddhism is not exempt from this type of struggle, according to Daiun, for Buddha Shakyamuni himself had conquered demons in the course of rea-

Shaku Sōen.

Sawaki Kōdō.
Photo courtesy of *Daihōrin* magazine

D. T. Suzuki.

Nantembō.

Uchiyama Gudō.

An image of Buddha Shakyamuni
carved by Uchiyama Gudō.

Daiun Gikō in 1943,
shortly before he was
drafted and sent
to China.

Seki Seisetsu sweeping his temple garden.

Cover of Seki Seisetsu's book The Promotion of Budō, *showing Roosevelt and Churchill as demons being subjugated by the Japanese fairy-tale hero Momotarō.*

*Lieutenant Colonel
Sugimoto Gorō.*

Yamazaki Ekijū.

Harada Daiun Sōgaku.

Yanagida Seizan.

Yamada Mumon.

Asahina Sōgen.

Ichikawa Hakugen.

Yasutani Hakuun. (Photo by Francis Haar, courtesy of Tom Haar.)

Ōmori Sōgen.

lizing enlightenment. Thus, "without plunging into the war arena, it is totally impossible to know the Buddha Dharma." Daiun then went on to point out that "in all phenomena of either the ordinary world or the spiritual world, there is not one where war is absent. How could Zen alone be free of this principle? . . . It is impermissible," he wrote, "to forget war for even an instant."[31]

In fairness to Daiun, aside from his initial praise for Japan's military success, he used the term "war Zen" to describe what he believed should be the appropriate mental attitude of Zen practitioners in their search for enlightenment. The enemy Daiun advocates conquering is the practitioner's ignorance and desire. Even this, he noted, was not the ultimate expression of Zen, for "in the Great Way of the Buddhas and [Zen] patriarchs there is neither war nor peace."[32]

While Daiun's initial use of "war Zen" may have been metaphoric, by 1934 this was clearly no longer the case. In March of that year he wrote the following in an article appearing in the March 1934 issue of the magazine *Chūō Bukkyō*:

> The spirit of Japan is the Great Way of the [Shinto] gods. It is the substance of the universe, the essence of the Truth. The Japanese people are a chosen people whose mission is to control the world. The sword which kills is also the sword which gives life. Comments opposing war are the foolish opinions of those who can only see one aspect of things and not the whole.
>
> Politics conducted on the basis of a constitution are premature, and therefore fascist politics should be implemented for the next ten years. . . . Similarly, education makes for shallow, cosmopolitan-minded persons. All of the people of this country should do Zen. That is to say, they should all awake to the Great Way of the Gods. This is Mahayana Zen."[33]

By 1939 Daiun no longer found it necessary to even discuss antiwar thought. In "The One Road of Zen and War," an article appearing in the November 1939 issue of the magazine *Daijō Zen,* he wrote:

> [If ordered to] march: tramp, tramp, or shoot: bang, bang. This is the manifestation of the highest Wisdom [of Enlightenment]. The unity of Zen and war of which I speak extends to the farthest reaches of the holy war [now under way]. Verse: I bow my head to the floor in reverence of those whose nobility is without equal.[34]

By the beginning of 1943 the tide of war had clearly turned against Japan. The government called on Buddhist leaders to do their utmost to mobilize the entire civilian population in the war effort. Under these circumstances Daiun wrote the following in the February 1943 issue of the periodical *Zen no Seikatsu:*

> It has never been as necessary as it is today for all one hundred million people of this country to be committed to the fact that as the state lives and dies, so do they. . . . We must devote ourselves to the practice of Zen and the discernment of the Way. We must push on in applying ourselves to "combat zazen," the king of meditation.[35]

By the latter part of 1944 the outlook for Japan had become bleak. The unthinkable was becoming thinkable. The home islands might be invaded. In this situation every able-bodied citizen, both young and old, armed often with no more than bamboo spears, was being trained to repel the invaders. In response, Daiun wrote the following article entitled, "Be Prepared, One Hundred Million [Subjects], for Death with Honor!" which appeared in the July issue of that year's *Daijō Zen:*

> It is necessary for all one hundred million subjects [of the emperor] to be prepared to die with honor. . . . If you see the enemy you must kill him; you must destroy the false and establish the true—these are the cardinal points of Zen. It is said that if you kill someone it is fitting that you see his blood. It is further said that if you are riding a powerful horse nothing is beyond your reach. Isn't the purpose of the zazen we have done in the past to be of assistance in an emergency like this?[36]

Japan's surrender was a year away. By early 1945 most Buddhist-related publications had closed down as part of the overall effort to funnel all available resources to the military effort. Buddhist leaders, Zen and otherwise, lost their printed voice. Newspapers were still being published, however, and on occasion Buddhist viewpoints were still to be found.

Masunaga Reihō One of the last Zen-related voices to be heard was that of Dr. Masunaga Reihō (1902–81), a Sōtō Zen priest and scholar who in the postwar years published substantial works in English.[37] From May 25 to June 1, 1945, Masunaga wrote a series of articles in the Buddhist newspaper

Chūgai Nippō entitled "The Source of the Spirit of the Special Attack Forces." He put forth the following argument:

> The source of the spirit of the Special Attack Forces lies in the denial of the individual self and the rebirth of the soul, which takes upon itself the burden of history. From ancient times Zen has described this conversion of mind as the achievement of complete enlightenment.[38]

In equating the suicidal spirit of *kamikaze* pilots of the Special Attack Forces with the complete enlightenment of Buddhism, Masunaga had taken Zen to the militaristic extreme.

ZEN SECTARIAN ACTIVITIES

The Zen school has long stressed the importance of uniting knowledge with practice. What kind of actions did the Zen sect take to actualize the positions that its leaders took on the war? For the most part, the war-related activities of Japan's two major Zen sects closely paralleled those of other sects. We have already discussed social relief at home and missionary work abroad, but the Zen sect carried out other activities as well.

One example of Zen war-related action was the holding of special religious services designed to ensure victory in battle. The belief in the efficacy of such services had been a part of Mahayana Buddhism prior to its introduction to Japan. It was related to the belief that "merit," a kind of spiritual compensation or reward, was created as a result of meritorious acts, for example, the copying or recitation of sutras, or the construction of temples. Such merit could be transferred to others. In the Mahayana tradition, merit transference was regarded as part of the perfection of morality, one of six such perfections, and an important part of a bodhisattva's practice.[39]

In Japan, these special services were conducted by all Buddhist sects. The Zen tradition had originally been opposed to such services, regarding them as prayers for worldly favors. However, from the time of Hōjō Tokiyori (1227–63) and Hōjō Tokimune (1215–84), the nobility and warrior classes, chief patrons of the Zen sect, demanded prayers and services for all sorts of matters and occasions, including the most trivial. Long before the advent of the modern period, Zen temples had been turned into "a sort of seminary of prayers."[40]

The most common practice in Zen temples came to be the recitation, in whole or in part, of the Perfection of Wisdom Sutras. As Rinzai Zen sect–affiliated Imai Fukuzan pointed out in the January 1938 edition of *Zenshū*, these sutras were thought to be particularly efficacious "because they teach that wherever these sutras are circulated, various disasters and demons will disappear, to be replaced by good fortune."[41] These sutras consisted, in their Japanese version, of some six hundred volumes, and it was typical in ceremonial use to read only a limited number of passages from the total collection. As an alternative, the entire collection might be divided up among the assembled monks and ceremonially "fanned" in grandiose fashion with only the titles being read.

Sōjiji The following passage describes one such service held at Sōjiji, the second of the two head monasteries of the Sōtō Zen sect. It appeared on the front page of the November–December 1944 issue of the *Sōtō Shūhō*, the sect's administrative organ. In this case, the focus of the service was on the completion of a sectwide effort to make millions of handwritten copies of the very short Heart Sutra, which was considered to contain the essence of the teachings. As already noted, copying sutras was regarded as a merit-producing act, especially when done on such a massive scale. The highlights of the article, beginning with its title, are as follows:

> *The Service to Pray for Certain Victory [Based on the Completion of] the Consecrated Copying of Ten Million Heart Sutras* . . . .
> The great victory that was recently achieved off the coasts of Taiwan and the Philippines astonished the world. Yet, in spite of that, the severity of the terrific counterattack by the American and British enemy, who depend on massive amounts of materials, increases day by day. Outside the country, extremely fierce fighting is taking place on the Philippine island of Leyte. Within the country, the ugly enemy lawlessly dares to bomb the imperial capital and reconnoiter our imperial land. The national crisis on the war front is unprecedented. There has never been a fall as severe as this one, nor has there ever been a greater need for all one hundred million imperial subjects to rouse themselves.
> It was our sect that first proposed zealously uniting together for the purpose of the consecrated copying of ten million copies of the Heart Sutra. The goal of this effort is our fervent prayer for certain victory. Burning with enthusiasm, our whole sect, clerics and lay

followers alike, applied themselves to this project with the result that they greatly exceeded the planned ten million copies by some one million three hundred and eighty thousand. Some of the copies were written in blood and others were sealed in blood. Some of the copies were written in braille by wounded soldiers who had lost their sight.

We were also deeply moved by the unsurpassed honor to have copies bestowed on us by members of the imperial family. For seven days beginning from September 1, [1944,] the Great Prayer Service was solemnly held at the great monastery of Sōjiji. Reverently we prayed for the health of His Majesty, the well-being of the imperial lands, and the surrender of the enemy countries.[42]

The war situation was tightly woven into the description of this "religious service." Even soldiers who had lost their sight in battle were given a prominent role. Leaders of both the Rinzai and Sōtō Zen sects also actually changed elements of the concluding "merit transfer verse" *(ekōbun)* of the service to reflect the nation's war priorities and thereby apply the merit generated by the service or other good works to the realization of military goals. According to the April 15, 1942 edition of the *Sōtō Shūhō*, that sect's newly approved *ekōbun* included such phrases as: (1) unending military fortune and health for the officers and men at the front; (2) continuing victory in the holy war; and (3) enhancement of national prestige. The verse also included the wish, "May the sacred life of His Majesty the emperor extend for ten thousand years and may he be in good health."[43]

Rinzai Zen Imai Fukuzan, mentioned above, pointed out: "In our sect, religious services have been performed during wartime for more than six hundred years with the goal of enhancing military power."[44] It was only after the beginning of the Meiji period, he further noted, that this custom had momentarily fallen into disuse, and only because the old-style military verses were considered to be disloyal to the newly established central government by some senior officials. These officials knew of these verses' original association with the local armies of feudal lords, who had often doubled as temple patrons. They seemed inappropriate for the new regime, since they were not dedicated to the person and the army of the new emperor.

Imai pointed out that there was no longer any reason to be hesitant about resurrecting the military-flavored *ekōbun* of the past. On the contrary, nothing could be more appropriate in light of the outbreak of war with China. A comparison of the pre-Meiji verse he proposed as a model for the Rinzai sect with that subsequently adopted by the Sōtō sect reveals little substantive difference.

Except for one. The bodhisattva of compassion, Avalokiteshvara (Kannon or Kanzewon in Japanese) was transformed into a martial figure. Avalokiteshvara was "elevated" in the Rinzai verse to the rank of shogun or generalissimo, with the full title Kanzeon Shōgun Bodhisattva.[45] Given the miraculous powers Avalokiteshvara was believed to possess, Japan's military leaders readily welcomed this most well-known of bodhisattvas into their ranks. In the fall of 1939, imperial army general Matsui Iwane (1878–1948) personally ordered the construction of the Kōa Kannon temple on a hillside outside of the city of Atami in Shizuoka Prefecture. The temple's connection to Japan's wartime effort is apparent in its name: "Avalokiteshvara for the Development of Asia." At the temple's formal dedication on February 24, 1940, General Matsui said:

> The China Incident [of 1937] has resulted in massive lost of life through the mutual killing of neighboring friends. This is the greatest tragedy of the last one thousand years. Nevertheless this is a holy war to save the peoples of East Asia. . . . Invoking the power of Avalokiteshvara, I pray for the bright future of East Asia.[46]

In addition to the statue of Avalokiteshvara enshrined in the main worship hall, Matsui also had a second and larger ceramic statue of the same figure placed on the temple grounds. This latter statue was approximately six feet tall and made out of the blood-soaked earth the general had brought back from his battlefields in China. He regarded it as a memorial to "console the spirits" of both Japanese and Chinese war dead. These noble sentiments notwithstanding, after the war General Matsui was sentenced to death by the International Military Tribunal for the Far East for his role as commander of the Japanese forces involved in the December 1937 Rape of Nanjing.

Fund Raising   The conduct of religious services by the Zen sect was only a part of a much larger effort to support Japan's war effort. Leaders of both the Sōtō and Rinzai Zen sects, as well as other sects of Japanese Buddhism, engaged in fund-raising activities to provide aircraft to the military. The Sōtō Zen sect began its fund-raising efforts on the fourth anniversary of full-scale war in China, July 7, 1941. Within two weeks, sufficient funds were raised to buy one fighter plane "of the latest model" for the imperial navy and two hospital transport planes for the imperial army. These planes were named *Sōtō No. 1, Sōtō No. 2*, and so forth. The September 1, 1941 issue of *Sōtō Shūhō* contained the following comments about this effort:

> In accordance with the national policy of constructing a fully-armed state, our sect, united as one, has contributed [airplanes named] *Sōtō* with the hope that the sincerity of this act will be manifested in the majestic form of these planes flying high in the sky of the Greater East Asia Co-prosperity Sphere . . . and believing this will contribute greatly to the stimulation and growth of the people's spirit.[47]

The Rinzai Zen sect, specifically the Myōshinji branch, made an even greater effort. Although this branch was considerably less than one-third the size of the unified Sōtō sect, by war's end it had contributed three fighter aircraft to the imperial navy. The last of these fighters, contributed in April 1945, bore the inscription "[Emperor] Hanazono Myōshinji."

The donation of a few aircraft was not a significant material contribution to the war effort, of course. But these fund-raising efforts were designed primarily as a method to raise the Japanese people's spirit, the focus of the bulk of the Zen and overall Buddhist effort at home and abroad, and within the military itself.

Training   In June 1942 the Sōtō sect established The Wartime Center for the Development of an Instructor Corps to Train Imperial Subjects. The November 1, 1943 issue of *Sōtō Shūhō* used its front page to describe the principles upon which this center was based. The main principle or goal was "the increase of fighting power," under which a total of sixteen subprinciples were arranged in a hierarchy. The first eight subprinciples were, broadly speaking, all war related: (1) Promotion of Belief in Certain Victory; (2) The Establishment of Wartime Life; (3) The Practice of Volunteering Oneself for Public Duty; (4) Clarification of [the Concept of] Our National Polity; (5) Guard and Maintain the Prosperity of the Imperial Throne; (6) Respect the [Shinto] Deities and Revere One's Ancestors; (7) Train the Subjects of the Emperor; and (8) Recompense the Debt of Gratitude Owed the Emperor.

These subprinciples, especially (3) through (8), show the unmistakable influence of the themes first developed in the National Doctrine of the Meiji period. Zen priests, like all Buddhist priests in Japan, were simply being called upon to continue their role as Doctrinal Instructors, with the added duty of promoting belief in certain victory.

Zen priests did, of course, have a unique methodology for the training of imperial subjects: the practice of zazen. Zazen was used not only to train officers and soldiers but also workers—known at the time as "industrial warriors" *(sangyō senshi)*—in war-industry factories. The training sessions were held either in the factory dormitory or in a nearby Zen temple, and they lasted for up to one week. Participants would seek "to discover, through a thorough-going examination of the self, the origin of the power which enabled them, in their various work capacities, to serve the emperor." They were urged not to forget that "the merit resulting from their practice of zazen would enable them to realize infinite power."[48]

As Japan's situation gradually grew more critical, Zen priests were called upon to do more than just engage in what was popularly called "thought war" *(shisōsen)*. In January 1944, Zen priests who had not been drafted, or were not serving as military chaplains or continental missionaries, were called upon to abandon their "Dharma castles," take up factory work, and "aid in the increased production of military goods."[49] This call appeared in the February 1, 1944 issue of *Sōtō Shūhō*, but had been issued by the multisect Great Japan Buddhist Federation (Dainihon Bukkyō Kai). It applied to all Buddhist priests between the ages of sixteen and forty-five. The heart of the announcement read:

> As has been said, "The buildup of military power comes from spiritual power." It is for this reason that we ask for a total of approximately ten thousand leading priests from each of the sects to come forth as volunteers and directly engage in production in important industrial factories. At the same time they will be expected to provide spiritual training and guidance to the industrial warriors [in these factories].[50]

To the war's bitter end, the Way of the Warrior played an important role in all aspects of Japanese society. As the spiritual advocates of this code, Zen priests and the priests of other sects continued to discharge their duties even as they joined the ranks of the "industrial warriors."

PART III

POSTWAR TRENDS

CHAPTER TEN

THE POSTWAR ZEN RESPONSES TO
IMPERIAL-WAY BUDDHISM,
IMPERIAL-STATE ZEN, AND SOLDIER ZEN

J apan's surrender on August 15, 1945, marked the end of imperial-way Buddhism, imperial-state Zen, and soldier Zen. In the wake of Japan's defeat and the Allied Occupation, the sects of institutional Buddhism quickly changed aspects of their daily liturgies to reflect the demise of these movements. Buddhist leaders were faced with the question of how to explain their wartime conduct. Had their actions been a legitimate expression of Buddha Dharma or a betrayal of it?

D. T. SUZUKI'S RESPONSE

D. T. Suzuki was probably the first Buddhist leader in the postwar period to address the moral questions related to Buddhist war support. He first broached the topic of Buddhist war responsibility in October 1945, in a new preface for a reprint of *Japanese Spirituality (Nihonteki Reisei)*, originally published in 1944. He began by assigning to Shinto the blame for providing the "conceptual background" to Japanese militarism, imperialism, and totalitarianism. He then went on to discuss the Buddhist role as follows:

> It is strange how Buddhists neither penetrated the fundamental meaning of Buddhism nor included a global vision in their mission. Instead, they diligently practiced the art of self-preservation through their narrow-minded focus on "pacifying and preserving the state." Receiving the protection of the politically powerful

figures of the day, Buddhism combined with the state, thinking that its ultimate goal was to subsist within this island nation of Japan.

As militarism became fashionable in recent years, Buddhism put itself in step with it, constantly endeavouring not to offend the powerful figures of the day. Out of this was born such things as totalitarianism, references to [Shinto] mythology, "imperial-way Buddhism," and so forth. As a result, Buddhists forgot to include either a global vision or concern for the masses within the duties they performed. In addition, they neglected to awake within the Japanese religious consciousness the philosophical and religious elements, and the spiritual awakening, that are an intrinsic part of Buddhism.

Although it may be said that Buddhism became "more Japanese" as a result of the above, the price was a retrogression in terms of Japanese spirituality itself. That is to say, the opportunity was lost to develop a world vision within Japanese spirituality that was sufficiently extensive or comprehensive.[1]

Suzuki also attached a large portion of the blame for the militarization of Zen to both Zen priests and the Zen establishment. In an article written in 1946 for the magazine *Zengaku Kenkyū* entitled "Renewal of the Zen World" *(Zenkai Sasshin)*, Suzuki called for a "renewal" of Japanese Zen: "Generally speaking, present-day Zen priests have no knowledge or learning and therefore are unable to think about things independently or formulate their own independent opinions. This is a great failing of Zen priests."[2] One result of this "great failing" had been Zen's collaboration with the war, including mouthing government propaganda during wartime and then suddenly embracing world peace and democracy in the postwar era. As far as Suzuki was concerned, "it would be justifiable for priests like these to be considered war criminals."[3]

Interestingly, Suzuki did not deny that the Zen priests he criticized were enlightened, but rather that being enlightened was no longer sufficient for Zen priests:

With *satori* [enlightenment] alone, it is impossible [for Zen priests] to shoulder their responsibilities as leaders of society. Not only is it impossible, but it is conceited of them to imagine they could do so. . . . In *satori* there is a world of *satori*. However, by itself *satori* is unable to judge the right and wrong of war. With regard to disputes in the ordinary world, it is necessary to employ intellectual discrimination. . . . Furthermore, *satori* by itself cannot determine whether something like communism's economic system is good or bad.⁴

One reason Suzuki gave for this regrettable state of affairs was that Zen had developed under the "oppression" of a feudal society and had been forced to utilize that oppression in order to advance its own interests. It is only human nature, Suzuki pointed out, "to lick the hand that feeds you."⁵ In addition, Japanese Zen priests had failed to realize that a world existed outside of their own country. Suzuki concluded his article as follows:

> In any event, today's Zen priests lack "intellectuality" *(J. chisei)*. . . . I wish to foster in Zen priests the power to increasingly think about things independently. A *satori* which lacks this element should be taken to the middle of the Pacific Ocean and sent straight to the bottom! If there are those who say this can't be done, those persons should confess and repent all of the ignorant and uncritical words they and others spoke during the war in their temples and other public places.⁶

In all the passages above Suzuki seems to except himself from the need to confess or repent, but in the preface to *Japanese Spirituality*, he alludes obliquely to his own responsibility: "I believe that a major reason for Japan's collapse was truly because each one of us lacked an awareness of Japanese spirituality."⁷ If Suzuki accepts any personal responsibility for Japan's collapse, it is responsibility shared equally with each and every Japanese.

Suzuki apparently regarded his active promotion of the unity of Zen and the sword, the unity of Zen and Bushido, as having had no connection to Japan's militarism, and he had very little to say about the possibility that any of his wartime writings may have influenced the course of events. He did, however, refer rather mysteriously to a deficiency in *Japanese Spirituality:* "This work was written before Japan's unconditional surrender to the Allies. I was therefore unable to give clear expression to the meaning of Japanese spirituality."⁸ Is Suzuki suggesting that he distorted or censored his own writings in order to publish them under Japan's military government? Apparently not, since later in the same preface he explains the lack of clarity was due to the book's "academic nature," coupled with its "extremely unorganized structure."

Suzuki spoke again of his own moral responsibility for the war in *The Spiritualizing of Japan* (*Nihon no Reiseika*), published in 1947. This book is a collection of five lectures that he had given at Shin sect–affiliated Ōtani University in Kyoto during the month of June 1946. The focus of his talks was Shinto, for by this time he had decided that Shinto was to blame for Japan's militaristic past. According to Suzuki, Shinto was a "primitive religion" that "lacked spirituality." These factors had led to Japan's "excessive nationalism" and "military control."9 The solution to this situation was, in Suzuki's eyes, quite simple: "do away with Shinto."10 But Suzuki also spoke of his own responsibility for events:

> This is not to say that we were blameless. We have to accept a great deal of blame and responsibility. . . . Both before and after the Manchurian Incident [of 1931] all of us applauded what had transpired as representing the growth of the empire. I think there were none amongst us who opposed it. If some were opposed, I think they were extremely few in number. At that time everyone was saying we had to be aggressively imperialistic. They said Japan had to go out into the world both industrially and economically because the country was too small to provide a living for its people. There simply wasn't enough food; people would starve.
>
> I have heard that the Manchurian Incident was fabricated through various tricks. I think there were probably some people who had reservations about what was going on, but instead of saying anything they simply accepted it. To tell the truth, people like myself were just not very interested in such things.11

Even in the midst of Japan's utter defeat, Suzuki remained determined to find something praiseworthy in Japan's war efforts. He described the positive side of the war as follows:

> Through the great sacrifice of the Japanese people and nation, it can be said that the various peoples of the countries of the Orient had the opportunity to awaken both economically and politically. . . . This was just the beginning, and I believe that after ten, twenty, or more years the various peoples of the Orient may well have formed independent countries and contributed to the improvement of the world's culture in tandem with the various peoples of Europe and America.12

Here, in an echo of his wartime writings, Suzuki continued to praise the "great sacrifice" the Japanese people allegedly made to "awaken the peoples of Asia."

To his English-reading audience, Suzuki offered a different interpretation of the war. The following appeared in an essay entitled "An Autobiographical Account," included in the commemorative anthology *A Zen Life: D.T. Suzuki Remembered:*

> The Pacific War was a ridiculous war for the Japanese to have initiated; it was probably completely without justification. Even so, seen in terms of the phases of history, it may have been inevitable. It is undeniable that while British interest in the East has existed for a long time, interest in the Orient on the part of Americans heightened as a consequence of their coming to Japan after the war, meeting the Japanese people, and coming into contact with various Japanese things.[13]

Added to the awakening of the peoples of Asia, Suzuki tells us that another positive side of the "inevitable" war was the increased American presence and interest in Japan. In sum, it would seem that both friend and foe alike benefited in some way from Japan's "great sacrifice."

It is also noteworthy that Suzuki did not find war itself "ridiculous" but only the Pacific War, which was "probably" unjustified. Nowhere in Suzuki's writings does one find the least regret, let alone an apology, for Japan's earlier colonial efforts in such places as China, Korea, or Taiwan. In fact, he was quite enthusiastic about Japanese military activities in Asia. In an article addressed specifically to young Japanese Buddhists written in 1943 he stated: "Although it is called the Greater East Asia War, its essence is that of an ideological struggle for the culture of East Asia. Buddhists must join in this struggle and accomplish their essential mission."[14] One is left with the suspicion that for Suzuki things really didn't go wrong until Japan decided to attack the United States. What was it that made this particular war so "ridiculous"?

I suggest the answer is that Suzuki, having previously lived for more than a decade in the United States, knew Japan would be defeated. In support of this conclusion I point to a guest lecture Suzuki presented at Kyoto University in September 1941, just three months before Pearl Harbor. His ostensible topic was "Zen and Japanese Culture," but after finishing the formal part of his presentation, Suzuki added:

Japan must evaluate more calmly and accurately the awesome reality of America's industrial productivity. Present-day wars will no longer be determined as in the past by military strategy and tactics, courage and fearlessness alone. This is because of the large role now played by production capacity and mechanical power.[15]

Some observers, including Suzuki's former student Hidaka Daishirō, who recorded these remarks, interpret them as "antiwar" statements. Another way to view them is as simple common sense, without any moral or political intent: Don't pick a fight with someone you can't beat! Suzuki did not continue to make such statements of common sense after Pearl Harbor, when Japan had already engaged the United States in combat. Much more important, however, is the fact that he never criticized Japan's long-standing aggression against the peoples of Asia. Suzuki thought that punishing the "unruly heathens" was all right as long as Japan was strong enough to do so.

DECLARATIONS OF WAR RESPONSIBILITY BY JAPANESE BUDDHIST SECTS

In the postwar years there have only been four declarations addressing war responsibility or complicity by the leaders of traditional Buddhist sects in Japan's war effort. None of these statements was issued until more than forty years after the end of the war. By comparison, Japan's largest Protestant organization first issued a statement, "A Confession of Responsibility During World War II by the United Church of Christ in Japan," in 1967, twenty years before any Buddhists spoke up—though even that statement was more than a generation in the making. Most leading Japanese Buddhist sects remain silent to this day. None of the branches of the Rinzai Zen sect, for example, has formally addressed this crucial issue, which institutional Japanese Buddhism is only beginning to face.

The first of the four Buddhist sects to make an admission of war responsibility was the Higashi Honganji branch of the Shin sect in 1987. Koga Seiji, administrative head of the branch, read the statement aloud as part of a "Memorial Service for All War Victims" held on April 2, 1987. It read in part:

As we recall the war years, it was our sect that called the war a "sacred war." It was we who said, "The heroic spirits [of the war dead] who have been enshrined in [Shinto's] Yasukuni Shrine have served in the great undertaking of guarding and maintaining the prosperity of the imperial throne. They should therefore to be revered for having done the great work of a bodhisattva ." This was an expression of deep ignorance and shamelessness on our part. When recalling this now, we are attacked by a sense of shame from which there is no escape. . . .

Calling that war a sacred war was a double lie. Those who participate in war are both victims and victimizers. In light of the great sin we have committed, we must not pass it by as being nothing more than a mistake. The sect declared that we should revere things that were never taught by Saint [Shinran]. When we who are priests think about this sin, we can only hang our heads in silence before all who are gathered here.[16]

The Nishi Honganji branch followed suit four years later, in 1991. The following statement was issued by the administrative assembly of the Nishi Honganji branch on February 27, 1991. It was entitled "The Resolution to Make Our Sect's Strong Desire for Peace Known to All in Japan and the World." The central focus of this declaration, however, was the Gulf War coupled with the question of nuclear warfare mentioned in the second and third paragraphs. The sect's own wartime role did not rate mention until the fourth paragraph:

Although there was pressure exerted on us by the military-controlled state, we must be deeply penitent before the Buddhas and patriarchs, for we ended up cooperating with the war and losing sight of the true nature of this sect. This can also be seen in the doctrinal sphere, where the [sect's] teaching of the existence of relative truth and absolute truth was put to cunning use.[17]

In 1992 the Sōtō sect published a "Statement of Repentance" (sanshabun) apologizing for its wartime role. If the Rinzai Zen sect has been unwilling to face its past, it cannot be claimed that the postwar leadership of the Sōtō Zen sect was any more anxious to do so. Yet, a series of allegations concerning human rights abuses by this sect had the cumulative effect of forcing it to do so in spite of its reluctance. Unquestionably, the single most important event in this series of allegations was the sect headquarters' publication in 1980 of *The History of the Sōtō Sect's Overseas Evangelization and Missionary Work (Sōtō Shū Kaigai Kaikyō Dendō Shi).*

In the January 1993 issue of *Sōtō Shūhō*, the sect's administrative head-quarters announced that it was recalling all copies of the publication:

> The content of this book consists of the history of the overseas mis-sionary work undertaken by this sect since the Meiji period, based on reports made by the persons involved. However, upon investiga-tion, it was discovered that this book contained many accounts that were based on discriminatory ideas. There were, for example, words which discriminated against peoples of various nationalities. Furthermore, there were places that were filled with uncritical adu-lation for militarism and the policy to turn [occupied peoples] into loyal imperial subjects.[18]

Immediately following the above announcement was the Statement of Repentance issued by the administrative head of the sect, Ōtake Myōgen. The statement contained a passage which clearly shows how the preceding work served as a catalyst for what amounted to the sect's condemnation of its wartime role. The statement's highlights are as follows:

> We, the Sōtō sect, have since the Meiji period and through to the end of the Pacific War, utilized the good name of overseas evange-lization to violate the human rights of the peoples of Asia, espe-cially those in East Asia. This was done by making common cause with, and sharing in, the sinister designs of those who then held political power to rule Asia. Furthermore, within the social climate of ceasing to be Asian and becoming Western, we despised the peo-ples of Asia and their cultures, forcing Japanese culture on them and taking actions which caused them to lose their national pride and dignity. This was all done out of a belief in the superiority of Japanese Buddhism and our national polity. Not only that, but these actions, which violated the teachings of Buddhism, were done in the name of Buddha Shakyamuni and the successive patri-archs in India, China, and Japan who transmitted the Dharma. There is nothing to be said about these actions other than that they were truly shameful.
>
> We forthrightly confess the serious mistakes we committed in the past history of our overseas missionary work, and we wish to deeply apologize and express our repentance to the peoples of Asia and the world.

Moreover, these actions are not merely the responsibility of those people who were directly involved in overseas missionary work. Needless to say, the responsibility of the entire sect must be questioned inasmuch as we applauded Japan's overseas aggression and attempted to justify it.

To make matters worse, the Sōtō sect's publication in 1980 of the *History of the Sōtō Sect's Overseas Evangelization and Missionary Work* was done without reflection on these past mistakes. This meant that within the body of the work there were not only positive evaluations of these past errors, but even expressions which attempted to glorify and extol what had been done. In doing this, there was a complete lack of concern for the pain of the peoples of Asia who suffered as a result. The publication involved claimed to be a work of history but was written from a viewpoint which affirmed an imperial view of history, recalling the ghosts of the past and the disgrace of Japan's modern history.

We are ashamed to have published such a work and cannot escape a deeply guilty conscience in that this work was published some thirty-five years after the end of the Pacific War. The reason for this is that since the Meiji period our sect has cooperated in waging war, sometimes having been flattered into making common cause with the state, and other times rushing on its own to support state policies. Beyond that, we have never reflected on the great misery that was forced upon the peoples of Asia nor felt a sense of responsibility for what happened.

The historian E. H. Carr has said: "History is an endless conversation between the past and the present." Regretfully, our sect has failed to engage in that conversation, with the result that we have arrived at today without questioning the meaning of the past for the present, or verifying our own standpoint in the light of past history. We neglected to self-critically examine our own war responsibility as we should have done immediately after having lost the war in 1945.

Although the Sōtō sect cannot escape the feeling of being too late, we wish to apologize once again for our negligence and, at the same time, apologize for our cooperation with the war. . . . We recognize that Buddhism teaches that all human beings are equal as children of the Buddha. And further, that they are living beings with a dignity that must not, for any reason whatsoever, be impaired by others. Nevertheless, our sect, which is grounded in the belief of the transference of Shakyamuni's Dharma from master to disciple, both supported and eagerly sought to cooperate with a war of aggression against other peoples of Asia, calling it a holy war.

Especially in Korea and the Korean peninsula, Japan first committed the outrage of assassinating the Korean Queen [in 1895], then forced the Korea of the Lee Dynasty into dependency status [in 1904–5], and finally, through the annexation of Korea [in 1910], obliterated a people and a nation. Our sect acted as an advance guard in this, contriving to assimilate the Korean people into this country, and promoting the policy of turning Koreans into loyal imperial subjects.

All human beings seek a sense of belonging. People feel secure when they have a guarantee of their identity deriving from their own family, language, nationality, state, land, culture, religious belief, and so forth. Having an identity guarantees the dignity of human beings. However, the policy to create loyal imperial subjects deprived the Korean people of their nation, their language, and, by forcing them to adopt Japanese family and personal names, the very heart of their national culture. The Sōtō sect, together with Japanese religion in general, took upon itself the role of justifying these barbaric acts in the name of religion.

In China and other countries, our sect took charge of pacification activities directed towards the peoples who were the victims of our aggression. There were even some priests who took the lead in making contact with the secret police and conducting spying operations on their behalf.

We committed mistakes on two levels. First, we subordinated Buddhist teachings to worldly teachings in the form of national policies. Then we proceeded to take away the dignity and identity of other peoples. We solemnly promise that we will never make these mistakes again. . . .

Furthermore, we deeply apologize to the peoples of Asia who suffered under the past political domination of Japan. We sincerely apologize that in its overseas evangelism and missionary work the Sōtō sect made common cause with those in power and stood on the side of the aggressors.[19]

Of all the Japanese Buddhist sects to date, the Sōtō sect's statement of apology is certainly the most comprehensive. Yet, it almost totally ignores the question of the doctrinal and historical relationship between Buddhism and the state, let alone between Buddhism and the emperor. Is, for example, "nation-protecting Buddhism" an intrinsic part of Buddhism or merely a historical accretion? Similarly, is the vaunted unity between Zen and the sword an orthodox or heretical doctrine? Is there such a thing as a physical "life-giving sword" or is it no more than a Zen metaphor that Suzuki and others have terribly misused?

The most recent statement by a Japanese Buddhist sect concerning its wartime role was issued on June 8, 1994 by the Jimon branch of the Tendai sect, the smallest of that sect's three branches. Its admission of war responsibility amounted to one short phrase contained in "An Appeal for the Extinction of Nuclear [Weapons]." It read: "Having reached the fiftieth anniversary of the deaths of the atomic bomb victims, we repent of our past cooperation and support for [Japan's] war of aggression."[20]

In spite of the positive good that has issued from the Sōtō sect's statement of apology, including the posthumous reinstatement of the priestly status of Uchiyama Gudō in 1983, Zen scholars such as Ichikawa Hakugen make it clear that the rationale for Zen's support of state-sponsored warfare in general, and Japanese militarism in particular, is far more deeply entrenched in Zen and Buddhist doctrine and historical practice, especially in its Mahayana form, than any Japanese Buddhist sect has yet to publicly admit.

ICHIKAWA HAKUGEN AND OTHER COMMENTATORS

Far more has been written on the relationship of the Zen school to war than on any other school or sect of Japanese Buddhism. This is due to the voluminous writings of one man, the late Zen scholar and former Rinzai Zen priest, Ichikawa Hakugen (1902–86). In the postwar years he almost single-handedly brought this topic before the public and made it into an area of scholarly research. His writing, in turn, has sparked further investigation of this issue within other sects as well.

Before examining Ichikawa's writings, however, it would be helpful to look at comments made by other Zen adherents to get some idea of the overall tenor of the discussion and to bring the breadth and depth of Ichikawa's contribution into clearer focus. Several Zen scholars after Ichikawa continued to pursue this theme, coming to some remarkable conclusions, and a review of their writings closes out this chapter.

Yanagida Seizan Yanagida Seizan (b. 1922) started life as the son of a Rinzai Zen priest in a small village temple in Shiga Prefecture. As an adult he became the director of the Institute for Humanistic Studies at Kyoto University. Following retirement, he founded and became the first director of the International Research Institute for Zen Buddhism located at Hanazono University. In 1989 he presented a series of lectures on Zen at both Stanford University and the University of California, Berkeley.

In 1990 Seizan published a book entitled *Zen from the Future (Mirai kara no Zen)*. This book, containing a number of lectures he had presented in the United States, included material that was both personal and confessional in nature, making it relatively unusual among Zen scholarship. In the book Seizan speaks of his experience as a young Rinzai Zen priest during and immediately after the war:

> When as a child I began to become aware of what was going on around me, the Japanese were fighting neighboring China. Then the war expanded to the Pacific region, and finally Japan was fighting the rest of the world. When Japan surrendered on August 15, 1945, I had experienced two major wars. As someone who was brought up while these wars were expanding, I did not have the luxury of thinking deeply about the relationship between the state as a sovereign power engaged in war and Zen Buddhism. No doubt this was largely due to the fact that I had neither the opportunity to go to the battlefield nor directly engage in battle. Furthermore, having been brought up in a remote Zen temple, I was completely ignorant of what was happening in the world. In the last phase of World War II, I was training as a Zen monk at Eigenji, proud of being away from the secular world and convinced that my total devotion to Zen practice would serve the state.
>
> At any rate, with Japan's defeat I became aware of my own stupidity for the first time, with the result that I developed a deep sense of self-loathing. From 1945 to 1950 I did not see any point to human life, and I was both mentally and physically in a state of collapse. I had lost many of my friends; I alone had been left behind. We had fought continuously against China, the home country of Zen. We had believed, without harboring the slightest doubt, that it was a just war. In a state of inexpressible remorse, I could find rest neither physically nor mentally, and day after day I was deeply disturbed, not knowing what to do.

There is no need to say how complete is the contradiction between the Buddhist precepts and war. Yet, what could I, as a Buddhist, do for the millions upon millions of my fellow human beings who had lost their lives in the war? At that time, it dawned on me for the first time that I had believed that to kill oneself on the state's behalf is the teaching of Zen. What a fanatical idea!

All of Japan's Buddhist sects—which had not only contributed to the war effort but had been one heart and soul in propagating the war in their teachings—flipped around as smoothly as one turns one's hand and proceeded to ring the bells of peace. The leaders of Japan's Buddhist sects had been among the leaders of the country who had egged us on by uttering big words about the righteousness [of the war]. Now, however, these same leaders acted shamelessly, thinking nothing of it. Since Japan had turned itself into a civilized [i.e., democratic] nation overnight, their actions may have been unavoidable. Still, I found it increasingly difficult to find peace within myself. I am not talking about what others should or should not have done. My own actions had been unpardonable, and I repeatedly thought of committing suicide.[21]

Seizan did not, of course, commit suicide, but it is bracing to meet a Japanese Buddhist who was so moved by his earlier support for the war that he entertained the idea of killing himself. The irony is that by comparison with the numerous Zen and other Buddhist leaders we have heard from so far, Seizan bore very little responsibility for what had happened. Yet in the idealism of youth he felt obliged to take the sins of his elders on his own shoulders. He neither sought to ignore what had happened nor place the blame on anyone else.

Seizan's disdain for the way in which the previously prowar leaders of the various sects had so abruptly abandoned their war cries and become "peacemakers," coupled with his overall dissatisfaction with Rinzai Zen war collaboration, led him to stop wearing his robes in 1955:

I recognized that the Rinzai sect lacked the ability to accept its [war] responsibility. There was no hope that the sect could in any meaningful way repent of its war cooperation. . . . Therefore, instead of demanding the Rinzai sect do something it couldn't do, I decided that I should stop being a priest and leave the sect. . . . As far as I'm concerned, [Zen] robes are a symbol of war responsibility.

It was those robes that affirmed the war. I never intend to wear them again."[22]

Seizan's return to lay life did not, however, signal a lessening of his interest in Zen, for he became one of Japan's preeminent contemporary scholars of Buddhism, earning an international reputation for his research into the early development of Chinese Zen, or Chan Buddhism.

Masanaga Reihō   Ichikawa Hakugen recorded numerous statements made by these instant converts to peace, Masanaga Reihō prominent among them. During the war, as we noted earlier, Reihō extolled the virtues of Japan's kamikaze pilots. On September 15, 1945, exactly one month after Japan's surrender, Reihō wrote the following:

> The cause of Japan's defeat . . . was that among the various classes within our country there were not sufficient capable men who could direct the war by truly giving it their all. . . . That is to say, we lacked individuals who, having transcended self-interest, were able to employ the power of a life based on moral principles. . . . It is religion and education that have the responsibility to develop such individuals. . . .
>
> We must develop patriotic citizens who understand [the Zen teaching] that both learning and wisdom must be united with practice. They will become the generative power for the revival of our people . . . and we will be able to preserve our glorious national polity. . . . It is for this reason that religionists, especially Buddhists, must bestir themselves.[23]

In peace as well as war, it would seem, the national polity required Buddhists to bestir themselves. Reihō certainly did. He became vice-president of Komazawa University.

Yamada Mumon   Rinzai Zen master Yamada Mumon was the editor in 1942 of the strongly prowar book by his teacher Seki Seisetsu entitled *The Promotion of Bushido.* As already noted, in postwar Japan Mumon became both president of Hanazono University and chief abbot of Myōshinji, the largest branch of the Rinzai Zen sect.

In 1964 a collection of Mumon's sayings was published in English under the title *A Flower in the Heart.* Although Mumon did not intend it to be a scholarly work, he nevertheless made some noteworthy observations about both modern Buddhist history and Japan's participation in the Pacific War:

The only time when Buddhism in Japan met a suppression by the hand of a government was during the Meiji Restoration. Then, its teachings were denounced and its sacred images desecrated. Only the desperate efforts of its leaders saved it from the fate of an utter extinction, but the price they had to pay for its survival was high, for the monks, they agreed, would take up arms at the time of national emergencies. The dealing was surely regrettable. If those celebrated priests of the Meiji era were deceived by the name of loyalty and patriotism, we of today were taken in by the deceitful name of holy war. As a consequence, the nation we all loved lost its gear and turned upside down. This teaches us that we must beware not so much of oppression as of compromise.[24]

Interestingly, Mumon described the events from what is basically a third party's point of view. Nowhere does he take personal responsibility for what happened. Later, however, he did broach this topic:

For a long time I have entertained a wish to build a temple in every Asian nation to which we caused so much indescribable sufferings and damages during the past war, as token of our sincere penitence and atonement, both to mourn for their deads and ours and to pray for a perpetual friendship between her and our country and for further cultural intercourses.[25] [English as in original]

Here Mumon does at least admit to a collective responsibility for what happened, though he still does not discuss any personal role. Later, however, Mumon tries to justify the war, at least to some degree:

The sacrifices listed above were the stepping stones upon which the South-East Asian peoples could obtain their political independence. In a feeble sense, this war was a holy war. Is this observation too partial? . . . "If it were for the sake of the peace of the Far East," a phrase in one of the war-time songs, still rings in my ears.[26]

In the face of all these contradictions, it is difficult indeed to identify Mumon's true views. This is made even more challenging by a subsequent statement made in Japanese and distributed at the inaugural meeting of the "Association to Repay the Heroic Spirits [of Dead Soldiers]" (Eirei ni Kotaeru Kai) on June 22, 1976. Mumon was one of the founders of this association, whose purpose was to lobby the Japanese Diet for reinstatement of state funding for Yasukuni Shrine, the Shinto shrine in Tokyo dedicated to the veneration of the "heroic spirits" of Japan's war dead. Mumon's statement was entitled "Thoughts on State Maintenance of Yasukuni Shrine." It contained the following passage:

> Japan destroyed itself in order to grandly give the countries of Asia their independence. I think this is truly an accomplishment worthy of the name "holy war." All of this is the result of the meritorious deeds of two million five hundred thousand heroic spirits in our country who were loyal, brave, and without rival. I think the various peoples of Asia who achieved their independence will ceaselessly praise their accomplishments for all eternity.[27]

To his English-speaking audience Mumon described the war as having been in some "feeble sense" a holy war. To his Japanese audience, however, he invokes "meritorious deeds," "heroic spirits," and the "ceaseless praise" of a Southeast Asia liberated by the Japanese imperial forces. Now the real Mumon speaks up—at least to his Japanese audience. In the introduction to *A Flower in the Heart*, Umehara Takeshi described Mumon as "one of those rare monks from whose presence emanates a sense of genuine holiness."[28] Questions of "genuine holiness" aside, Mumon clearly persisted in his belief in Japan's holy war even into the postwar period, a belief that has been a credo for conservative Japanese politicians to this day.

Asahina Sōgen Asahina Sōgen (1891–1979) was the chief abbot and administrative head of the Engakuji branch of the Rinzai Zen sect. It will be recalled that Shaku Sōen had earlier been the abbot of this same temple, and though Sōgen had never been his disciple, their thinking was quite similar. Furthermore, like Yamada Mumon, Sōgen was active in conservative causes in the postwar years, most notably as one of the founders of the "Association to Protect Japan" (Nihon o Mamoru Kai).

In 1978 Sōgen published a book entitled *Are You Ready? (Kakugo wa Yoi ka)*, the last part of which was autobiographical in nature and included extensive comments about the war, its historical background, and his own role in it. Sōgen began his discussion, as so many others had, by praising the thirteenth-century military ruler Hōjō Tokimune and his Chinese Zen master Mugaku Sogen. According to Sōgen, the roots of both Zen involvement in prayer services and the subsequent close relationship between Zen and the state can be traced back to this period:

> The reason that Japanese Zen began to chant sutras in both morning and evening services was due to the Mongol invasion. Although other temples were making a big fuss of their prayers [to protect the country], Zen priests were only doing zazen. They were out of step [with the other sects] and said to be indifferent to the affairs of state. The result was that they began to recite sutras.[29]

Jumping more than six hundred years to the nineteenth century, Sōgen wrote that the Sino-Japanese War had been caused by China, which tried "to put Japan under its thumb" in Korea.[30] The subsequent Russo-Japanese War was, in his opinion, due entirely to Russian actions. "Russia rapidly increased its armaments and intended to destroy Japan without fighting. It was decided that if Japan was going to be destroyed without fighting, it might as well have a go at it and be destroyed."[31]

These remarks were only a warm-up for Sōgen's lengthy discussion of the Pacific War. He began this discussion with the following comments:

> Shortly after the [Pacific] War started, I realized that this was one we were going to lose. That is to say, the civil and military officials of whom the Japanese were so proud had turned into a totally disgusting bunch. . . .
>
> I'm not going to mince words—the top-level leadership of the navy was useless. I know because living in Kamakura as I did, I had met many of them. . . . For example, two close friends of [Admiral] Yamamoto Isoroku [1884–1943] told me the following story: After the great victory Yamamoto achieved in the air attack on Pearl Harbor, he had a meeting with [General] Tōjō Hideki. Yamamoto told him that this was no longer the era of battleships with their big guns. Rather, it was unquestionably the era of the airplane. Therefore every effort should be made to build more airplanes. Yamamoto was right, of course, in having said this.
>
> Tōjō, however, being the kind of person he was, in addition to being an army general, was consumed with jealousy, for, unlike the navy, the army had yet to achieve any major victories. The result

was that, due to his stubbornness, Tōjō told Yamamoto that he refused to accept orders from him because the latter was merely the commander-in-chief of the combined fleet while he [Tōjō] was the nation's prime minister. They were like two children fighting. Yamamoto's two friends claimed that because Japan wasn't building more airplanes, it was losing the war.

I [Sōgen] said to them, "Why wasn't Yamamoto willing to risk his position in opposing him? Why didn't he tell Tōjō he would resign his position as combined fleet commander?" . . . If I had been there, I would have let go with an explosive "Fool!" . . . The army and the navy don't exist for themselves, they exist to defend the country. . . . With people like these at the top how can they accomplish what is expected of them? We're already losing. With people like them as commanders, we cannot expect to win. . . . They're only thinking about themselves.[32]

Even though Sōgen claimed to have realized that Japan faced defeat at an early stage of the war with the Allies, he did not withdraw his support for the nation's war effort. On the contrary, he wrote that on numerous occasions he had given lectures and led "training camps" *(rensei kai)* to help maintain the people's morale. One of his earliest efforts (omitted from his book) was given on national radio (NHK) in July 1939. Speaking in support of the government's newly issued order for a general mobilization of the civilian population, he said:

> Lieutenant Colonel Sugimoto Gorō was revered as a god of war, having undergone Zen training. . . . Had he possessed a weak spirit, or lacked the ability to carry out [what needed to be done], he would have been held in contempt by the people, given today's emergency situation. Let us be inspired by the [Zen] expression: "A day without work is a day without eating." If we were to carry this over into every aspect of our daily lives, that is to say, if we were to dedicate ourselves totally to repaying the debt of gratitude we owe the nation, we would have a splendidly coherent life. Though we found ourselves on the home front and not on the battlefield, we would have nothing to be ashamed of.[33]

A second lecture, which Sōgen did choose to write about, was given at the Naval Technical Research Institute in Tokyo. With evident pride, he twice mentioned that all the members of this institute were university graduates and that it was the most important center for naval technology in Japan. His lecture was given to all two hundred workers at the institute and lasted for a full three hours and twenty minutes. Perhaps embarrassed by its content (within the context of the postwar era), he did not give the details of his talk, but he claimed there was not so much as a cough from his audience the entire time. "I'll be satisfied if what I've said has been of even a small benefit to the state," he concluded.[34] As an example of one of the training camps he led, Sōgen described a military-sponsored visit of some forty-four wounded war veterans to Engakuji. They underwent Zen training as best they could for a one-week period. When it came time for them to leave, Sōgen addressed them:

> Even though you have sustained injuries to your eyes or to your hands, you are still brave and seasoned warriors. This is now a time when the people must give everything they have to the state. You, too, have something precious to give. That is to say, transfer your spirit to the people of this nation, hardening their resolve. You were not sent to a place like this to be pampered. I took charge of you because I wanted you to have the resolve and the courage to offer up the last thing you possess [to the state].[35]

"They cried," Sogen reported, "all of them."[36]

Sōgen was not critical of all those in leadership positions during the war. There was one institution, or figure, for whom he had unwavering respect both during and after the war, the emperor: "The debt of gratitude owed the emperor . . . is so precious that there is no way to express one's gratitude for it or to repay it."[37] Although Sōgen didn't discuss Emperor Hirohito's wartime role, he had nothing but praise for his actions following Japan's defeat. It was the emperor's "nobility of spirit," Sōgen maintained, that so moved General Douglas MacArthur, head of the Allied Occupation Forces, that he decided to treat Japan leniently, maintaining its integrity as a single country. It was in this spirit that Sōgen left his Japanese readers with the following parting thought: "The prosperity and everything we enjoy today is completely due to the selflessness and no-mindedness of the emperor's benevolence. I want you to remember this. Human beings must never forget the debt of gratitude they owe [others]."[38] Though the terms "imperial-state Zen" and "soldier Zen" may have ceased being rallying cries in postwar Japan, Sōgen, like Yamada Mumon, demonstrates that their spirit

Sōgen master (handwritten margin note)
Zen master (handwritten margin note)

Cf (handwritten margin note)
Seto (handwritten margin note)

lived on. He was far from the only postwar Zen master to maintain this attitude, a fact which explains, at least in part, why even today not a single
branch of the Rinzai Zen sect has ever publicly discussed, let alone apologized
for, its wartime role. To do so would call into question not only the modern
history of that sect but much of its seven-hundred-year history in Japan.

Ichikawa Hakugen   While the Rinzai Zen sect has spawned some of the
strongest advocates of imperial-state Zen and soldier Zen, it has also produced some of its most severe critics. Yanagida Seizan may be considered
one, though his was at best a limited critique. The Rinzai Zen–affiliated
priest and scholar Ichikawa Hakugen took up this challenge on a much
broader scope and a much deeper level.

Hakugen's classic statement on the role of Buddhism, particularly Zen,
in the wartime era is *The War Responsibility of Buddhists (Bukkyōsha no Sensō
Sekinin)*, published in 1970. Three years before, in 1967, he had begun to
examine this issue in *Zen and Contemporary Thought (Zen to Gendai Shisō)*.
He developed his ideas still further in a series of articles and books including *Religion Under Japanese Fascism (Nihon Fashizumu Ka no Shūkyō)*, published in 1975, and a major article entitled "The Ideology of the Military
State" *(Kokubō Kokka Shisō)* included in *Buddhism During the War (Senji Ka
no Bukkyō)*, published in 1977 and edited by Nakano Kyōtoku.

In *Religion Under Japanese Fascism*, Hakugen justified his call for a critical evaluation of the relationship between Buddhism and Japanese
militarism:

> In recent times, Japanese Buddhists talk about Buddhism possess-
> ing the wisdom and philosophy to save the world and humanity
> from collapse. However, I believe Buddhism first has to reflect on
> what, if any, doctrines and missionary work it advocated during the
> Meiji, Taishō, and Shōwa periods to oppose exploitation and op-
> pression within Japan itself, as well as Korea, Taiwan, Okinawa,
> China, and Southeast Asia. Beyond that, Buddhism has the duty and
> responsibility to clarify individual responsibility for what happened
> and express its determination [never to let it happen again].39

In the preceding work, as well as many of his other works, Hakugen set
out to do just what he said needed to be done. He not only clarified individual responsibility but also looked at those doctrinal and historical aspects
of both Zen and Buddhism which he believed lent themselves, rightly or

wrongly, to abuse by supporters of Japanese militarism. One of the individuals whom Hakugen felt was most responsible for the development of imperial-way Zen was D. T. Suzuki.

Hakugen felt that Suzuki's position as expressed in *A Treatise on the New [Meaning of] Religion* in the latter part of the Meiji period helped form the theoretical basis for what followed. In justification of this assertion, he quoted the same passage from that treatise introduced in chapter 2. He stated that Suzuki had been speaking of China when he mentioned a "lawless country" in this treatise. Hakugen then went on to say:

> [Suzuki] considered the Sino-Japanese War to be religious practice designed to punish China in order to advance humanity. This is, at least in its format, the very same logic used to support the fifteen years of warfare devoted to "The Holy War for the Construction of a New Order in East Asia." Suzuki didn't stop to consider that the war to punish China had not started with a Chinese attack on Japanese soil, but, instead, took place on the continent of China. Suzuki was unable to see the war from the viewpoint of the Chinese people, whose lives and natural environment were being devastated. Lacking this reflection, he considered the war of aggression on the continent as religious practice, as justifiable in the name of religion. . . .
>
> The logic that Suzuki used to support his "religious conduct" was that of "the sword that kills is identical with the sword that gives life" and "kill one in order that many may live." It was the experience of "holy war" that spread this logic throughout all of Asia. It was Buddhists and Buddhist organizations that integrated this experience of war with the experience of the emperor system.[40]

Needless to say, Suzuki was not the only Zen adherent who Hakugen believed shared responsibility for the war. Mention has already been made, for example, of Harada Daiun Sōgaku, whom Hakugen identified as a "fanatical militarist." Hakugen went on to point out that yet another of Harada's chief disciples and Dharma successors, Yasutani Hakuun (1885–1973) was, in postwar years, "no less a fanatical militarist and anticommunist" than his master.[41]

Specifically, in 1951, Hakuun established a publication known as *Awakening Gong (Gyōshō)* as a vehicle for his religious and political views. The following passage is typical of his political views:

Those organizations which are labeled right-wing at present are the true Japanese nationalists. Their goal is the preservation of the true character of Japan. There are, on the other hand, some malcontents who ignore the imperial household, despise tradition, forget the national polity, forget the true character of Japan, and get caught up in the schemes and enticements of Red China and the Soviets. It is resentment against such malcontents that on occasion leads to the actions of young [assassin] Yamaguchi Ojiya or the speech and behavior of [right-wing novelist] Mishima Yukio.[42]

Coupled with Hakuun's admiration for Japan's right wing was his equal distaste for Japan's labor movement and institutions of higher learning. Less than a year after the above, he wrote:

It goes without saying the leaders of the Japan Teachers' Union are at the forefront of the feebleminded [in this country]. . . . They, together with the four opposition political parties, the General Council of Trade Unions, the Government and Public Workers Union, the Association of Young Jurists, the Citizen's League for Peace in Vietnam, and so forth, have taken it upon themselves to become traitors to the nation. . . .

The universities we presently have must be smashed one and all. If that can't be done under the present constitution, then it should be declared null and void just as soon as possible, for it is an un-Japanese constitution ruining the nation, a sham constitution born as the bastard child of the allied occupation forces.[43]

As for the theoretical basis of Hakuun's political views, he shared the following with his readers six months later: "All machines are assembled with screws having right-hand threads. Right-handedness signifies coming into existence, while left-handedness signifies destruction."[44] When Hakuun went to the United States to lead meditation training on seven different occasions between 1962 and 1969, sentiments like the above were noticably missing from his public presentations. It would appear that they were for domestic consumption only. Yet Hakuun did not hesitate to tell his American students what the true cause of conflict in the world was. In a 1969 essay entitled "The Crisis in Human Affairs and the Liberation Found in Buddhism," he wrote:

Western-style social sciences have been based on a deluded misconception of the self, and they attempt to develop this "I" consciousness. This is dichotomy. As a result, they have reinforced the idea of dichotomy between human beings which has lead to conflicts and fighting. They have even created a crisis which may destroy all of mankind.[45]

Naturally, Hakugen was sharply critical of "god of war" Sugimoto Gorō and his Zen master and eulogist Yamazaki Ekijū:

First, Sugimoto and Yamazaki used Zen as nothing more than a means for the practice of the imperial way. Not only that, but by forcing the meaning and tenets of Zen to fit within the context of a religion centered on the emperor, Zen itself was obliterated.[46]

Hakugen also pointed out that the Sōtō Zen sect had gone so far as to actually change its fundamental principles in order to place itself squarely behind the state's war efforts. In 1940 this sect revised its creed to read: "The purpose of this sect is . . . to exalt the great principle of protecting the state and promoting the emperor, thereby providing a blessing for the eternal nature of the imperial throne while praying for the tranquillity of a world ruled by his majesty."[47] In its new creed promulgated following Japan's defeat, the Sōtō sect dropped the preceding paragraph in its entirety, as it was clearly no longer politically acceptable.

Hakugen was the first postwar Zen and Buddhist scholar to try to determine what Buddhist doctrines or pre-Meiji historical developments might have either contributed to or facilitated Buddhist war collaboration. He identifies one example of a contributing historical development in *Zen and Contemporary Thought:*

In the Edo period [1600–1867] Zen priests such as Bunan [1603– 76], Hakuin [1685–1768], and Tōrei [1721–92] attempted to promote the unity of Zen and Shinto by emphasizing Shinto's Zen-like features. While this resulted in the further assimilation of Zen into Japan, it occurred at the same time as the establishment of the power of the emperor system. Ultimately this meant that Zen lost almost all of its independence, the impact of the High Treason Incident on the Zen world representing the final stage of this transformation.[48]

Hakugen also looked for those Buddhist tenets that seem to have made Buddhism susceptible to militaristic manipulation. One example he gave of such an idea concerned the Buddhist teaching of *wago* (harmony). Out of harmony, he postulated, had come Buddhism's "nonresistance" and "tolerance":

> With what has modern Japanese Buddhism harmonized itself? With State Shinto. With the power of the state. With militarism. And therefore, with war. To what has modern Japanese Buddhism been nonresistant? To State Shinto. To the power of the state. To militarism. To wars of aggression. Toward what has modern Japanese Buddhism been tolerant? Toward the above mentioned entities with which it harmonized. Therefore, toward its own war responsibility.
>
> And I should not forget to include myself as one of those modern Japanese Buddhists who did these things.[49]

Hakugen's self-indictment was, in fact, quite appropriate, for during the war years he had indeed been a strong advocate of Japan's "holy war." For example, in September 1942, he published an article in *Daihōrin* entitled, "War, Science, and Zen." He began his article with the following observation:

> Pacifistic humanitarism, which takes the position that all conflicts are inhumane crimes, is the sentiment of moralists who don't know the true nature of life. We, on the other hand, know of numerous instances in which peace is far more unwholesome and evil than conflict. In this regard, Nietzsche, who taught the logic of war instead of peace, was a man with a firm grip on living truth rather than the abstractions of pacificists.[50]

Hakugen went on to relate these ideas to Zen:

> The words [of Zen master Dōgen] discuss the "falling away" of body and mind of both oneself and others. A truly solemn battle must be one in which one conquers not only the evil within the enemy, but within one's own side as well. A conflict which thoroughly incorporates within itself defense, penitence, and liberation, is one that is worthy of the name "holy war."

By protecting oneself one can truly save others, and through saving others one can undoubtedly be saved oneself. It is in such a war that the "sword which kills" can, at the same time, be the "sword which gives life." It is the creativity which emerges from tragedy that gives the title "holy war" its appropriateness.[51]

And finally Hakugen becomes quite concrete and specific: "The current war is a fight for 'eternal peace in the Orient.'"[52]

Motivated by his awareness of his wartime complicity, Hakugen tenaciously uncovered layer after layer of factors that had facilitated or caused Buddhism, and Zen in particular, to unite with militarism. Nowhere is this clearer than in his examination of the historical character of Japanese Buddhism that was included in his book *The War Responsibility of Buddhists*. Hakugen outlined twelve historical characteristics which, developing over the centuries, produced in Japanese Buddhism a receptiveness to authoritarianism.[53]

The first of these characteristics was the subservience of Buddhism to the state. Hakugen pointed out that there were a number of Mahayana sutras originating in India that emphasized the role of Buddhism as "protector of the state." These sutras had been particularly welcomed in Japan, where this aspect of Buddhism became even more pronounced. During the Edo period Buddhism came under complete government control and, mixed together with Shinto, evolved into what was essentially a state religion.

As a state religion, Buddhism became a mere shell of its former self. Its attention was now focused on ancestor veneration in the form of funerals and memorial services, making it a religion with a limited social nexus, the extended family. It was antagonistic to Christianity because of the latter's transnational and modern character. Furthermore, the Meiji government's opposition to Christianity and socialism only reinforced Buddhism's opposition to those movements. Buddhism sought to protect itself by ever greater subservience to the state, including opposition to any group or movement that threatened nationalism based on the emperor system and military expansionism.

Hakugen's second characteristic concerned Buddhist views on humanity and society. On the one hand, Buddhism emphasizes the equality of human beings based on their possession of a Buddha nature, the innate potential to realize Buddhahood. On the other hand, the doctrine of karma, with its corollary belief in good and bad karmic retribution, tends to serve as a kind of moral justification for social inequality. Differences in social status, wealth, and happiness are seen as just rewards for good or bad conduct both in this and previous lives, having nothing to do with the political or social structure of society.

Understood in this light, social inequality is not only just, but represents true equality. It is, furthermore, only natural for Buddhism to protect a society with clear differences in social status since such a society facilitates the working out of past karma. Socialism, on the other hand, advocates the purposeful leveling of these social differences, thus becoming the proponent of "evil equality." As such, it must be rejected.

The third characteristic was concerned with the question of social morality, the encouragement of good and the punishment of evil. In this context Hakugen discussed one of Japan's oldest quasi-legal documents, the Seventeen Article Constitution of Prince Regent Shōtoku, allegedly promulgated in 604. This Constitution contained the following warning: "If you receive an imperial command, it must be obeyed without fail. The sovereign is heaven, and imperial subjects are the earth. . . . Should the earth seek to overthrow heaven, there will only be destruction."

Hakugen maintained that as a semistate religion from this period onwards, Buddhism sought to protect not only the state but its hierarchical social structure as well. On the basis of having completely internalized this essentially Confucian logic over the centuries, Buddhism readily became a faithful servant of the Meiji government's conservative social policies, working to create the ideal imperial subject.

The fourth characteristic concerned both human rights and justice. Hakugen first introduced the Buddhist doctrine of dependent co-arising or causality, explaining that all phenomena are regarded as being in a constant state of flux, born and dying without any permanent substance to them, empty. When this doctrine is applied to the self, it produces the concept of egolessness or no-self, leaving no room for the independence of the individual.

According to Hakugen, this doctrine prevented the development of the Western principle of Natural Law within Buddhism, leaving the modern concepts of human rights and justice without a foundation. In the Seventeen Article Constitution, there is an admonition to "turn one's back on self-interest and embrace the public good." Hakugen believed there existed a direct connection between this and the wartime slogan "exterminate the self and serve the public" *(messhi hōkō)*. The "public" referred to, he maintained, was none other than the state and the emperor. Thus, "The teaching of 'no-self' became both a theory and ethic serving mikado imperialism."54

The lack of Buddhist dogma was the fifth characteristic Hakugen identified. Lacking a transcendent, personal God who had to be worshiped and defended, Buddhism failed to establish the type of compelling basic dogma a believer would fight to preserve. In Japan, this resulted in the neglect of both discursive thought and logical theory. Instead, Buddhism concentrated on the inner self, giving the central role to the individual's subjective feelings. There was little concern for the results of external actions.

The sixth characteristic was the concept of *on*. Forming the heart of Mahayana Buddhist ethics, *on* is the teaching that a debt of gratitude is owed to those from whom favors are received. Traditionally, *on* was owed to four classes or types of individuals: (1) one's parents; (2) the ruler; (3) all sentient beings; and (4) either heaven and earth, or the Three Treasures of Buddhism, the Buddha, Dharma, and Sangha. Hakugen argued that in Japan the debt of gratitude owed one's parents had converged with that owed one's sovereign, the emperor, who assumed the role of the head of the entire Japanese family. This produced a corresponding weakening of the sense of universal indebtedness to all sentient beings.

The Buddhist belief in the mutual interdependence of all things was the seventh characteristic. Hakugen stated that this belief led in modern Japan to an organic view of the state coupled with a feeling of intimacy towards it. Encompassed within this viewpoint was the recognition of the preeminence of the state, with the individual being no more than a constituent element. In similar fashion, it meant that capitalists, too, were preeminent, with workers being subsumed beneath them in an extended family system that emphasized harmony and cooperation.

Hakugen's eighth characteristic focused on the doctrine of the Middle Way. He maintained that the Middle Way doctrine of early Buddhism in India had become the operating principle for social development in modern Japanese Buddhism. This did not manifest itself as some type of compromise between extreme left-wing and right-wing political ideology. Instead, it took the form of a constant search for compromise with the aim of avoiding confrontation before it occurred. This lead to an unwillingness to take clearcut positions on social issues as well as very hazy ideas about social reform.

The ninth characteristic centered on the tradition of ancestor veneration. As "nation-protecting Buddhism" assimilated itself to Japan, it promoted the customs and virtues of ancestor veneration. The entire nation came to be regarded as one large family in which loyalty between subject and sovereign was the chief virtue. This logic was extended and employed as a support mechanism for the sacred war as voiced by the wartime slogan "the whole world under one roof" [*hakkō ichiu*].

The tenth characteristic was the idea of "aging." The Middle Ages in Japan gave rise to a culture in which old and mature things were valued. Out of this came such aesthetic concepts as *wabi* (rustic antiqueness) and *sabi* (ancient solitariness). According to this way of thinking, society was based on a set of ancient and immutable laws, especially as regarded its hierarchical structure. To challenge those laws and to suggest new social structures was seen as the act of an immature person who had not fully grasped the laws. The mature person, in contrast, would dismiss proposals for social change, especially those threatening the existing social order, while remaining accepting, obedient, and uncritical of the status quo.

The eleventh characteristic involved Buddhism's emphasis on inner peace rather than justice. Lacking a God as the author of transcendental principles, Buddhism was not compelled to build a Kingdom of God based on justice here on earth. Furthermore, because Buddhism is a religion based on the idea of the emptiness of things, it had almost no basis for maintaining an antagonistic attitude towards State Shinto. Buddhism's focus on the inner peace of the individual also contributed to its failure to encourage and justify the will to reorganize society.

Hakugen's twelfth and final characteristic concerned the Buddhist logic of *soku*, a copula that means "just as it is" and is related to the Buddhist concepts of suchness and nonduality. Ichikawa contended that the logic of *soku*, appearing as it does throughout Buddhist thought, leads to a static, aesthetic perspective, a detached, subjective harmony with things. In Hakugen's view, Buddhism lacks a dynamic theoretical basis for either confronting reality or promoting social change.

Each one of the twelve characteristics identified by Hakugen is, certainly, open to debate. Nevertheless, his critique strongly suggests that the issue of Buddhism's collaboration with Japanese militarism is one with very deep roots in Buddhist history and doctrine, by no means limited to Japan alone. For this insight, and much more, future students of this topic will remain indebted to this pioneering scholar.

Hakamaya and Matsumoto   The Sōtō Zen sect has made a beginning in addressing some of the many issues involved in the modern historical relationship between the sect and the Japanese state and militarism. This work continues even now through the ongoing research and writings of such contemporary Sōtō Zen scholars at Komazawa University as Hakamaya

Noriaki (b. 1943) and Matsumoto Shirō (b. 1950). Both of these scholars, like Ichikawa Hakugen before them, have undertaken an in-depth look at some of the doctrinal underpinnings of Zen which facilitated, if not prompted, its support for Japanese militarism. They have reached some surprising and radical conclusions.

Matsumoto discusses the relationship of patriotism to Buddhism:

> I believe that to love Japan is to love one's self. To me "Japan" is an extension of my own mind and body. As I love my own body, so I love Japan. Self-love, or narcissism, is very enticing and sweet. . . . However, love is something which should be directed to others; if it is directed at one's self, it becomes self-attachment.
>
> On the basis of the Buddhist teaching of no-self, I have come to the following conclusions: (1) one should disdain oneself; and (2) one should love only the absolute other (God or Buddha). Therefore, as a Buddhist, based on the teaching of no-self, I must not love Japan, since it is an extension of my self.
>
> Even if I believe I should not love myself, it is certainly true that I am always loving myself; even if I believe I should not love Japan, I cannot avoid loving Japan. However, the teaching of the Buddha is absolute. . . . A Buddhist must not love Japan [i.e. one's own country].[55]

Hakamaya's conclusions are no less dramatic. In his 1990 book *Critical Buddhism (Hihan Bukkyō)*, Hakamaya echoed Ichikawa Hakugen's earlier critique of the Buddhist concept of "harmony" *(wa)*:

> True Buddhists must, having disavowed the Law of the Sovereign, believe in the Law of the Buddha. They must draw a sharp distinction between Buddhist teachings and anti-Buddhist teachings, using both intellect and language to denounce the latter. . . .
>
> In the present age dominated by a harmony which is ever ready to compromise, to be opposed to war means to reject harmony.[56]

Hakamaya also directed his attention to those Sōtō Zen masters who supported Japan's war effort. He had the following to say about Sawaki Kōdō, whose wartime writings have been previously introduced:

> When one becomes aware of Sawaki Kōdō's [wartime] call to "Invoke the power of the emperor; invoke the power of the military

banner," it is enough to send shivers down one's spine. . . . Not only was Sawaki not a Buddhist, but he took up arms against [Sōtō Zen Master] Dōgen himself. . . .⁵⁷

This is very strong criticism coming from a Sōto Zen–affiliated scholar, for even today that sect continues, on the whole, to regard Kōdō as one of its great scholar-priests of this century. But Hakamaya is driven by the belief that Buddhists "must draw a sharp distinction between Buddhist and anti-Buddhist teachings."

Even more surprising, Hakamaya and Matsumoto are ready and willing to subject traditional, nearly sacrosanct Zen doctrines to the test of Buddhist versus anti-Buddhist teachings. Nowhere is this better seen than in Hakamaya's assertion that the doctrine of the original or inherent enlightenment of all sentient beings, which forms a crucial part of East Asian Buddhism in general and Zen in particular, is not a Buddhist concept at all. It is this assertion that serves as the basis of his attack on harmony, claiming that it, too, is "not Buddhism."⁵⁸

Hakamaya's basic position is that the doctrine that all beings are inherently, therefore originally enlightened (hongaku shisō), violates the fundamental Buddhist teaching of causality, the twelvefold chain of dependent arising said to have been discovered by Buddha Shakyamuni through his enlightenment experience. Hakamaya sees the doctrine of original enlightenment as affirming an eternal, substantial, underlying essence, often referred to as Buddha nature, on which everything else in the phenomenal world depends or arises from. The teaching of causality, on the other hand, describes a temporal sequence from cause to effect, and is predicated on the logic that if B exists, then A has existed; if A does not exist, then B will not exist. In other words, each precondition is dependent on the one before it, with a total of twelve preconditions linked together and forming an indivisible circle, typically represented in Buddhist art as the Wheel of Life. In this scheme, there is no place for an unchanging substratum such as original enlightenment beneath or behind the phenomenal world.

For a similar reason both Hakamaya and Matsumoto criticize the doctrine of tathagatagarbha (J. nyoraizō), a second foundation of East Asian Buddhism. Unlike original enlightenment, which lacks a Sanskrit equivalent and may well be a later Chinese creation, the latter doctrine is a clear if relatively minor part of the Indian Mahayana tradition.⁵⁹ In this compound term, tathagata denotes the Eternal Buddha and therefore can also be translated as "suchness," "thusness," or "the absolute." The word garbha literally means a "seed" or "embryo," and refers to the receptacle or womb in which the absolute resides. As a compound, this term refers to the absolute residing as a constituent element, though in embryonic form, within sentient beings—the universal potential for enlightenment waiting to be realized. While the phenomenal world is regarded as ultimately unreal (i.e. non-existent), being devoid of any unchanging self-nature, the realm of the unconditioned absolute, of suchness, is real (existent).

In Japan the doctrine of original enlightenment was expanded over time to embrace the idea that all things, animate and inanimate alike, were inherently enlightened. Hence the famous phrase, often encountered in Japanese literature, that "mountains and rivers, plants and trees, all attain Buddhahood" *(sansen sōmoku shikkai jōbutsu)*. On the surface this appears to an optimistic, even democratic idea, for enlightenment becomes equally and inherently open to all, regardless of wealth, sex, age, education, or nationality, and embraces even the objects of the inanimate world.

The question is, of course, what these abstract doctrinal arguments have to do with Hakamaya's and Matsumoto's social critiques. They discovered that in historical practice these two doctrines produced what they regard as very undesirable consequences, a major one of which is a philosophy of discrimination. They argue that if a single, unchanging reality underlies all phenomena, then everything in the phenomenal world becomes essentially the same. This includes, of course, such moral distinctions as right and wrong and good and bad, and such social distinctions as rich and poor and strong and weak. Accordingly, there is no longer any need or reason to fight injustice or to right wrongs. Discrimination and injustice come to be regarded as no more than the way things are and ought to be. The moral imperative to act selflessly, to reach out to those in need, disappears.

Hakamaya further argues that original enlightenment functions as an authoritarian idea because suchness is seen as being ineffable, with no place for either words or concepts, let alone faith or intellect. This in turn leads to those Zen terms so beloved by Suzuki and other Zen masters, terms such as "no reliance on words or letters" *(furyū monji)*, "direct intuition" *(chokkan)*, and especially, "no-thought" and "no-reflection." In this connection it may be helpful to recall Suzuki's comments concerning the way of the sword:

> In the *Kendō* ("the Way of the Sword"), what is most essential to attain besides its technique is the spiritual element controlling the art throughout. It is a state of mind known as *munen* or *musō*, "no-thought" or "no-reflection." . . . It means letting your natural

faculties act in a consciousness free from thoughts, reflections, or affections of any kind. . . . When this is understood, your art is perfect. Finally, Zen and the Sword's Way are one in this, that both ultimately aim at transcending the duality of life and death.[60]

Matsumoto identified this type of thinking as a philosophy of death and rejected it categorically.

Hakamaya rejected the idea of harmony, calling it an enemy of Buddhism because it inevitably promotes compromise and tolerance—tolerance that is exploited by the powerful in society to maintain the *status quo,* no matter how unjust it may be. At the same time, it is used to stifle internal dissent, thereby making people easy prey for political propaganda. In one of his strongest statements on this issue, Hakamaya said:

> The previous Greater East Asia War was prosecuted in accord with the concept of harmony utilizing [such slogans as] "The Greater East Asia Co-Prosperity Sphere" and "The Whole World Under One Roof." The sons of Japan, unable to become traitors, silently and obediently took their bodies to the battlefield, regarding it as a virtue to do so. If we reflect on this for but a moment, it is clear that it is through faith one becomes a true Buddhist. Should there be an occasion when the Law of the Sovereign and the Law of the Buddha come into conflict, then . . . the Law of the Buddha should be chosen. One must never allow oneself to be reduced to a mere physical entity. Instead, the intellect must be used to its utmost to clearly distinguish what is right, and words used to their utmost to criticize what is wrong. I believe this is the way in which faith becomes an activity opposed to war.[61]

Needless to say, statements like the above have not gone unchallenged within Japanese Buddhist circles. For one, critics want to know what these two scholars consider Buddhism *is* if the preceding doctrines are dismissed as invalid. Their reply has been to present what they consider to be true Buddhism's three defining characteristics. Briefly, they are: (1) Buddha Shakyamuni's teaching of the law of causality, which denies the existence of any underlying or unchanging substance in the world, including the self; (2) the duty of those who would call themselves Buddhist to act altruistically, or "selflessly," to benefit others; and (3) the use of words and the intellect in making a conscious decision to believe in the law of causality.

Though the positions set forth by Hakayama and Matsumoto are certainly not impervious to criticism (for example, the teaching of the universal possession of the Buddha nature, "with neither superior nor inferior," was a catalyst for Uchiyama Gudō's social activism, which battled social repression and discrimination), the willingness of these two scholars to call into question some long held and cherished tenets of both Japanese Buddhism in general and Zen in particular augurs well for an intellectual revitalization of Japanese Buddhist thought, not least of all within the Zen tradition. It also demonstrates how far Japanese Buddhism has come in the half century since its leaders claimed that it was the only Buddhist country in Asia, the country in which pure Mahayana Buddhism was to be found.

Hirata Seiko   As noted above, not one of the numerous branches of the Rinzai Zen sect has ever formally admitted or examined its own war complicity.[62] (Ichikawa Hakugen's critique was personal, not official.) It is difficult to escape the conclusion that this inability to come to grips with its past is due to the fact that the Rinzai sect's complicity was even more thoroughgoing than that of the Sōtō sect.

In the absence of any formal statement from official Rinzai spokesmen, let us conclude this chapter with a look at the most contemporary statement on Zen war responsibility made by a Rinzai Zen–sect priest, Hirata Seikō (b. 1924). Chief abbot of Tenryūji temple in Kyoto, former Professor of Buddhism at Hanazono University, and a disciple of Seki Seisetsu, Seikō responded to this issue in an article entitled "Zen Buddhist Attitudes to War" which is included in *Rude Awakenings (Zen, the Kyoto School, & the Question of Nationalism)*.

At first glance, Seikō seems to take a position not unlike that of Ichikawa Hakugen. For example, he frankly admitted that Japan's war efforts were, at least in part, "a self-serving attempt on the part of certain Japanese political and economic leaders to jump onto the imperialist bandwagon and carve out a piece of the Asian mainland for themselves." He further stated that "the Pacific War can only be seen as a reckless undertaking that simply reflected the military leaders' ignorance of the international situation."[63]

Seikō was no less frank in admitting Zen complicity in Japan's wartime activities:

The Zen priesthood is made up of individuals, and as in any religion during times of war, there were among them many who appear to have abandoned the ideals of their faith to embrace the

narrower ideals of their country. Not a few Zen priests joined
hands with State Shinto and its imperialist view of history in order
to promote the war. None of the historical arguments brought
forth in their defense (for example, the indignation at the West's
colonization of the East . . .) can justify their simple failure to
speak out on the Buddhist ideal of nonbelligerence, much less their
active support of the war effort.[64]

There is also another, more subtle, apologist dimension to Seikō's admissions. On the secular level this is manifest in such statements as "the
Russo-Japanese War of 1904–5 can be seen as a defensive strategy by Japan
to halt the southward advance of the Russian Empire," or "as the leading
power of Asia it was incumbent on Japan to stand up to the [Western] colonizers."[65] That neither the Korean nor Chinese people ever asked to be
defended or colonized by Japan seems to have eluded Seikō's grasp.

Seikō's most questionable statements, however, are reserved for his description of the wartime activities of his own Zen teacher, Seki Seisetsu.
According to Seikō, Seisetsu was one representative of "domestic criticism
of the trend toward militarism." Thus, at the time of an extreme ultranationalist rebellion led by junior imperial army officers on February 26, 1936,
Seisetsu wrote a letter to the minister of the army, Terauchi Hisaichi, "urg-
[ing] him take what action he could to check the reactionary elements in the
officer corps." Terauchi was, we are told, "a frequent visitor of the master."[66]

What Seikō fails to mention, however, is that in spite of the major policy differences between them, the leaders on both sides of the rebellion were
ultranationalists, equally committed to the maintanence and expansion of
Japan's empire. As far as foreign policy was concerned, the conflict between
them was over the best strategy for accomplishing their shared expansionist goals. From the viewpoint of Japan's colonial subjects, it made little difference which side prevailed. In the words of the colloquial Japanese expression, the only difference was whether they [the colonial peoples] were to be
"broiled and eaten or boiled and eaten."

Seikō goes on to admit that "Unfortunately, the effort bore no fruit, for
whatever reason, and Japan continued its downslide into military rule." The
reason it bore no fruit, of course, is that it was little more than a factional
dispute in the officer corps, both sides of which supported Japan's overseas
empire. This is further attested to by the fact that once the central government succeeded in putting down the rebellion (as Seisetsu had requested),
Terauchi went on, the following year, to become the commander of the

North China area army and lead Japan's full-scale invasion of that country. By the end of the war this "frequent visitor of the master" would rise to the rank of field-marshal and command the entire southern area army in Southeast Asia.

Seisetsu went on, as previously described, to write *The Promotion of Bushido* in 1942. Even earlier, in September 1937, Seisetsu had gone on national radio to say:

> Showing the utmost loyalty to the emperor is identical with engaging in the religious practice of Mahayana Buddhism. This is because Mahayana Buddhism is identical with the Law of the Sovereign. The truth is that when the ego has been thoroughly destroyed, that which manifests itself is identical with the Buddha nature. The truth is that when the ego has been thoroughly discarded, that which springs forth is identical with the spirit of Japan. It is the red devils [i.e., Communists] who seek to throw our noble national polity into disarray. We must seek to exterminate the devils at home, while stamping out the devils abroad. This can be accomplished by uniting together as one, working harmoniously, being loyal, and serving the emperor.[67]

And finally, to what did Seikō attribute the willingness of Zen leaders to support Japanese militarism? Was its cause to be found deeply embedded in Japanese or Chinese Zen doctrines, as Hakugen and Hakamaya have asserted? Could it be connected to organizational Buddhism's early willingness to protect the nation, or Zen's willingness to assert the identity of Zen and the sword? In Seikō's view it could not, for it was all much simpler than that. Just as "the Pacific War can only be seen as a reckless undertaking that simply reflected the military leaders' ignorance of the international situation," so too "the Zen priesthood can be faulted for its ignorance of the international situation at the time of the Pacific War."[68] Some fifty years after the end of the war, this Rinzai leader had come to the conclusion that Zen complicity in the wartime deaths of millions upon millions could be explained by ignorance of the international situation.

CHAPTER ELEVEN:

Corporate Zen in Postwar Japan

D uring World War II, we have seen, Zen was used a a method to train not only officers and soldiers but "industrial warriors" as well. In postwar Japan, when the "infinite power" supposedly derived from zazen was no longer needed on the battlefield, some Japanese businessmen decided it could be put to use in the rebuilding of Japan's devastated industrial base. The Occupation had introduced democracy and education reform, including a new emphasis on individual rights, to Japanese society. In addition, the terrible postwar poverty had encouraged the growth of leftist forces, including militant labor unions. Some in the business community saw Zen as a way of restoring the traditional values of discipline, obedience, and loyalty to superiors.

CORPORATE TRAINING PROGRAMS

One form the corporate response took was the creation of training programs for their new employees. An article entitled "Marching to the Company Tune," appearing in the June 1977 issue of *Focus Japan,* an English-language magazine published by the semigovernmental Japan External Trade Organization (JETRO), describes the history of these programs:

> [These programs] were developed in the late 1950s when companies realized that schools were no longer emphasizing the old virtues of obedience and conformity. Living and training together, sometimes for as long as a month, are designed to artificially recreate the old neglected virtues.[1]

What better place than a Zen monastery for the artificial recreation of the old neglected virtues? Here monk and lay trainees rise at 3:30 A.M. to meditate, eat rice gruel for breakfast, and endure the winter cold with only tiny charcoal braziers for heat. Extended periods of sitting in the traditional cross-legged lotus posture can be quite painful even for an experienced meditator, let alone a novice. If even the slightest movement is detected, the meditator will be "encouraged" to remain immobile by one or more blows of a long wooden stick known as a *kyōsaku* wielded by a senior monk-monitor. After being struck, the offending meditator is required to place the palms of his hands together and bow as an expression of his appreciation for the blows.

There can be no doubt that this Spartan life style does increase the ability to withstand adversity; and, as George A. DeVos has pointed out, endurance has long been a highly desirable virtue in Japanese business organizations.[2] It is, however, in the social rather than the physical environment of a Zen monastery that there is the greatest emphasis on obedience and conformity. To be allowed to enter a monastery as a trainee, a monk is expected to prostrate himself in supplication before the entrance gate for hours, if not days, depending on the monastery. When asked why he wishes to enter the monastery, the monk should reply, "I know nothing. Please accept my request!" indicating that his mind is like a blank sheet of paper, ready to be inscribed by his superiors as they wish. If a monk fails to give the proper answer, he is struck repeatedly with the *kyōsaku* until his shoulders are black and blue and the desired state of mind is achieved.

Once permitted to enter the monastery, the monk finds that everyone is his superior. Even a fellow monk who was admitted only a few hours before him will automatically precede him on any formal or semiformal occasion, including meals, and exercise some degree of authority over him. Those senior monks who have been in training for more than one or two years seem, to the new entrant, to be superior beings. They not only wield the *kyōsaku* but also determine whether or not the novice's work assignments are performed satisfactorily. These senior monks wear finer and more colorful robes than their juniors and live in more spacious quarters. They also have the official privilege of leaving the monastery for short periods of time and the unofficial privileges of surreptitiously eating meat, drinking alcohol, and keeping petty monetary and in-kind gifts made to the monastery.

There are striking parallels between Zen monastic life and training, and military life and training. During the war Sōtō Zen master Sawaki Kōdō noted that Zen monasteries and the military "truly resemble each other closely." Among other things, this was because both required communal life styles. Kōdō continued:

> The first thing required in communal life is to discard the self. . . .
> In battle those who have been living together communally can
> work together very bravely at the front. . . . Today the state requires
> that we all follow a communal life style wherever we are, thus
> repaying the debt of gratitude we owe the state. The spirit of Zen
> monastic life does not belong to Zen priests alone but must be
> learned by all the people.[3]

The prospect of incoming employees learning a communal life style to "repay the debt of gratitude" owed their company is, of course, no less attractive to Japan's business world than it was to the imperial military. Not surprisingly, therefore, corporate Zen training is often conducted in tandem with or in place of so-called "temporary enlistment" *(kari nyūtai)* in the Japanese Self-Defense Forces. In the case of Zen monasteries, senior monks act very much like drill sergeants, and novice monks are their recruits. As one new salesman who had just completed his company's training program noted: "My work has much in common with that of a soldier."[4]

If senior monks are the drill sergeants, then it is the Zen master or masters who act as the generals or corporate heads. They enjoy the real authority in a Zen monastery and are ultimately responsible for directing the training programs for both monks and lay persons. In the talks they give to incoming trainees, one of the most frequently recurring themes is the Zen phrase *daishu ichinyo,* which means that all members of the monastic community *(daishu)* should act as one *(ichinyo).* When it is time to do zazen, everyone sits. When it is time to eat, engage in long, silent hours of manual labor, or sleep, everyone acts together as if they were one body. To do otherwise is called *katte na kōdō* or "self-willed action" and condemned as the very antithesis of the Zen life. In a Zen monastery, complete conformity is by no means an old, neglected virtue.

Discipline, obedience, conformity, and physical and mental endurance in the face of hardship are not the only features of monastic life attractive to corporate Japan. The traditional Buddhist teaching of the non-substantiality of the self has also been given a unique corporate twist. This twist is well illustrated by Ozeki Sōen (b. 1932), the abbot of Rinzai Zen–sect affiliated Daisen'in temple and one of the best-known of the Zen priests conducting employee-training courses. In a collection of his sermons delivered during such training courses, he stated:

> Employing your vital life force, you should exert yourselves to the utmost, free of any conceptual thought. . . . This is what it means to be alive. That is to say, at every time and in every place, you should work selflessly.[5]

Sakai Tokugen　A further example of Zen's corporate twist is provided by Sakai Tokugen (1912–96), another leading Zen master involved with employee-training programs. Tokugen, a disciple of Sawaki Kōdō, was also a former professor of Buddhist Studies at Komazawa University. In the May 1974 issue of *Daihōrin*, he lamented the lack of sincerity in carrying out the orders of one's superiors in postwar Japan:

> Sincerity [in carrying out orders] means having feelings and actions of absolute service, giving one's all [to the task at hand]. In doing this there can be no thought of personal loss or gain. . . . By carrying out our [assigned] tasks, we become part of the life of the entire universe; we realize our original True Self. . . . This is the most noble thing human beings can do.[6]

For Tokugen, then, selfless devotion to the accomplishment of one's assigned duties is none other than enlightenment itself. Is it any wonder that he has also been a popular leader of employee-training programs? How many Western companies can promise enlightenment as an added employee benefit? Here, certainly, the Protestant work ethic, with eternal salvation as its reward, has met its match.

It should be clear by now that, at its most basic, the same spirit of self-renunciation characterizes both Tokugen's exhortations to be a good worker and those of D. T. Suzuki, Yamazaki Ekijū, Harada Sōgaku, and others to be a good soldier. The only difference between them is the object of loyalty and devotion. In premodern Japan, absolute loyalty was owed to one's feudal lord. From the Meiji period onward the focus shifted to the central government and its policies as embodied in the person of the emperor. In postwar Japan the focus shifted once again, this time to the corporation and its interests—which are of course very closely connected in Japan with those of the state.

There is one further aspect of Zen training that is very attractive to corporate Japan, the practice of zazen itself. The *samadhi* power supposedly derived from the practice of zazen was originally utilized in Zen training to give the practitioner a deeper insight into his or her own nature and the nature of reality itself. Yet this same power, facilitating as it does complete absorption into the present moment, can be applied to any work, from wielding a samurai sword with lightning swiftness, to fighting selflessly on the battlefield, to manufacturing computer components with flawless precision. What could be more attractive to a Japanese company?

In reality, Japan's defeat meant not the demise of imperial-way Zen and soldier Zen but only their metamorphosis and rebirth as corporate Zen. Perhaps Zen's newest incarnation is more benign than its past variants, in that it does not seem to require loyalty even unto death. But in the mid-1970s, a new phenomenon was detected among Japan's corporate warriors: *karōshi, or* "death from overwork." At least some part of postwar Japan's economic miracle must be assigned to the willingness of company employees to work themselves to death.

Katsuhira Sōtetsu The emergence of corporate Zen in postwar Japan was not entirely without its critics. Perhaps the most prominent of these was Katsuhira Sōtetsu (1922–1983), head of the Nanzenji branch of the Rinzai Zen sect. In his posthumous 1988 book *Enlightenment of a Pickle-pressing Stone (Takuan Ishi no Satori)* Sōtetsu wrote:

> Of late there has been a Zen boom, with various companies coming to Zen temples saying they wish to educate their new employees. But it is clear what kind of education they are seeking. They want to educate their employees to do just as they are told. They claim that Zen is good at this. However, their claim is a bunch of rubbish! Zen is not as paltry as all that. It is not so small-minded as to restrict a person to such a limited framework. This said, the responsibility for having sanctioned such a Zen boom lies with the Zen temples themselves.[7]

During the war years, as a young Zen priest, Sōtetsu had volunteered to become a pilot in a special-attack, or kamikaze unit. He frequently begged his unit commander to send him on a mission, but the war ended before he got his wish. Sōtetsu wrote about this: "Without entertaining the slightest doubt, I believed I should die for my country, killing even a single enemy. I now recognize that, as a priest, there could be no greater contradiction than this. I will carry this contradiction with me to the day I die."[8] In November 1983, at sixty-one years of age, Sōtetsu committed suicide.

ZEN AND THE POSTWAR JAPANESE MILITARY

Zen remains influential in Japanese military circles as well. The reconstituted Japanese military, the Self-Defense Forces, with a budget in 1996 second only to the United States military, continue to call on Zen masters for spiritual guidance despite Japan's so-called "Peace Constitution" of the postwar era.

Sugawara Gidō In his 1974 book, *If I Die, So What! (Shinde Motomoto)* Sugawara Gidō (1915–78), the chief abbot of Rinzai Zen sect–affiliated Hōkoku Zenji temple, writes with evident pride of his more than ten years of service as an adjunct instructor for the Self-Defense Forces.[9] Gidō goes on to draw a parallel between the "unwavering faith" displayed by both Fleet Commander Admiral Tōgō Heihachirō (1848–1934) and Army General Nogi Maresuke during the Russo-Japanese War, and Zen enlightenment.[10] As for the Pacific War, he wrote:

> There is no doubt that all those involved in the Greater East Asia War had discarded their self-centeredness and, sacrificing their lives, acted on what they believed was right for their country.[11] I think they attained the path of Truth *[makoto]*. If you believe that something is right, that it is the path of Truth, you should rush forward towards it.[12]

Gidō also discussed Bushido, remarking that it was such Kamakura period (1185–1333) Zen masters as Eisai and Dōgen who helped develop the samurai spirit, which "regarded the body as of no more value than so many goose feathers and was ever willing to sacrifice life itself in the service of one's lord."[13] Gidō argued that the ultimate spiritual beauty of Bushido was to be found in two of its uniquely Japanese practices, which he believed continue to course through the veins of the Japanese people: ritual disembowelment *(seppuku)* and seeking revenge on one's enemies *(ada uchi)*. What made these two acts so compelling was that their practitioners "were well-acquainted with shame, propriety, and Truth." Moreover, the "selfless mind" embodied in these practices was the equivalent of the classical Zen koan

Mu. Needless to say, Gidō regarded these acts as being "incomprehensible to foreigners."[14]

In Gidō's eyes, one of the most persistent problems facing the Self-Defense Forces was that their members were subjected to various forms of social discrimination at the hands of those Japanese, including local government officials, who were opposed to the reestablishment of a military force. According to Gidō, however, there was no need for Self-Defense Forces soldiers to be concerned about whether they were loved or hated. "Just silently continue polishing your machine guns and cleaning your tanks, even if you don't have to use them for the next two, three, or even five hundred years. . . . This is where your true life lies."[15]

Ōmori Sōgen Ōmori Sōgen (1904–94) began his Zen practice in 1925 as a lay disciple of Seki Seisetsu, abbot of Tenryūji. Sōgen claimed to have realized enlightenment at the age of twenty-nine, after having meditated intensely for eight years on the koan *Mu.* His breakthrough occurred as follows:

> I finished zazen and went to the toilet. I heard the sound of the urine hitting the back of the urinal. It splashed and sounded very loud to me. At that time I thought, "Aha!" and I understood. I had a deep realization.[16]

In 1966 Sōgen published a book with a familiar ring to its title, *Sword and Zen (Ken to Zen)*. Sōgen opened his book by admitting that he didn't know when the phrase "The sword and Zen are one" *(ken Zen ichinyo)* had first been used.[17] Nevertheless, he had no hesitation in stating "there can be doubt that with regard to their ultimate goals and aims, the sword and Zen are identical."[18] He described the nature of this unity:

> Zen is the sword of the mind while the sword is the Zen of the sword blade. . . . For a warrior to discharge his duties he must necessarily clarify the origin of life, and transcend life and death in order to reach the absolute realm. . . . This is the reason the destiny of the sword is inevitably connected to Zen.[19]

Abstract as this quotation may seem, Sōgen was prepared to cut through the metaphorical rhetoric when it came justifying the use of the sword in the defense of "peace and justice":

Can someone tell me just how justice is to be protected and peace preserved? Are there any concrete ways of protecting justice and maintaining peace other than resolutely making evil submit and eliminating those who threaten peace? In order to accomplish this, those [who do such things] must be harmed, even though in one respect it is, I dare say, wrong to do so.[20]

Sōgen was well aware that "protecting justice and maintaining peace [in East Asia]" was precisely the rationale given to justify Japan's wartime actions; he had formerly been an ardent supporter of those same actions. In August 1945, Sōgen made plans to preempt the broadcast of the emperor's announcement of Japan's surrender and fight till the end.[21] He would have had to have very powerful friends indeed to even know in advance of the emperor's radio broadcast, let alone its contents. But in fact Sōgen was very well connected, for he enjoyed the patronage of the Tōyama family, the patriarch of which, Tōyama Mitsuru (1855–1944), was a central figure in two of Japan's most infamous ultranationalist secret societies, the Genyōsha (Dark Ocean Society) and Kokuryūkai (Black Dragon Society). The historian David Bergamini described Tōyama as the Lord High Assassin of these two secret societies.[22] A second historian, E. H. Norman, noted that the two secret societies that Tōyama helped run formed "the advance guard of Japanese imperialism . . . mold[ing] public opinion in favor of aggression."[23]

Sōgen also praised the elder Tōyama for providing him with the wisdom necessary to endure his life of hardship amidst the poverty of the immediate postwar period. Tōyama, he wrote, had once told him that "Since ancient times there has never been a person who starved from doing the right thing. If you are doing what is right, heaven will surely provide food. Therefore, even if you starve and die, do the right thing.[24] What Sōgen conveniently omitted from his account is that, for Tōyama, doing the right thing had meant a lifetime of assassinations, drug dealing, and terrorism in Japan's colonies, coupled with political blackmail, intimidation, and backstairs intrigue at home.

Just how close Sōgen was to the Tōyamas is demonstrated by the fact that Tōyama Mitsuru's son, Ryusuke, served as an advisor to the martial arts hall, Jiki Shin Dōjō, that Sōgen founded in 1933 and headed through the end of the war. For Sōgen, Tōyama Ryusuke's most attractive feature was his utter fearlessness:

During his [Ryusuke's] student days at Dōbun Shoin, a very good friend had tuberculosis. Seeing this person who was depressed and in despair vomit blood, Tōyama Sensei said, "Tuberculosis is nothing. Watch this!" and drank down the blood.[25]

According to Sōgen, Ryusuke was "a great man that one can meet only once in a lifetime."[26]

Because Japan lost the war, Sōgen decided "according to the Way of the Samurai," to formally enter the Rinzai Zen priesthood.[27] He then went on to become a professor at Rinzai-affiliated Hanazono University in 1970 and its president in 1978. Six years earlier, in 1972, he had established Chozenji International Zen Dōjō, complete with a martial arts training hall, in Hawaii. In material published in 1988, Sōgen's American disciples described him as having earlier been an antiwar activist. They wrote:

> Ōmori Roshi was influential in government circles before the outbreak of World War II and strenuously appealed to [Prince] Konoe, who was to be the next prime minister, to appoint either Ugaki or Mazaki to the post of Commander of the Army instead of Tōjō. He hoped to avert Japan's war with the United States. He blamed his own spiritual weakness for his failure.[28]

As with D. T. Suzuki and others, the question must be asked as to whether Sōgen was opposed to war in principle or merely opposed to fighting a losing war with the United States. The two generals whom Sōgen supported, Ugaki Kazushige (1869–1956) and Mazaki Jinzaburō (1876–1956), were both longstanding supporters of Japan's colonial expansion. Ugaki, for example, had willingly accepted appointment as governor general of Korea in 1931. Similarly, there is nothing in the record to suggest that Sōgen himself was opposed to the subjugation of Taiwan, Korea, or Manchuria. Thus, even if his "strenuous appeal" to Prince Konoe had been successful, it would have done little or no good for the millions of Chinese, Koreans, and other Asian peoples who became the victims of Japanese aggression, supported by such doctrines as the identity of the sword and Zen.

While corporate Zen is the primary manifestation of imperial-way Zen and soldier Zen in postwar Japan,[29] Zen's connection to the Japanese military, and to the sword, has by no means disappeared. Yasutani Hakuun was another of those Zen masters leading retreats for members of the Self-Defense Forces, specifically for officer-candidates at the elite Self-Defense

Academy.[30] In fact, thanks to the writings and missionary activities of numerous postwar and small numbers of prewar Zen leaders like Yasutani, it can be argued that modern-day variations of imperial-way Zen and soldier Zen are now to be found in the West as well as in Japan, although often without the knowledge or support of their Western adherents. As these Zen variations settle into their new home in the West, the critical question is simply this: Will the doctrine of the unity of Zen and the sword, with all this implies historically, settle in with them?

CHAPTER TWELVE

Was It Buddhism?

Introduction

This book has explored the relationship between institutional Japanese Buddhism, primarily Zen, and the state from 1868 to 1945. Now we turn to the broader issue of the relationship between Zen and war in light of the historical development of Buddhism.

In answering the question "Was it Buddhism?" I contend that both Imperial Way–Buddhism and Imperial State/Soldier–Zen can only be understood in the context of their historical and doctrinal antecedents in Japan and East Asia as a whole, extending as far back as the life of Buddha Shakyamuni himself (if not before). Therefore, this chapter surveys 2,500 years of Buddhist social thought and practice, beginning with an introduction to the "social consciousness" of the Buddha and extending through the emergence of modern Japan. In attempting this ambitious sweep in only a few pages, no one is more aware than I that what follows is but the first step in explaining this vast and complex topic.

Buddha Shakyamuni's Social Consciousness

The basic teachings of Buddha Shakyamuni are well-known, so suffice it to say, there is nothing in either the Four Noble Truths or the Holy Eightfold Path to suggest support for the use of violence, let alone warfare. On the contrary, two admonitions in the Holy Eightfold Path—"right action" and "right livelihood"—clearly indicate the very opposite.

Right action promotes moral, honorable, and peaceful conduct. It admonishes the believer to abstain from *destroying life*, from stealing, from dishonest dealings, and from illegitimate sexual intercourse. Instead, the believer should help others lead peaceful and honorable lives.

Right livelihood means that one should abstain from *making one's living through a profession that brings harm to others*, such as selling arms and lethal weapons, providing intoxicating drink or poisons, or *soldiering*, killing animals, or cheating. Instead, one should live in a way that does not cause harm or do injustice to others.

Together with right speech, right action and right livelihood form the basis for Buddhist ethical conduct. Underlying all Buddhist ethical conduct is a broad conception of universal love and compassion for all living beings, both human and nonhuman. Thus, based on these fundamental teachings of Shakyamuni, Buddhist adherents could *in theory* no more participate in that form of mass human slaughter known as "war" than they could purposely take the life of another. Yet ideals and practice often parted ways, as we will explore next.

LIFE OF THE BUDDHA

In accordance with the religious norms of his day, Shakyamuni offered advice on secular as well as purely spiritual matters. One example concerns a dispute that arose over the division of water from the drought-stricken Rohini River, which flowed between two kingdoms, one of them his own homeland of Kapilavastu. It is recorded that when the quarrel reached the point where a battle seemed imminent, Shakyamuni proceeded to the proposed battlefield and took his seat on the riverbank. He asked why the princes of the two kingdoms were assembled, and when informed that they were preparing for battle, he asked what the dispute was about. The princes said that they didn't know for sure, and they, in turn, asked the commander-in-chief. He also didn't know and sought information from the regent; and so the enquiry went on until it reached the husbandmen who related the whole affair. "What then is the value of water?" asked Shakyamuni. "It is but little," replied the princes. "And what of princes?" "It cannot be measured," they said. "Then would you," said Shakyamuni, "destroy that which is of the highest value for the sake of that which is worth little?" Reflecting on the wisdom of his words, the princes agreed to return peaceably to their homes.[1]

Another example of Shakyamuni's political intervention is said to have occurred in his seventy-ninth year, shortly before his death. King Ajatasattu of Magadha wished to make war on the tribal confederation of Vajji, so he sent an emissary to ask Shakyamuni what his chances of victory were. Shakyamuni declared that he himself had taught the Vajjians the conditions of true welfare, and as he was informed that the Vajjians were continuing to observe these conditions, he foretold that they would not be defeated. Upon hearing this, Ajatasattu abandoned his plan to attack.

Significantly, the first of the seven conditions Shakyamuni had taught the Vajjians was that they must "hold frequent public assemblies." Secondly, they must "meet in concord, rise in concord, and act as they are supposed to do in concord."[2] As a noted scholar pointed out, these conditions represent "a truly democratic approach," and "any society following these rules is likely to prosper and remain peaceful."[3]

A. L. Basham suggests that incidents like these demonstrate Shakyamuni's clear support for a republican form of government, though with the caveat that we are speaking of a form of governance in which there was an executive—sometimes elected, sometimes hereditary—supported by an assembly of heads of families that gathered periodically to make decisions relating to the common welfare.[4] Restated in more contemporary terminology, Shakyamuni advocated a political model approaching a small-scale, direct democracy, though it is also clear that he did not deny his counsel to the kings of the rising monarchies of his day.

Other elements of Shakyamuni's stance on violence are illustrated in the lead-up to an attack on his homeland by King Vidudabha of Kosala, the most powerful of the sixteen major kingdoms of his time. Shakyamuni recognized that this time the nature of the feud was such that his words would not be heeded, and he did not attempt to intervene. But even when the very existence of his homeland was at stake, Shakyamuni, his warrior background notwithstanding, refused to take up arms in its defense.

Shakyamuni's teaching on warfare and violence is perhaps best clarified in the *Dhammapada*, a Pali canonical work. In chapter 1, stanza 1, for example, Shakyamuni states: "For never does hatred cease by hatred here below: hatred ceases by love; this is an eternal law." And again, in chapter 15, stanza 201: "Victory breeds hatred, for the conquered is unhappy. The person who has given up both victory and defeat, that person, contented, is happy." In chapter 10, stanza 129, he says: "All persons tremble at being harmed, all persons fear death; remembering that you are like unto them, neither strike nor slay." And finally, in chapter 8, stanza 103: "If someone conquers in battle a thousand times a thousand enemies, and if another conquers himself, that person is the greatest of conquerors."[5] While scholars doubt these admonitions came directly from Shakyamuni's lips, the admonitions are, nevertheless, entirely consistent with his earliest and most fundamental teachings.

Two further aspects of Shakyamuni's teachings are worthy of mention. First, he was concerned about what we would today call social justice. For example, in the Pali *Cakkavattisihanada Sutta* of the *Digha Nikaya* (no. 26), Shakyamuni clearly identified poverty as the cause of violence and other social ills:

> As a result of goods not being accrued to those who are destitute, poverty becomes rife. From poverty becoming rife, stealing, ... violence, ... murder, ... lying, ... evil speech, ... adultery, ... incest, till finally lack of respect for parents, filial love, religious piety and lack of regard for the ruler will result.

Likewise, in the *Kutadanta Sutta* of the same *Nikaya* (no. 5), Shakyamuni praised a king named Mahavijita who, faced with an upsurge of robbery in his impoverished kingdom, provided his subjects with the economic means to improve their lives rather than imprisoning and executing the wrongdoers.[6]

The Early Buddhist Sangha and the State

Also important is the political or social dimension of the religious organization that Buddha Shakyamuni founded, the Sangha, that is, the community of monks and nuns (organized separately) dedicated to practicing his teachings. Primarily religious in nature, it embodied his concept of an ideal society.

The Sangha was based on noncoercive, nonauthoritarian principles by which leadership was acquired through superior moral character and spiritual insight, and monastic affairs were managed by a general meeting of the monks (or nuns). Unlike a modern business meeting, however, all decisions required the unanimous consent of those assembled. When differences could not be settled, a committee of elders was charged with finding satisfactory solutions.

Ideally, the Sangha was to be an organization that had no political ambitions and in whose ranks there was no striving for leadership. It sought by example and exhortation to persuade men and women to follow its way, not by force. Further, by his completely eliminating the then-prevalent caste system from its ranks, Shakyamuni may rightly be considered one of recorded history's first leaders to practice his belief in the basic equality of all human beings. He clearly hoped that the religious and social ideals of the Sangha would one day permeate the whole of society. This said, the historical subordination of the female Sangha to the male Sangha, through the imposition of eight additional precepts for nuns, betrays the ideal of human equality and points to the existence of a sexist attitude that may date back to Shakyamuni himself.

It is also true that even during the Buddha's lifetime, his Sangha became a wealthy landowner, though the lands referred to were held as the communal property of the various monastic communities.[7] The lands themselves had all been donated by the faithful, initially kings, princes, and rich merchants. This raises the question as to what the donors expected of the Sangha *in return for* their material support. The classic answer is that they expected to acquire "merit," that spiritual reward that promises rebirth in a blessed state to all those who perform good deeds. As one Pali sutra relates, however, the accumulation of merit by the laity can also lead to the more immediate and mundane goals of "long life, fame, heavenly fortune, and *sovereign power* [italics mine]."[8] The fact that King Ajatasattu also looked to Buddha Shakyamuni to forecast the likelihood of his victory against the Vajjians is significant here. Significant, in that it was already widely believed in ancient India that accomplished "holy men" possessed superhuman powers, including the ability to foresee the future.

Related questions are what effect the Sangha's collective possession of ever-greater amounts of land had on its own conduct, and equally important, whether as a major landholder it could fail in its actions and pronouncements to escape the notice and concern of state rulers. Would it be surprising to learn that these rulers also expected something in return for their material support of the Sangha, something approaching a moral endorsement of their rule, or the acquisition of merit, or the utilization of the supposed superhuman powers of Buddhist priests (and sutras) to protect the state from its enemies or ensure victory in battle?

KING ASHOKA—THE "IDEAL" BUDDHIST RULER?

If in the long run the Sangha willingly provided rulers with a moral endorsement, that endorsement was initially given only on the basis that rulers fulfill certain prerequisites or conditions. These conditions were contained in the *Jataka* stories, five hundred Indian folk tales that had been given a Buddhist didactic purpose and were incorporated into the Pali Buddhist canon sometime before the beginning of the Christian era. Among these tales we find a description of the "Ten Duties of the King," which include, among other things, the requirement that rulers abstain from anything that involves violence and destruction of life. Rulers are further exhorted to be free from selfishness, hatred, and falsehood, and to be ready to give up all personal comfort, reputation, fame, and even their very life if need be to promote the welfare of the people. Furthermore, it was the responsibility of kings to provide (1) grain and other facilities for agriculture to farmers and cultivators, (2) capital for traders and those engaged in business, and (3) adequate wages for those who were employed. When people are provided with sufficient income, they will be contented and have no fear or anxiety. Consequently, their countries will be peaceful and free from crime.9

It was, of course, one thing to present kingly duties in the abstract and another to find kings who actually practiced them. Buddhists discovered one such ruler in the person of King Ashoka (ca. 269–32 B.C.E.), who already controlled much of India at the time of his accession to the throne. Prior to converting to Buddhism, Ashoka is said to have engaged in wars of expansion until the bloodiness of his conquest of the kingdom of Kalinga caused him to repent and become a Buddhist layman, forswearing the use of violence. He then embarked upon a "Reign of Dharma" in which he advocated such moral precepts as nonharming, respect for all religious teachers, and noncovetousness.

In addition to renouncing aggressive warfare, Ashoka is said to have urged moderation in spending and accumulation of wealth, kind treatment of servants and slaves, cessation of animal sacrifices for religious purposes, and various other maxims, all carved as inscriptions and royal edicts on cliff faces and stone pillars throughout his vast realm, which extended almost the entire length and breadth of the Indian subcontinent. Further, he appointed officers known as Superintendents of Dharma for the propagation of religion, and arranged for regular preaching tours. Realizing the effectiveness of exhortation over legislation, he is said to have preached the Dharma on occasion. Ashoka become the archetypal Buddhist ruler, an ideal or Universal Monarch (see chapter 7).

As opposed to this idealized portrait, Indian historian A. L. Basham has pointed to another side of King Ashoka. For example, Ashoka maintained an army and used force against tribal groups that clashed with his empire. Beyond that, one Buddhist description of his life, the Sanskrit *Ashokavandana*, records that he ordered *eighteen thousand* non-Buddhist adherents, probably Jains, executed because of a minor insult to Buddhism on the part of a single one. On another occasion, he forced a Jain follower and his entire family into their house before having it burnt to the ground. He also maintained the death penalty for criminals, including his own wife, Tisyaraksita, whom he executed. In light of these and similar acts, we can say that Ashoka was an archetypal "defender of the faith" who was not averse to the use of violence.

Nor did King Ashoka's remorse at having killed over 100,000 inhabitants of Kalinga lead him to restore its freedom or that of any other of his earlier conquests. Instead, he continued to govern them all as an integral part of his empire, for "he by no means gave up his imperial ambitions."[10] In fact, inasmuch as many of his edicts mention only support for *Dharma*, (a pan-Indian, politico-religious term) and not the *Buddha Dharma*, it is possible to argue that he used Dharma not so much out of allegiance to the Buddhist faith and its ideals, but as a means to centralize power, maintain unity among his disparate peoples, and promote law and order throughout the empire.

At the very least, in promoting Buddhism throughout India, Ashoka was clearly also promoting his own kingship and establishing himself.[11] That is to say, an alliance of politics and religion had been born. This is important to note because while Ashoka may have been the first to use Buddhism and the (Buddha) Dharma for what we would today identify as political purposes, he was hardly the last, as we shall see shortly when we examine the development of Buddhism in China and Japan.

A noted Indian political philosopher, Vishwanath Prasad Varma, pointed out that due to King Ashoka's royal patronage, "the Sangha became contaminated with regal and aristocratic affiliations."[12] Similarly, the pioneer Buddhist scholar T. W. Rhys Davids remarked that it was the Sangha's close affiliation with King Ashoka that was "the first step on the downward path of Buddhism, the first step on its expulsion from India."[13]

What is certain is that Ashoka enjoyed a great deal of power over the Sangha. For example, a second Buddhist record of Ashoka's life, the Pali *Mahavamsa*, states that Ashoka was, with the aid of the great elder Moggaliputta Tissa, responsible for defrocking sixty thousand Sangha members who were found to harbor "false views."[14] Ashoka had the power to prescribe passages from the sutras that Sangha members were required to study. Those who failed to do so could be defrocked by his officers.[15] In fact, it became necessary to receive Ashoka's permission even to enter the priesthood.[16] In short, during Ashoka's reign, if not before, the Raja Dharma (Law of the Sovereign) became deeply involved in, if not yet in full command of, the Buddha Dharma. This too was a harbinger of things to come.

In this connection, both Basham and Rhys Davids identified the concept of a so-called Universal Monarch, or *Cakravartin* (Wheel-Turning King), as coming into prominence within Buddhist circles only after the reign of Ashoka's father, Candragupta, who ascended the throne sometime at the end of the fourth century B.C.E.[17] Thus, the idea of a Universal Monarch, who served as the protector of the Buddha Dharma and as the recipient of the Dharma's protection, did not originate as a teaching of Buddha Shakyamuni himself. Instead, it is best understood as a later accretion that "'was an inspiration to ambitious monarchs, . . . some [of whom] claimed to be Universal Monarchs themselves."[18] It is also significant that as a Universal Monarch and Dharma Protector, Ashoka was accorded the personal title of Dharma Raja (Dharma King), a title he shared with Buddha Shakyamuni.[19] This "sharing of titles" would play an important role in China.

BUDDHISM IN CHINESE SOCIETY

Confucian Critique of Early Buddhism in China

Buddhism entered China by way of Central Asia at the beginning of the Christian era. By this time China already had a sophisticated culture of its own that included two well-developed, indigenous, religious-oriented belief systems: Taoism and Confucianism. Buddhist advocates eventually reached an uneasy truce with both Taoists and Confucians, who initially opposed the introduction of this foreign religion.

Chinese Buddhist monks appeased the Taoists by discussing Buddhism in a Taoist vocabulary and proposing Buddhist solutions to unresolved Taoist doctrinal disputes, such as the relationship of the "holy man" to the world. However, it was the compromise reached with the Confucians that was to have the most far-reaching effects on the subsequent development of Buddhism throughout East Asia, including Japan.

The compromise concerned the relationship of the Sangha with the state. As propagators of a universal Dharma, Chinese monks of the Eastern Chin dynasty (317–420 C.E.) asserted they had no need to kowtow (show obeisance) to the emperor. From the popular Confucian viewpoint, this was a heretical doctrine that undermined Confucian advocacy of social harmony derived from a strictly hierarchical conception of society, in which nothing was higher than the "Son of Heaven."

Subordination of Buddhism to the State

While Buddhist monks in southern China (under the Chin dynasty) successfully maintained independence from the state, their northern counterparts did not fare as well. Faced with the non-Chinese rulers of the Northern Wei dynasty (386–534 C.E.), Buddhist monks offered their services as political, diplomatic, and military advisers. They claimed to be able to prophesy not only the outcome of battles and entire military campaigns, but even the rise and fall of empires. According to Kenneth Ch'en, in "offering their technical services to the rulers, these imperial monk advisers were able to persuade them to become staunch supporters of Buddhism."[20]

In justifying the decision of northern monks to reverence the emperor in accordance with Confucian tradition, Fa-kuo, chief of monks from 396 to 398, came up with an "ingenious solution." Namely, he claimed that then Emperor T'ai-tsu was a living Buddha, the Tathagata himself. Therefore, when a monk bowed down to him, he was not doing obeisance to an emperor but was worshipping the Buddha, an entirely fit and proper act for all faithful.[21]

Fa-kuo, it should be noted, had been appointed to his position by Emperor T'ai-tsu. Although the effect this had on Fa-kuo's views is unknown, it is significant that a Chinese emperor possessed the authority to make such an appointment over the Sangha. This said, it must also be remembered that Fa-kuo's innovation was based on such Indian precedents as the "sharing of titles" in the Buddhist records of King Ashoka's reign. Furthermore, there was, by this time, scriptural justification for Fa-kuo's position in the *Suvarnaprabhasa* [Golden Light] *Sutra*. This Indian Mahayana sutra took the view that while a king is not a god in his own right, he does hold his position by the authority of the gods and is therefore entitled to be called a "son of the gods." It can readily be seen that this position, which is Brahmanical (not Buddhist) in origin, dovetails nicely with the Chinese doctrine of a ruler's Mandate of Heaven. Further paralleling the Chinese doctrine, there is an implicit admission in this sutra (and in its Chinese variant) that revolt against a wicked or negligent king is morally acceptable.

Whatever motives one may ascribe to these northern Buddhist monks, the fact remains they established a pattern that was to characterize Chinese Buddhism down through the ages. That is to say, in return for imperial patronage and protection, Buddhism was expected to serve and protect the interests of the state and its rulers, including the attainment of victory on the battlefield. Thus was the foundation laid for what came to be known in Japan as "Nation Protecting–Buddhism." It can be argued, of course, that this was but an extension of the Sangha's subservience to the state as first observed in India.

Be that as it may, when a subsequent emperor—Wen (r. 581–604) of the Sui dynasty (c. 581–618)—decided to enlist the spiritual aid of Buddhist monks in his military campaigns, he was doing no more than extending a precedent that had already existed for more than two hundred years, at least in northern China. Specifically, Wen constructed temples at sites where he and his father had won important battles, ordering temple priests to hold commemorative services for the spirits of his fallen soldiers. Already in the midst of planning future military campaigns, the emperor wanted to assure his followers that should they fall on some future battlefield, their spirits, too, would be looked after.[22]

Emperor Wen's innovation was his determination to use Buddhism as a method of unifying all of China. Presenting himself as a Universal Monarch, soon after establishing the Sui dynasty in 581 C.E. he declared:

With the armed might of a Cakravartin King, We spread the ideals of the ultimately benevolent one [that is, the Buddha]. With a hundred victories and a hundred battles, We promote the practice of the ten Buddhist virtues. Therefore *We regard weapons of war as having become like incense and flowers* [presented as offerings to the Buddha] and the fields of this visible world as becoming forever identical with the Buddha land [italics mine].[23]

To secure his position still further, Wen gave himself the title Bodhisattva Son of Heaven, and proceeded to have hundreds of stupas built throughout China to enshrine Buddhist relics. This conveyed the unity of king and empire through faith in Buddhism. In doing this, he was once again emulating pious acts by that other great empire builder, King Ashoka. Ashoka allegedly had eighty-four thousand stupas constructed throughout his empire.[24]

However, for the imperial support it enjoyed, the Sangha always paid a heavy price in the loss of its independence, even in internal affairs, and in increasing subservience to the state. Thus, after Emperor Yang succeeded to the throne in 604 (by killing his father, Emperor Wen), he issued a decree in 607 ending the exemption of monks in southern China from having to pay homage to the emperor and his officials. The Law of the Sovereign was now supreme in China and would remain so, as far as Buddhism was concerned, forevermore. One added "benefit" of this subservience was, however, that Buddhism gained at least a degree of acceptance by the Confucians.

The Sangha's support of state interests did not stop with prophesy, state ritual, and provision of a unifying ideology. By the time of the T'ang dynasty (c. 618–907), some monks had themselves begun to participate directly in politics. During the reign of Wu Tse-t'ien, for example, one monk by the name of Hsüeh Huai-i was actually commissioned as a "grand general sustaining the state." As such, he led a number of military expeditions to expel Turks who had invaded China's border regions. Later, Huai-i even attempted to usurp the throne for himself.[25]

Monks meddling in politics (and warfare) suggests, of course, that decadence had infiltrated the Sangha under imperial patronage. In fact, one official of the time complained that "present-day temples surpass even imperial palaces in design, embodying the last word in extravagance, splendor, artistry, and finesse."[26] Thus, when Emperor Hsüan-tsung ascended the throne in 712, he instituted a series of measures to control the Sangha's wealth and power, including limitations on the size of temple landholdings, defrocking of up to thirty thousand "unworthy monks," and requiring government permission before repairs to temples could be made. In order to control the number of entrants into the Sangha, the emperor also initiated a system of granting official "monk certificates" in 747.[27]

None of these acts, however, can begin to compare to the suppression of Buddhism that occurred at the hands of Emperor Wu-tsung in 845. At the time, the emperor claimed to have forced 260,500 monks and nuns to return to lay life, while destroying 44,600 monasteries, temples, and shrines, and confiscating their vast, tax-exempt lands and 150,000 slaves.[28] Although the emperor's death the following year marked the formal end of the persecution, Buddhism never regained its preeminent position in Chinese life and society. A long period of decline set in, extending to the present day. Only the Ch'an (Zen) and Pure Land schools maintained a certain degree of vitality.

Ch'an

Ch'an's resilience may have derived in part from its syncretism, for Ch'an had incorporated *both* Taoist and Confucian tenets into its practice and outlook. By the Sung period (960–1279) if not before, it was typical for Ch'an masters (like other Chinese Buddhists) to refer to Buddhism as one leg of a religious tripod that also included Confucianism and Taoism. Japanese Zen Master Dōgen, who trained in China from 1223 to 1227, described this syncretism:

Among present-day monks . . . not one of them, not even half of one of them, has understood that the Buddha's teachings are superior to those of the other two. It was only Ju-ching, my late master, who understood this fact and proclaimed it ceaselessly day and night.[29]

Ju-ching, it should be noted, also refused both an honorary purple robe and the title "Ch'an Master" from Emperor Ning-tsung. Further, in the context of explaining the differences between Buddhism and Confucianism, Dōgen characterized Confucianism as "merely teach[ing] *loyal service to the emperor and filial piety, the latter seen as a method of regulating one's household* [italics mine]."[30]

This syncretism on the part of nearly all Ch'an masters meant that Ch'an, like the rest of Chinese Buddhism, internalized Confucian values, including emphasis on a hierarchical social structure with the emperor at the pinnacle of the social pyramid. Confucians argued that such a configuration would produce social harmony when everyone knew their place in society and faithfully followed the dictates of their superiors.

Iconoclasm

Although based more on rhetoric than actual historical practice, Ch'an has a reputation for iconoclasm, dismissing, as it does, the need for scholastic study of Buddhist texts and dependence on Buddhist images and rituals. Coupled with Ch'an's emphasis on productive labor, this led, at least initially, to a certain degree of independence from, if not indifference to, the emperor and the imperial state. For example, consider Hui-neng, traditionally seen as the pivotal Sixth Patriarch of the Southern school of Ch'an. Although there are conflicting accounts of his life, the *Special Transmission of the Great Master from Ts'ao-ch'i* presents this master as being so unconcerned with worldly fame that he refused an invitation from the emperor to visit the imperial court. Notwithstanding this, the emperor still presented him with gifts, one of which was, significantly, a new name for his former residence, that is, Kuo-en-ssu (Temple to Repay the Debt of Gratitude Owed the State).

Hui-neng's disciple Shen-hui (684–758), however, maintained a much closer, if sometimes strained, relationship with the imperial court. Heinrich Dumoulin noted that Shen-hui first took up residence in Nan-yang, not far south of the imperial capital of Lo-yang, in 720 *in obedience to an imperial decree.* In 745, Shen-hui moved to a temple in Lo-yang, where large crowds were drawn to hear his exposition of Ch'an teachings. This led to charges, perhaps incited by his Northern Ch'an rivals, that he was fomenting social unrest, resulting in his banishment from the capital for three years (753–56).

In 755 when a major rebellion broke out in the northeastern part of the country, Shen-hui was recalled to the capital as a fundraiser for the imperial military. Offering his contributors exemption from both monetary taxation and the requirement to participate in yearly, government-sponsored labor battalions, Shen-hui proved an exemplary fundraiser, and the rebellion was suppressed. The emperor gratefully showered Shen-hui with honors, ensuring that his last days were spent "basking in the graces of the powers that be."[31]

In light of this and similar episodes, it is clear that Ch'an leaders also willingly served the state's needs, in war as well as peace. In fact, when the Sōtō and Rinzai sects raised funds to buy fighter aircraft for the Japanese military in the 1930s and 1940s, they were following a Ch'an and Zen precedent with a history of nearly 1,200 years! As for Shen-hui, he continued to be honored even after his death, and in 796 was formally recognized as the Seventh Patriarch, also *by virtue of an imperial decree.*[32] Inasmuch as Shen-hui had been an untiring advocate of the Southern Ch'an school and its doctrine of sudden enlightenment, this imperial recognition was destined to have a major impact on subsequent Ch'an history.

Shen-hui was but one figure in the long-term decline of the Buddhist tradition of nonviolence. Consider the following poem in a sixth-century treatise from the *Hsin-hsin Ming* by the Third Ch'an Patriarch, Seng-ts'an (d. 606):

> *Be not concerned with right and wrong*
> *The conflict between right and wrong*
> *Is the sickness of the mind.*[33]

Further, French scholar Paul Demiéville pointed out that according to the seventh-century Ch'an text "Treatise on Absolute Contemplation," killing is evil only in the event the killer fails to recognize his victim as empty and dream-like. On the contrary, if one no longer sees his opponent as a "living being" separate from emptiness, then he is free to kill him.[34] This antinomian license to kill with moral impunity is the most dangerous, *and deadly*, of Ch'an's many "insights."

This said, Ch'an's abandonment of Buddhist morality did not go unnoticed or unchallenged. As early as the eighth century, the famous writer Liang Su (753–93) criticized the Ch'an school as follows:

> Nowadays, few men have true faith. Those who travel the path of Ch'an go so far as to teach the people that there is neither Buddha nor Dharma, and that neither good nor evil has any significance . . . Such ideas are accepted as great truths that sound so pleasing to the ear. And the people are attracted to them just as *moths in the night are drawn to their burning death by the candle light* [italics mine].³⁵

In reading this critique, one is tempted to believe that Liang was also a prophet able to foresee the deaths over a thousand years later of millions of young Japanese men who were drawn to their own deaths by the Zen-inspired "light" of Bushido. All the more, the millions of innocent men, women, and children who burned with (or because of) them, and who must never be forgotten.

By the Sung dynasty (960–1279), Ch'an monasteries not only maintained friendly relations with the imperial court but had become involved in political affairs as well.³⁶ Emperors granted noted Ch'an masters purple robes and honorific titles such as "Ch'an Master of the Buddha Fruit" or "Ch'an Master of Full Enlightenment." Inevitably, however, imperial favors brought with them increased state control. One result was the establishment of the system of "Five Mountains [i.e., major monasteries] and Ten Temples." In the spirit of Confucian hierarchy, Ch'an temples were classified and ranked, those at the top being blessed with imperial favors. In this case, all of the privileged temples belonged to the Yang-ch'i line of the Lin-chi (J. Rinzai) school.

Among other things, Ch'an temples operating under imperial patronage were expected to pray for the emperor and the prosperity of the state. In describing this system, Yanagida Seizan wrote:

> Given the danger of foreign invasion from the north, Buddhism was used to promote the idea of the state and its people among the general populace. . . . Inevitably, the Ch'an priests residing in these government temples in accordance with imperial decree gradually linked the content of their teaching to the goals of the state. This is not unconnected to the fact that Zen temples [in Japan] in the Kamakura and Tokugawa periods had . . . a nationalistic character in

line with the traditional consciousness of the Chinese Ch'an school that advocated the spread of Ch'an in order to protect the nation.[37]

The succeeding Yüan period (c. 1280–1368) would bring even greater state control of Ch'an and other temples and monasteries. Gradually however, the syncretic tendencies already at work within Buddhism grew ever stronger until by the Ming period (c. 1368–1644) all Chinese Buddhist schools and sects fused into a loose amalgamation of the Ch'an and Pure Land schools. This brought the story of a distinct Ch'an school or movement to an end.

Preliminary Conclusion

In light of this discussion, I would like to make three additional points. First, while Ch'an's iconoclastic tendencies and economic self-reliance may have initially enabled it to maintain a certain distance from the state, over the long term there was a spiritual price for this freedom. That is to say, parallel-ing a heavy emphasis on the practice of meditation (J. zazen), intellectual stimulation from such activities as lively discussions on points of doctrine were strongly discouraged by Ch'an masters, who insisted on intuitive com-prehension and lightning-quick responses within an overall framework of anti-textualism and anti-scholasticism. To some extent, this can be seen as Ch'an's internalization of such Taoist values as *spontaneity, originality, para-doxy, innate naturalness,* and *the ineffability of Truth.*[38]

I am not suggesting that the strong emphasis on meditation or Taoist-influenced values was *necessarily* "un-Buddhist," but as Kenneth Ch'en pointed out:

> The strength and vigor of Buddhism rested on the principle of equal emphasis on all three aspects of the Buddhist discipline—moral conduct, [meditative] concentration, and wisdom. Special attention to one, to the neglect of the other two, would certainly result in the deterioration of the Dharma.[39]

The reader will recall that Hakamaya Noriaki also raised a related criticism of Japanese Zen when he said, "True Buddhists must draw a sharp distinction between Buddhist teachings and anti-Buddhist teachings, *using both intellect and language* to denounce the latter [italics mine]."

My second point is closely connected with the first. I refer to what might be called a "violence-condoning atmosphere" fostered as one dimension of

Ch'an's iconoclastic attitude. Historically, this atmosphere began as early as the second patriarch, Hui-k'o (c. 484–590), who, tradition states, cut off his left arm at the elbow to show how fervently he wished to become a disciple of Bodhidharma, the legendary fifth-century Indian founder of the Ch'an school in China. T'ang Ch'an Master Chü-chih is also recorded as having cut off his disciple's finger with a knife after discovering that the latter had been imitating his "one finger Ch'an" (though in doing so, Chü-chih allegedly precipitated the disciple's enlightenment).

Less dramatic, though far more widespread, was the Ch'an use of such training methods as physical blows from both fists and staffs, together with thundering shouts. Lin-chi I-hsüan (d. 866), founder of the Lin-chi school, is the preeminent example of such a "rough and tumble" master. It was this master who taught his disciples:

> Followers of the Way, if you wish to have a viewpoint that is in ac-cord with the Dharma, it is only [necessary] that you not be be-guiled by others. Whether you meet them within or without, kill them right away! When you meet the Buddha, kill him. When you meet a patriarch, kill him. When you meet an Arhat [enlightened person], kill him. When you meet parents, kill them. When you meet relatives, kill them. Thus you will begin to attain liberation. You will be unattached and be able to pass in and out [of any place] and become free.[40]

I do not suggest there is a direct link between Ch'an's physical and verbal vi-olence and the later emergence of Zen's support for Japanese militarism. All of the examples given above have legitimate didactic purposes within the Ch'an and Zen tradition. For example, in Lin-chi's oft-misunderstood admo-nition quoted above, the "killing" referred to is that of *detaching* oneself from dependency on authority figures, whether they be people or ideas, in order to achieve genuine spiritual liberation. It might be called a dramatic restatement of Buddha Shakyamuni's own final instructions to his disciples:

> You must be lamps unto yourselves. You must rely on yourselves and on no one else. You must make the Dharma your light and your sup-port and rely on nothing else.[41]

Lin-chi's statement, like that of Shakyamuni, is basically antiauthoritarian in that it aims to free the trainee from dependence on anyone or anything outside of his own mind and apart from his own direct experience of the Dharma. Nevertheless, Ch'an's verbal and physical violence, didactic though it be, *lent itself* to misuse and abuse by later practitioners, especially in Japan. It provided the link that facilitated the connection made between Zen and the sword in feudal Japan, and in turn, between Zen and total war in modern Japan. Note too, that it was Ch'an Master Kuei-shan Ling-yu (771–853) who first referred to the interplay between action and silence in Ch'an as "sword-play."[42] Lin-chi was also fond of referring to "swords" and "sword-blades," but the reference was to the "sword of *wisdom*," a common Buddhist metaphor referring to wisdom that can "cut through" (i.e., eliminate) all discriminating thought and conceptualization, *not* human flesh!

D. T. Suzuki's application of the Zen phrase "the sword that gives life" (J. *katsujin-ken*) to the modern battlefield is a particularly pernicious example of the abuse of Zen terminology. This phrase together with its twin, that is, "the sword that kills" (J. *satsujin-tō*), is found in the famous Sung dynasty collection of one hundred Zen koans known as the *Blue Cliff Record*. In introducing the twelfth koan of the collection, Ch'an master Yüan Wu K'e Ch'in (1063–1135) wrote:

> The sword that kills people and the sword that gives life to people is an ancient custom that is also important for today. If you talk of killing, *not a single hair is harmed*. If you talk of giving life, body and life are lost [italics mine].[43]

Although phrased paradoxically, it is obvious that the above does not refer to anyone's physical death. Rather, Yüan Wu, once again using the sword as a metaphor for Buddhist wisdom, dramatically restates the classical Zen (and Buddhist) position that the destruction (i.e., the "killing") *of the illusory self* does not result in the least injury to the true self (hence, "not a single hair is harmed"). Or, expressed in reverse order, "giving life" *to the true self* inevitably involves the destruction of the illusory self (hence, "body and life are lost"). Thus, whichever sword is spoken of, no one physically dies!

One can only marvel at the fact that the transference of these terms to the real battlefield by later generations, Suzuki and his ilk included, has for so long escaped criticism and condemnation. At least part of the responsibility for this must be laid at the feet of those Ch'an pioneers, like Lin-chi, who chose to incorporate "life-giving" blows and shouts, coupled with a vocabulary of violence, into their instructional regimen. In the hands of lesser men (especially those aided and abetted by the state) these methods became, as has been seen, lethal in the extreme.

Finally, I would point out that the subordination of the Buddha Dharma to the state continues to exert a significant impact on Chinese Buddhism to this very day. In his book *Buddhism under Mao*, Holmes Welch noted that in 1951–52, Chinese Buddhists raised money for a fighter aircraft named *Chinese Buddhist* to be used against UN (mainly American) forces in the Korean War. In justifying Buddhist support for the Chinese government's policy of military intervention, a Buddhist leader named Hsin-tao addressed a meeting of Nan-ch'ang Buddhists as follows:

> We know that the People's Government absolutely guarantees the freedom of religious belief. We Buddhists must unite as quickly as possible and, with the followers of other religions, completely support the Chinese Volunteer Army and the Korean People's Army. The best thing is to be able to join the army directly and to learn the spirit in which Shakyamuni, as the embodiment of compassion and our guide to Buddhahood, killed robbers *to save the people and suffered hardship on behalf of all living creatures*. To wipe out the American imperialist demons who are breaking world peace is, according to Buddhist doctrine, not only blameless but actually *gives rise to merit* [italics mine].[44]

Once again, America and its allies were fighting "Buddhism," if not necessarily at sea, then at least on the ground and in the air. Once again, Buddhists themselves took up arms, out of a *spirit of compassion*, to fight the American "demons." As in wartime Japan, scriptural justification was also used in the Buddhist campaign to raise funds for weapons. Chü-tsan, another Buddhist leader wrote,

> The [*Mahapari*]*nirvana Sutra* advocates wielding the spear and starting battle. Therefore there is nothing contrary to Buddhist doctrine in a Buddhist responding to the appeal to contribute towards fighter planes, bombers, cannons and tanks.[45]

Ironically, when Tibetan monks revolted against the Communist Chinese Army's occupation of Tibet in 1959, they used the same scriptural evidence to justify their armed resistance.

The Chinese government's political use of Buddhism is by no means at an end, most especially in relation to Tibet. As recently as May 1996, the Chinese government donated a large memorial plaque to a Tibetan temple that read "Protect the State; Benefit the People."[46] In doing this, the state (albeit communist) sought to portray itself once again as a patron of Buddhism, but on the same condition as always, that is to say, that Buddhism agree to protect the state. In this instance there was an added "Tibetan twist" to the state's munificence, for clearly Tibetan Buddhists were also expected to protect *the unity of* the state from those alleged "splittists" (like the Dalai Lama and his supporters) who continued to seek some form of Tibetan autonomy.

In Taiwan, on the other hand, the Nationalist Chinese government has supported Buddhism far more strongly, receiving in return Buddhist leaders' endorsement of that government's longstanding dream to militarily retake the mainland. In light of this, it is not surprising to learn that Taiwanese monks share the same attitude toward Buddhist-endorsed violence as their mainland brethren. One such monk, a disciple of the modern Buddhist reformer T'ai-hsü (1890–1947), said,

> According to the Mahayana it is guiltless to kill from compassion. If I kill you, the objective is not to kill you, but to save you, because if I do not kill you, you will kill a great many other people, thus causing great suffering and incurring great guilt. By killing you, I prevent you from doing this, so that I can save both you and them. To kill people from compassion in such a way is not wrongdoing.[47]

There was, of course, one difference between the refugee monks on Taiwan and in Hong Kong and those on the mainland: the former wished Buddhist-condoned violence to be used *against* the Communists, instead of on their behalf. As always, the one constant is that the Law of the Sovereign, or in other words, the state and its rulers, is supreme!

Buddhism in Japanese Society

Prince Shōtoku and the Introduction of Buddhism to Japan

In his *History of Japanese Religion*, Anesaki Masaharu noted that the Buddha Dharma was closely identified with the state and its interests from its first introduction into Japan from Korea in the sixth century. He wrote, "A close alliance was established between the throne and the [Buddhist] religion, since the consolidation of the nation under the sovereignty of the ruler was greatly supported by the fidelity of the imported religion to the government."[48]

This development was far from being uniquely Japanese. On the contrary, it was only a replication of the relationship between Buddhism and the state that already existed on the Korean peninsula. As S. Keel pointed out,

> Buddhism [in Korea] was available as the politico-religious ideology which would serve the cause of building a powerful centralized state with a sacred royal authority.... [It] was understood primarily as the state-protecting religion, *hoguk pulgyo* [J. *gokoku Bukkyō*] not as the supra-mundane truth of salvation for individuals.[49]

The subservience of Buddhism to the state in Japan was nothing more than a copy of its Korean counterpart that, in turn, differed little from its Chinese antecedent. In fact, when Emperor Wen had hundreds of stupas built throughout China at the start of the seventh century, envoys from the three Korean kingdoms of Koguryo, Paekche, and Silla requested, and received, relics to take back to their own countries. Prince Shōtoku was also greatly impressed by this display of imperial support for Buddhism.[50]

In Japan, the Sangha's subservience to the state is made clear in the so-called Seventeen Article Constitution of 604, traditionally ascribed to Prince Shōtoku. In article 2 of the constitution, Shōtoku called on his subjects to "faithfully respect the 'Three Treasures,' i.e., the Buddha, Dharma, and Sangha." However, in article 3, he wrote:

> Respect the Imperial commands. The ruler is analogous to heaven, the subjects to the earth. The heaven covers the earth, and the earth supports heaven; if the four seasons pass smoothly, everything functions well. But if the earth tries to dominate heaven, it crumbles into powder. For this reason heaven commands and the earth receives, and for the same reason *the ruler commands and the subjects obey*. Therefore, every subject should respect the Imperial commands, if not there will be confusion [italics mine].[51]

Although a number of distinctly separate Buddhist sects would later develop in Japan, the one thing they always agreed on was that "the ruler commands and subjects obey." It may be argued that given the fragile nature of Shōtoku's only recently unified central government, his emphasis on the supremacy of the ruler was necessary. Thus, it may also be argued that Buddhism made a positive contribution to the subsequent development of Japanese civilization by providing the newly formed state with a highly moral unifying ideology that transcended the clan divisions (and clan deities) of Shōtoku's day. What cannot be disputed, however, is that this emphasis on the supremacy of the ruler also set the stage for the historical subservience of Buddhism to the Japanese state.

The Japanese ruler who made the most blatant political use of the Buddha Dharma was probably Emperor Shōmu, whose reign lasted from 724 to 748. He focused on the teachings of the *Avatamsaka Sutra*, particularly its doctrine of a central celestial, or cosmic, Buddha (i.e., *Mahavairocana*) surrounded by an infinite number of Bodhisattvas. *Mahavairocana*'s mind was believed to pervade all of reality and to be present in all things, the latter being ranked in harmonious interdependence.

With this imagery in mind, Emperor Shōmu built the giant central cathedral of Tōdaiji in Nara and enshrined there a sixteen-meter-high statue of *Mahavairocana* (J. *Dainichi*). As Anesaki described it, this cathedral "was to be a symbolic display of the Buddhist ideal of universal spiritual communion centered in the person of the Buddha, parallel to the political unity of national life centered in the monarch."[52] Devotion and loyalty to this Buddha became synonymous with the same virtues directed toward the person of the emperor and the state that he embodied. The use of *Mahavairocana* had the added benefit that as a celestial or Sun Buddha, the *Mahavairocana* also provided a symbolic link to the indigenous Shinto Sun goddess, Amaterasu Ōmikami, the mythical progenitor of the imperial house.

The State and Zen Masters Eisai and Dōgen

In order to discuss the relationship of Eisai (1141–1215) and Dōgen (1200–1253) to the state, it is necessary to start with a brief description of the political situation at the beginning of the Kamakura period (1185–1333). This can be summarized in one word, *turbulent*. On the one hand, there was a power struggle between the traditional nobility, including the emperor, and an increasingly more powerful warrior class. Due to the nobility's own decadence, this struggle was one it was bound to lose, though the emperor would be retained as an important national symbol, albeit with increasingly limited powers.

The nobility's decadence was matched by that of the competing monastic institutions, which by then had accumulated large, tax-free estates defended by monk-soldiers (*sōhei*). Holmes Welch alluded to this situation when he noted, "In China fighting monks were rare; in Japan they became a national institution."[53] One caveat to this, however, is that many, if not most, of these monk-soldiers were in the nature of a hired mercenary force doing the bidding of their clerical masters, many of whom were court nobles themselves.

In any event, it was not unusual for major Buddhist monasteries to use their standing armies not only in power struggles with rival Buddhist institutions, but to press their demands on the government itself. The government, that is, the nobility, had no choice but to turn to the warrior class for protection, thus hastening the demise of its own political power. What power the reigning emperor had left was often exercised by a former emperor who had ostensibly retired to become a Buddhist monk but who continued to exercise power from behind monastic walls.

With the establishment of the Kamakura Shogunate (military government) in 1192, real political power came to be exercised by the leaders of the warrior class. Though there would be many internal upheavals, betrayals, and battles along the way, it was this class that continued to hold power through the Meiji Restoration of 1868. And it was to this class that the straightforward, vigorous, and austere doctrines and practice of Zen appealed. In addition, Zen had the advantage of being a direct import from China, thereby offering the new government an opportunity to escape the embrace of the large, nobility-dominated monastic institutions in the Kyoto area.

The Rinzai Zen sect introduced by Eisai would find greater acceptance in the new and former political power centers of Kamakura and Kyoto respectively. In fact, thanks to its powerful benefactors in these two centers, the Rinzai Zen sect would itself become a major landholder by the Muromachi period (1333–1573). Dōgen's Sōtō Zen, on the other hand, found its major benefactors among provincial warrior lords. It was for this reason that the popular designations Rinzai Shōgun (Rinzai of the Shōgun) and Sōtō *Domin* (Sōto of the Peasants) came to characterize the difference in social status of the two Zen sects.

With this background in mind, we can now examine Eisai's and Dōgen's attitudes to the state. In his famous treatise *Kōzen Gokoku-ron* (A Treatise on Protecting the Nation by Spreading Zen), Eisai argued that it was through the universal adoption of Zen teachings that the nation could be protected. In identifying Zen with the state, Eisai had an immediate concern in mind, that is, the need to seek state assistance in overcoming the strong opposition of other monastic institutions—especially the Tendai sect headquartered on Mount Hiei—to the introduction of new *and competing* sects into Japan.

Eisai's appeal did eventually succeed, with the result that the Kamakura Shogunate had the temple of Jufukuji built for him in Kamakura in 1200, and two years later the emperor had the temple of Kenninji built for him in Kyoto. However, this victory was tempered by the fact that the emperor also ordered him to erect shrines within Kenninji honoring both the Tendai and esoteric Shingon sects. In this connection, it is noteworthy that toward the end of his life, Eisai focused more and more on the conduct of esoteric rituals associated with the Tendai sect embodying, as they did, the promise of immediate, "this-worldly" benefits for his benefactors.

In the following years, the Rinzai Zen sect's connection to, and patronage by, the state would grow only stronger. To give but one example, the famous Rinzai master Musō Soseki (1275–1351) successfully sought Shogunal patronage to have one Ankokuji (Temple to Pacify the State) built in each of Japan's sixty-six regions and two islands. Musō himself was rewarded for his efforts by having the unique title of State Teacher (*Kokushi*) bestowed on him by no less than seven successive emperors.

On the Sōtō Zen side, Dōgen designated the first temple he established in Japan upon his return from China as Kōshō-gokokuji (Temple to Protect the State by Propagating the Holy Practice). Dōgen also wrote a treatise titled *Gokoku-shōbōgi* (The Method of Protecting the State by the True Dharma). Although the contents of this latter treatise are no longer extant, its title, and Dōgen's other writings on the same topic, suggests a similar position to that of Eisai (and probably for the same reason). For example, in the *Bendōwa* section of his masterwork, the *Shōbōgenzō* (Treasury of the Essence of the True Dharma), Dōgen wrote, "When the true Way is widely practiced in the nation, the various Buddhas and heavenly deities will continuously protect it, and the virtue of the emperor will exert a good influence on the people, thereby bringing peace."[54]

Dōgen, unlike Eisai, did not conduct esoteric rituals seeking worldly benefits, but this did not stop those who followed in his footsteps from introducing a similar element into Sōtō Zen. Even Zen practice, especially the practice of zazen, came to take on supposedly magical powers. As William Bodiford noted:

> For powerful *warrior patrons who prayed for military victories* [italics mine] and economic prosperity, the purity of [Sōtō] monks ensured the efficacy of simple religious prayers (*kitō*). For local villagers who expected the Zen masters to pacify evil spirits,

summon rain, or empower talismans, the meditative powers (*zenjōriki*) of the monks energized simple folk magic.[55]

The chief abbots of Sōtō Zen head temples also quickly acceded to the custom of receiving the title of Zen master (*Zenji*) from the emperor, though it must be admitted that Dōgen had himself accepted the gift of a purple robe from retired Emperor Gosaga (1220–72). Dōgen did, however, refuse to accept it the first two times it was offered, and tradition states that he never wore the robe even after finally accepting it. The following poem, attributed to Dōgen, is thought to express his sentiments in this regard:

> *Though the valley below Eiheiji is not deep,*
> *I am profoundly honored to receive the emperor's command.*
> *But I would be laughed at by monkeys and cranes*
> *If I, a mere old man, were to wear this purple robe.*[56]

During the Kamakura period, the same hierarchically ranked system of Five Mountains and Ten Temples (J. *Gozan Jissetsu*) was introduced into the Japanese Rinzai Zen sect as the system had been first established in China. By the Muromachi period there would be two such systems, one in Kyoto (which was superior in rank) and the second in Kamakura. As in China, however, the government expected something in return for its patronage. For example, Zen monks, with their knowledge of Chinese, were sent on diplomatic and commercial missions to China. They were also used to suppress unruly elements among the populace. In short, as Dumoulin noted, "The organization of the *gozan* temples of the Rinzai sect made immeasurable contributions to the political, social, and economic power of the state apparatus."[57]

Development of "Samurai Zen"

The reader will recall earlier discussions by D. T. Suzuki and others of how Shōgun Hōjō Tokimune (1251–84) sought strength from Zen to deal with the threat of a second Mongol invasion. Tokimune went for guidance to his spiritual mentor, Chinese Zen Master Sogen (Ch. Tsu-yüan, 1226–86), shortly before the expected invasion in 1281.

When Tokimune said, "The greatest event of my life is here at last," the master asked, "How will you face it?" Tokimune replied by merely shouting the exclamatory word *Katsu!* as though he were frightening all of his enemies into submission. Pleased with this show of courage, Sogen indicated his approval of Tokimune's answer by saying, "Truly, a lion's child roars like a lion."

A similar though somewhat lesser-known incident is recorded as having occurred at the time of the first Mongol invasion in 1274. This one involved a second Chinese Zen master by the name of Daikyū Shōnen (Ch. Ta-hsui Cheng-nien, 1214–89). At the time, Daikyū directed Tokimune to solve the koan concerning Chao-chou (J. Jōshū, 778–897) on whether or not a dog has the Buddha nature. Chao-chou's famous answer was *Mu* (literally, "nil" or "naught"). Tokimune is said to have solved this koan, "thereby releasing his mind to deal calmly with the grave issues of war and peace."[58]

Collectively, these two incidents appear to be the earliest indications of the unity of Zen and the sword in Japan, though it is noteworthy that neither of them involved Japanese Zen masters. That is to say, it was Chinese Zen masters who introduced the idea of the efficacy of Zen training in warfare, or at least in developing the right mental attitude for it. Both Daikyū and Sogen, themselves refugees from the Mongol conquest of China, were acting on the basis of a long Chinese tradition of Buddhist service to the state and the needs of its rulers.

Unlike China with its long history of government by civil administrators—that is, "Mandarins"—Japan, from the Kamakura period onward, was ruled by a warrior class composed of a Shōgun (generalissimo) at the top, lesser feudal lords (*daimyō*), and the samurai armies they commanded. These early warriors, however, were a far cry from the Bushido-inspired ideal of the Tokugawa period. Instead, as Hee-jin Kim noted, they were "greedy, predatory, ruthlessly calculating, a strict business dealing with little or no sense of absolute loyalty and sacrifice."[59] If Japan were ever to become *and remain* a unified nation at peace (albeit under warrior control), a code like Bushido *had to arise* and be relentlessly drilled into the heads of otherwise self-seeking warriors!

And who better to do the "drilling into" than Confucian-influenced Zen monks with their ethical system that emphasized unquestioning, selfless loyalty to one's superiors? A letter written by the famous Zen master Takuan (1573–1645) clearly reveals what Zen had to offer the samurai. The letter shows how the mind that has transcended discriminating thought, technically known in Zen as "no-mind" (*mushin*), can be identified with martial prowess, particularly in the use of the sword. Addressing the famous swordsman Yagyū Tajima no Kami Munenori (1571–1646), Takuan wrote:

"No-mind" applies to all activities we may perform, such as dancing, *as it does to swordplay*. The dancer takes up the fan and begins to stamp his feet. If he has any idea at all of displaying his art well, he ceases to be a good dancer, for his mind "stops" with every movement he goes through. In all things, it is important to forget your "mind" and become one with the work at hand.

When we tie a cat, being afraid of its catching a bird, it keeps on struggling for freedom. But train the cat so that it would not mind the presence of a bird. The animal is now free and can go anywhere it likes. In a similar way, when the mind is tied up, it feels inhibited in every move it makes, and nothing will be accomplished with any sense of spontaneity. Not only that, the work itself will be of a poor quality, or it may not be finished at all. Therefore, *do not get your mind "stopped" with the sword you raise; forget what you are doing, and strike the enemy* [italics mine].[60]

Takuan also placed stress on the warrior's acquisition of "immovable wisdom" (J. *fudōchi*). He viewed this not as a static concept or the absence of movement but, on the contrary, as the immovable ground in which existed the potential for movement in all directions. For this reason, it was as applicable to the swordfighter's art as it was to the life of the Zen priest. "When the mind freely moves forwards and backwards, to the left and to the right, in the four and eight directions, if it clings to nothing, this is 'immovable wisdom.'"[61]

In Fudō Myō-ō (Skt. *Acala-vidya-raja*), the fierce-looking Hindu god introduced into Zen via esoteric Buddhism, Takuan saw the incarnation of his ideal of immovable wisdom. He described this figure as follows:

Fudō Myō-ō holds a sword in his right hand and a rope in his left. His lips are rolled back revealing his teeth, and his eyes are full of anger. He thrusts violently at all evil demons who interfere with the Buddha Dharma, forcing them to surrender. He is universally present as a figure who protects the Buddha Dharma. He reveals himself to people as the embodiment of immovable wisdom.[62]

Although in Buddhism, Fudō's sword was originally a symbol of "cutting through" *one's own desire and illusion*, Takuan succeeded in transmuting this figure into a slayer of "evil demons who interfere with the Buddha Dharma," as well as into the embodiment of the swordsman's ideal of "immovable wisdom." In a short work titled *Taia-ki* (History of the Sword), Takuan also discussed the dual nature of the sword. He emphasized the "total freedom" of the Zen-trained swordsman "to give life or to kill."[63] Takuan further advocated the absolute necessity for the warrior to *sacrifice his self* in the process of acquiring this freedom.

In light of the above, it is hardly surprising that Takuan also had something to say about the ever-present, overriding virtue of loyalty. To the Mysteries of Immovable Wisdom (*Fudōchi Shinmyō-roku*) quoted above, Takuan added:

> To be totally loyal means first of all to rectify your mind, discipline your body, and be without the least duplicity toward your lord. You must not hate or criticize others, nor fail to perform your daily duties. . . . If the spirit in which the military arts are practiced is correct, you will enjoy freedom of movement, and though thousands of the enemy appear, you will be able to force them to submit with only one sword. This is [the meaning of] great loyalty.[64]

As one of the greatest Zen masters of the Tokugawa period, Takuan's thought, including his emphasis on complete and selfless devotion to one's lord, would have a deep and lasting effect on his and later times.

Takuan was by no means the only Tokugawa Zen figure to interpret Zen in this manner. The same emphasis can also be seen in the teachings of Zen monk Suzuki Shōsan (1579–1655). Shōsan, born into a samurai family in the old province of Mikawa (present-day Aichi prefecture), originally fought on behalf of Tokugawa Ieyasu (1542–1616), founder of the Tokugawa Shogunate, at the major battle of Sekigahara in 1600, and at the sieges of Osaka Castle in 1614 and 1615. In 1621, after a period of guard duty at Osaka Castle, Shōsan determined to enter the Zen priesthood and is thought to have been ordained by Rinzai master Daigu (1583–1668). His Rinzai ordination notwithstanding, Shōsan went on to become a vigorous champion of the Sōtō sect, though he was never formally affiliated with it.[65]

Like Takuan, Shōsan taught that selflessness was the critical element of both true service and true freedom. It was only in overcoming the fear of death that true selflessness could be realized. In addressing samurai, Shōsan urged them to practice *tokinokoe zazen*, that is, zazen in the midst of war cries. As the following quotation reveals, Shōsan maintained that meditation that could not be applied to the battlefield was useless:

It's best to practice zazen from the start amid hustle and bustle. A warrior, in particular, absolutely must practice a zazen that works amid war cries. Gunfire crackles, spears clash down the line, a roar goes up and the fray is on: and that's where, firmly disposed, he puts meditation into action. At a time like that, what use could he have for a zazen that prefers quiet? However fond of Buddhism a warrior may be, he'd better throw it out if it doesn't work amid war cries.[66]

In terms of the subsequent development of "soldier-Zen" previously introduced in this book, it is also significant that Shōsan clearly articulated the unity of *samadhi* power and the military arts. Shōsan stated,

It's with the energy of Zen *samadhi* that all the arts are executed. The military arts in particular can't be executed with a slack mind. . . . This energy of Zen *samadhi* is everything. The man of arms, however, is in Zen *samadhi* while he applies his skill.[67]

As the phrase "all the arts" suggests, Shōsan's admonitions were not reserved for warriors alone. In fact, Shōsan insisted that the truth of Buddhism was to be found in any form of work or activity whatsoever. As the following passage makes clear, he believed that work itself could be equated with religious practice:

You must work in extremes of heat and cold—work with all your heart and soul. When you toil, your heart is at peace. In this way you are always engaged in Buddhist practice. . . . Every kind of work is Buddhist practice. Through work we can attain Buddhahood. There is no occupation that is not Buddhist.[68]

In his religious affirmation of the value of all forms of work, Shōsan has come to be viewed in modern Japan as one of the major contributors to the development of a Japanese work ethic. While this may be true, as a Zen monk Shōsan, like Takuan, also laid the foundations of not only "soldier Zen" but "corporate Zen" as well. And it must not be forgotten that in a classic work on Bushido titled *Hagakure*, Shōsan is quoted as having said, "What is there in the world purer than renouncing one's own life for the sake of one's lord?"[69]

And speaking of the *Hagakure*, the reader will recall an earlier reference to this same work made by D. T. Suzuki. It was this work "that was very much talked about in connection with the Japanese military operations in China in the 1930's." The Zen monk Suzuki referred to as being involved in its creation was another former samurai by the name of Yamamoto Jōchō (1659–1719), a retainer of Kyushu Lord Nabeshima Mitsushige (1632–1700). In light of Jōchō's background, it is hardly surprising to find him extolling the unity of Zen and the sword. Further, Jōchō described the purpose of meditation as follows:

> Meditation on inevitable death should be performed daily. Every day when one's body and mind are at peace, one should meditate upon being ripped apart by arrows, rifles, spears and swords, being carried away by surging waves, being thrown into the midst of a great fire, being struck by lightning, being shaken to death by a great earthquake, falling from thousand-foot cliffs, dying of disease or committing *seppuku* [ritual suicide] at the death of one's master. And every day without fail one should consider himself as dead.
>
> There is a saying of the elders that goes, "Step from under the eaves and you're a dead man. Leave the gate and the enemy is waiting." This is not a matter of being careful. It is to consider oneself as dead beforehand.[70]

And finally, Jōchō demonstrates that Takuan, quoted above, was by no means unique in identifying the nondiscriminating "no-mind" of Zen with Bushido. He does this by relating the following exchange between his nephew, Yamamoto Gorōzaemon, and yet another Buddhist priest, Tetsugyū:

> When Yamamoto Gorōzaemon went to the priest Tetsugyū in Edo wanting to hear something about Buddhism, Tetsugyū said, "Buddhism gets rid of the discriminating mind. It is nothing more than this. . . . When a man attaches discrimination to his true mind, he becomes a coward. In [Bushido] can a man be courageous when discrimination arises?"[71]

By the middle of the Tokugawa period, Hakuin (1685–1768), one of Rinzai Zen's greatest masters and reformers, had reached the conclusion that the warrior's lifestyle was actually superior to that of a monk's for practicing Zen. This was because of the physical strength the warrior brought to his practice as well as his need to adhere to proper decorum at all times. More important, however, it was due to the opportunity for meditation that was afforded the warrior while he was "riding forth to face an uncountable horde of enemies." In a letter written to one of his warrior patrons, Hakuin continued this train of thought as follows:

> Meditating in this way [i.e., while on horseback], the warrior can accomplish in one month what it takes the monk a year to do; in three days he can open up for himself benefits that would take the monk a hundred days.[72]

As to the benefits accruing to the warrior-meditator, Hakuin agreed with Takuan, Suzuki Shōsan, Jōchō, and others that chief among them was fearlessness in the face of death. The death referred to, however, was not just any death, but rather death on the battlefield when "though but a hundred men facing ten thousand, . . . they will press forward as though piercing through the hardest stone." This was all made possible, according to Hakuin, when the "benevolence of the lord" was united with the "benevolence of the Buddha Dharma." In this case, "who would regret giving his life for his lord?"[73]

"Fossilization" of Buddhism and Zen

This book began with a brief description of the decline, or "fossilization," of Buddhism that took place during the Tokugawa period (1603–1868). As can now be seen, it would be more accurate to describe Buddhism's emergence as a de facto state religion in Tokugawa Japan as but one *further* stage of its decline. It should thus come as no surprise to learn that the Tokugawa Shogunate turned to a Zen priest, that is, Rinzai Zen priest Ishin Sūden (1569–1633), chief abbot of Nanzenji in Kyoto, to register and supervise all Buddhist temples and clergy, regardless of sect. One aspect of this task was the formulation of a decree proscribing Christianity. Additionally, from 1612 onward, Sūden served as a "shogunal diviner," determining "auspicious days" on which his warrior patrons could perform certain acts with confidence. Sūden was duly rewarded for his many services with the purple robe of honor and the title National Teacher (*Honkō Kokushi*).

As illustrated by Sūden's own career, institutional Buddhism's subjection to strict state control did bring with it both prestige and financial rewards. But it also brought with it a clear set of obligations. On the one hand, Buddhist priests effectively became government functionaries, acting as the police arm of the state by enforcing the government's absolute prohibition of Christianity as well as by suppressing those Buddhist sects that the government found unacceptable. More controversially, they aided in the maintenance and reinforcement of the traditional social discrimination that existed in Japanese society against so-called outcastes (*burakumin*). Although its members were physically indistinguishable from other Japanese, this pariah group had long been forced to live in separate villages and engage in what were considered lowly, if not "unclean," trades such as animal butchery, leather working, and refuse collection.

In a study done in 1989, Tomonaga Kenzō found that the Sōtō Zen sect had been one of the leading sects promoting social discrimination not only during the Tokugawa period but right up through the 1980s. Popular Sōtō sermons commonly included references to the Ten Fates Preached by the Buddha (*Bussetsu Jūrai*). These "fates" included:

Short life-spans resulting *from butchering animals.*
Ugliness and sickness resulting from ritual impurities.
Poverty and desperation resulting from miserly thoughts.
Being crippled and blind as coming from violating the Buddhist precepts [italics mine].[74]

Further doctrinal support for social discrimination came from the highly esteemed Mahayana work, the Lotus Sutra. Specifically, in chapter 28 we are informed that anyone slandering this scripture or those who uphold it will be stricken with blindness, leprosy, missing teeth, ugly lips, flat noses, crooked limbs, tuberculosis, evil tumors, stinking and dirty bodies, and more "for *life after life* [italics mine]."[75] Not only Sōtō Zen, but all of Tokugawa Buddhism engaged in the classic ruse of blaming the victims for their misfortunes. Thus, not only outcastes, but the sick and disabled as well were afflicted in their present lives as karmic retribution for the evil acts of their past lives. That is to say, they had it coming!

And this discrimination did not stop with their death, for Tomonaga discovered that 5,649 Sōtō temples (out of nearly 15,000) as late as 1983 maintained records indicating which families were or were not descended from outcastes, and that 1,911 temples identified such families on their tombstones. Such post-death discrimination has very real consequences for the descendants of outcastes who seek employment or hope to marry the son or daughter of a "good family." In these situations, at least until recently, many temples would cooperate with private investigators who were regularly hired to check into a person's personal background.

Having read this, the reader may recall Uchiyama Gudō's struggle in the

Meiji period against an interpretation of karma that provided a religious justification for both social discrimination and social privilege. The failure of his
struggle then meant it would not be until 1974 that the Sōtō sect would express a willingness to consider its role in sustaining this type of discrimination. Significantly, the sect's willingness to examine this issue did not come
from within but from without, that is to say, from demands made by social
activists associated with the Outcaste Liberation League (*Buraku Kaihō
Dōmei*). This led, in 1982, to the establishment of a Human Rights Division
within the sect's administrative headquarters, some 110 years after the Meiji
government had, at least *on paper*, emancipated the outcastes in an edict issued in 1872.

Although at first glance this issue may not seem to be directly relevant
to the question of (Zen) Buddhism and war, it is, in fact, quite relevant. If a
society succeeds in identifying a sizable segment of its own people as being
inferior to other citizens, justifying this on moral and religious grounds,
then it is not difficult to identify other religions, ethnic groups, nations, and
others as being even *more inferior*. In this book we have seen how this happened to Christians, Russians, Koreans, Chinese, and eventually to American and English "savages." In the same connection, it should be noted that
as early as 1611, Sōtō Zen documents referred to outcastes as *hinin*, that is to
say, "nonhumans."[76]

Needless to say, discrimination in its various guises is hardly limited to
either Japan or Buddhism. Indeed, it can be found to a greater or lesser degree, at one time or another, in all cultures and major world religions. But
this does not lessen the tragedy that in this instance it was found among the
adherents of a religion whose founder, Buddha Shakyamuni, so clearly advocated the equality of all human beings irrespective of their birth, lineage,
occupation, and so forth. For Shakyamuni, there was only one acceptable
standard for judging others: their words and actions.

It is also noteworthy that it was as a direct consequence of establishing
the Sōtō sect's Division of Human Rights that the Sōtō headquarters issued
its official war apology and, in 1993, reinstated Uchiyama Gudō's clerical
status. Both of these issues were seen as further examples of this sect's abuse
of human rights.

For more than two hundred and fifty years, Zen, and Japanese Buddhism in general, remained locked in the warm but debilitating embrace of
the Tokugawa Shogunate. Interestingly, the founder of the Tokugawa Shogunate, Tokugawa Ieyasu (1542–1616) was brought up in a Jōdo (Pure Land)
sect–affiliated family. Ieyasu himself regularly recited the name of Buddha

Amida (i.e., *Nembutsu*) though his was a warrior-oriented faith as evidenced by the five-foot statue of Buddha Amida he had constructed with its own specially designed carrying case. This made it possible for him to transport the statue directly to his many battlefields, where he prayed for victory in accordance with the advice he received in 1560 from the abbot of Daijuji temple, located in present-day Aichi prefecture. The abbot had said,

> Who can resist you, if you have the spirit of Amida with you? If a man is afraid of losing anything, he will certainly lose it, but if he is willing to give it up, he will gain it. So be willing to give up your life for the sake of your followers.[77]

This did not mean, however, that Ieyasu was either indifferent or opposed to Zen. On the contrary, his personal secretary was a Rinzai Zen monk by the name of Denchōrō, head of Nanzenji in Kyoto, which was and remains one of the Rinzai sect's greatest monastic complexes. Denchōrō's secretarial services included not only accompanying his master to the battlefield but, occasionally, going into battle himself. On one occasion, following the battle of Mikata-ga-hara, he presented Ieyasu with the severed heads of three enemies. As a reward, Ieyasu granted his secretary the right to use three black stars as the armorial bearings for Konchiji, a second temple headed by Denchōrō. Eventually, this Zen monk would be appointed superintendent of all religious institutions in Japan, both Buddhist and Shinto alike.

Despite his deep religious faith in Buddhism, however, Ieyasu was not prepared to brook resistance from any quarter to his authoritarian rule. Thus, he and his successors devised an elaborate system of controls that materially enriched the Buddhist clergy just as it sapped their religious vigor. In effect, the Buddhist clergy became petty government bureaucrats, dedicated to ensuring the continuation of the Tokugawa military dictatorship as well as the total eradication of Christianity. Thus, well before the end of this period in 1868, the transformation process that resulted in Buddhism's "fossilization" was complete. Commenting on this development, Hayashi Makoto of Aichi Gakuin University noted:

> The universalistic doctrines and moral discipline originally advocated by a world religion [like Buddhism] completely disappeared, and instead emphasis was placed on the rituals and religious ideas necessary for the stability and prosperity of particular social groups such as the nation, feudal domain (*han*), village, and household.[78]

It can be argued that, despite the sometimes brave, though largely futile, efforts of subsequent Buddhist reformers, institutional Japanese Buddhism remains even today in a state of "suspended fossilization." That is to say, it remains focused almost exclusively on the conduct of rites believed to benefit the dead, not the living. Generally unable and unwilling to critically evaluate Japanese Buddhism's past subservience to the state and its rulers, institutional Buddhist leaders end up paying no more than lip service to the universalistic doctrines and moral discipline that are so fundamental to their faith. In alleging this, I would happily be proven wrong.

DOCTRINAL SUPPORT FOR VIOLENCE AND WARFARE AS SEEN IN THE SUTRAS

Once Buddhism accepted the responsibility of protecting the state, the question naturally arose as to how this was to be accomplished. Accompanying the emergence of Mahayana Buddhism in India came the belief that merit could not only be generated by pious acts but that, once generated, it could be transferred to others for their benefit. Thus the idea of utilizing the merit generated by sutra recitation became one method of protecting the state. Inevitably, however, the state had to resort to violence to defend itself, even when this defense involved invading and conquering other people's lands. How did Buddhism respond to state-condoned violence? Did Buddhism really offer doctrinal justification for war?

The answer to the latter question, especially in the Mahayana tradition found throughout East Asia, is yes. Historically, this justification is found primarily in the doctrine of *upaya* or "skillful means." That is to say, it is permissible to effect certain changes in the teaching of the Dharma in the short term in order that the listener may gradually come to understand its true and deeper meaning in the long term, ultimately leading to salvation.

It is within the Mahayana Buddhist ideal of a bodhisattva that we meet the quintessential practitioner of skillful means. A bodhisattva, of course, is one who, instead of realizing Nirvana, vows to save all human beings and works compassionately on their behalf. In order to accomplish this compassionate mission, however, some Mahayana sutras teach that a bodhisattva may go as far as to break the traditional Buddhist precepts, even those forbidding the taking of human life.

The *Upaya-kaushalya Sutra*, for example, relates a story about Buddha Shakyamuni in a previous life when he was still a bodhisattva. While on board a ship, Shakyamuni discovers that there is a robber intent on killing all five hundred of his fellow passengers. Shakyamuni ultimately decides to kill the robber, not only for the sake of his fellow passengers but also to save the robber himself from the karmic consequences of his horrendous act. In Shakyamuni's so doing, the negative karma from killing the robber should have accrued to Shakyamuni but it did not, for as he explained:

> Good man, because I used ingenuity *out of great compassion* at that time, I was able to avoid the suffering of one hundred thousand *kalpas* of *samsara* [the ordinary world of form and desire] and that wicked man was reborn in heaven, a good plane of existence, after death [italics mine].79

Here we see one justification for the idea so often quoted by wartime Japanese Buddhist leaders that it is morally right "to kill one in order that many may live" (J. *issatsu tashō*).

The *Upaya-kaushalya* is by no means the only Mahayana sutra that has been historically interpreted as in some sense excusing, if not actually sanctioning, violence. The *Jen-wang-ching* (Sutra on Benevolent Kings) also states that one can escape the karmic consequences arising from such acts as killing others by simply reciting the sutra.

It is noteworthy that this latter sutra is also closely connected with the protection of the state. Section 5 of the sutra is, in fact, titled exactly that: "Section on the Protection of the State." This section claims to give Buddha Shakyamuni's detailed instructions to kings in order that they might ensure the protection of their kingdoms from both internal and external enemies. Armies, if needed, could be assembled and used with the assurance that the soldiers involved in the killing could later be totally absolved of the karmic consequences of their acts.

Although the above sutras provided a somewhat passive justification for Buddhist participation in warfare, this is not the case with the Sanskrit *Mahaparinirvana Sutra*, previously mentioned. In this sutra, Buddha Shakyamuni tells how he killed several Brahmins in a previous life in order to prevent them from slandering the Dharma. Once again, this is said to have been done out of compassion for the slain Brahmins, that is, to save them from the karmic consequences of their slander.

In a more aggressive vein, chapter 5 of the same sutra admonishes Mahāyāna followers to protect the Dharma at all costs, even if this means using weapons to do so and breaking the prohibition against taking life.

This injunction is similar to that found in the *Gandavyuha Sutra*. Here, an Indian king by the name of Anala is singled out for praise because he is "said to have made killing into a divine service in order to reform people through punishment."[80]

In his seminal article "Le Bouddhisme et la guerre" (Buddhism and War), Demiéville identified even further scriptural basis for Buddhist participation in killing and warfare. Demiéville also pointed out the paradox that exists in this regard between the Southern Hinayana (i.e., Theravada) and Northern Mahayana schools: the Hinayana, which tends to condemn life, has remained strict in the prohibition of killing; but it is the Mahayana, which extols life, that has ended up by finding excuses for killing and even for its glorification.[81]

Conclusion

State-Protecting Buddhism

As we have already seen, Buddha Shakyamuni himself praised a republic as the ideal form of the state. Further, Indian Buddhism prior to Ashoka was also clearly suspicious of monarchs, placing them in the same category as robbers, for both were capable of endangering the people's welfare. In this regard, Uchiyama Gudō's identification of Japan's imperial ancestors as people who "kill[ed] and rob[bed] as they went" harkens back to Buddhism's earliest attitudes.

According to early Buddhist legends, a ruler was to be selected by election, not by birth or divine right. Such an election represented a social contract between the ruler and his subjects in which the former was responsible for protecting the country and seeing to it that good was rewarded and evil punished. The underlying attitude expressed in these legends is consistent with Buddha Shakyamuni's own praise of the Vajjian state, for it provided its inhabitants with a voice in their governance.

It is noteworthy that in spite of various Mahayana sutras to the contrary, Japan's leaders were both well aware of, and adamantly opposed to, this earliest Buddhist attitude toward the state. The Shinto-influenced writer, Kitabatake Chikafusa (1293–1354) wrote:

The Buddhist theory [of the state] is merely an Indian theory; Indian monarchs may have been the descendants of a monarch selected for the people's welfare, but Our Imperial Family is the only continuous and unending line of family descending from its Heavenly Ancestors.[82]

Further, with regard to the Japanese nation, Kitabatake had this is say:

> Our Great Nippon is a Divine Nation. Our Divine Ancestors founded it; the Sun Goddess let her descendents reign over it for a long time. This is unique to Our Nation; no other nation has the like of it. This is the reason why Our Nation is called "Divine Nation"![83]

As this book has demonstrated, it was this Shinto-inspired attitude that was to find almost universal acceptance among Japanese Buddhists, especially among Zen masters. This said, it must also be recognized that the foundation for Buddhism's subservience to the state dates back to at least the time of King Ashoka in India, not to mention its even greater subservience in China and Korea. Unlike D. T. Suzuki's claim that Shinto alone was to blame for Japan's "excessive nationalism" in the modern era, the truth is that Shinto was no more than the proximate cause of a tendency in Buddhism that, by 1945, had been developing for more than two thousand years.

If historical developments in a religion may be judged according to their consistency with the avowed teachings of the founder of that religion, in this case, Buddha Shakyamuni, then the best scholarship to date strongly suggests that Buddhist subservience to the state is an accretion to the Buddha Dharma that not only does not belong to that body, but actively betrays it.

This is said knowing full well that had Buddhism remained faithful to its earliest teachings, it is quite possible that it would not have survived, let alone prospered, in those countries that adopted it. Its subsequent almost total disappearance from the land of its birth is but one indication of the dangers it faced. Yet, admitting this does not change one central fact: the historical phenomenon known as Nation-Protecting Buddhism (*Gokoku-Bukkyō*) represents the betrayal of the Buddha Dharma.

Samurai Zen

If Nation-Protecting Buddhism is a betrayal of the Buddha Dharma, it should come as no surprise that Samurai Zen is a particularly pernicious variation of the same aberration. What is perhaps surprising, however, is that confirmation of this assertion is contained in the Zen-inspired work already quoted extensively above, the *Hagakure*.

Returning to this work one last time, we find Jōchō quoting a Zen master about whom D. T. Suzuki had nothing to say. This was the Zen priest Tannen (d. 1680), under whom Jōchō himself had trained. What is so surprising about this priest is that Jōchō quoted him as saying, "It is a great mistake for a young samurai to learn about Buddhism." Tannen then went on to say, "It is fine for old retired men to learn about Buddhism as a diversion."[84]

What was it about Buddhism that made it a fit religion for old samurai to study but not young ones? In a word, it was Buddhism's teaching of compassion. Tannen explained that the feelings of compassion prompted by Buddhism could interfere with the most essential characteristic of a samurai, that is, his courage. According to Tannen, if a young samurai studied Buddhism, "he [would] see things in two ways." That is to say, he would be torn between the courage needed to fulfill his duties toward his lord, and feelings of compassion for his victims. Hence, "A person who does not set himself in just one direction will be of no value at all."[85]

In Tannen's eyes, a young samurai could ill afford to let compassion rule his conduct. Only an elderly samurai had that luxury. This is not to say, however, that a Buddhist priest had no need of courage as well as compassion. Still, a Buddhist priest's courage should be devoted to "things like kicking a man back from the dead, or pulling all living creatures out of hell." A Buddhist priest required courage to save dead or near-dead sentient beings. On the other hand, among warriors, "there are some cowards who advance Buddhism."[86]

In the end, Tannen attempted to resolve the conflict between courage and compassion by stating that priests and samurai had need of equal measures of both, though each of the parties should manifest them differently:

A monk cannot fulfill the Buddhist Way if he does not manifest compassion without and persistently store up courage within. And if a warrior does not manifest courage on the outside and hold enough compassion within his heart to burst his chest, he cannot become a retainer. Therefore, the monk pursues courage with the warrior as his model, and the warrior pursues the compassion of the monk.[87]

Leaving aside the appropriateness of the resolution of the conflict between courage and compassion for the moment, what is significant about the above is the recognition that there is any conflict at all between the teaching of Buddhist compassion and the courage expected of a samurai. In fact, the potential conflict between them is so severe that it is a "great mistake" for the young samurai to even learn about Buddhism, for to do so is to be turned into a "coward."

As for the proposed all-embracing resolution of the conflict, it should be noted that the compassion of the warrior is to be held "within his heart" and not acted upon. This corresponds to a very strong dichotomy manifested in Japanese society between duty (*giri*) to one's superiors and human feelings (*ninjō*) of kindness and compassion toward others. In classical Japanese drama there can be no question, in the end, which of these conflicting values will prevail. That is to say, nothing can be allowed to interfere with the accomplishment of one's duty. Buddhism, therefore, may be studied safely only by "retired old men."

As with Nation-Protecting Buddhism, it can be cogently argued that Buddhism would not have survived in a warrior-dominated society without compromising its ethical code as expressed in the Holy Eightfold Path, especially its prohibitions against the taking of life, pursuing a career as a soldier, or even selling weapons. Once again however, this does not alter the fact that all of these acts endorsed by Samurai Zen are a violation of the fundamental teachings of Buddhism.

In particular, advocates of the unity of Zen and the sword such as Takuan, Shōsan, and D. T. Suzuki have taken the very real power emanating from the concentrated state of mind arising out of Buddhist meditation, that is, *samadhi* power, and placed it in the service of men who can, in the final analysis, only be described as "hired killers." Especially when viewed in light of the innumerable atrocities perpetrated by the Japanese military during the Asia-Pacific war, including the systematic, institutionalized killing and raping of civilians, D. T. Suzuki's statements that "the enemy appears and makes himself a victim," or that "the swordsman turns into an artist of the first grade, engaged in producing a work of genuine originality," and so forth must be clearly and unequivocally recognized as desecrations of the Buddha Dharma. As we have amply seen, Suzuki was far from being the only one to say or write such things.

Experienced Zen practitioners know that the "no-mind" of Zen does in fact exist. Equally, they know that *samadhi* (i.e., meditative) power also exists. But they also know, or at least *ought to know*, that these things, in their original Buddhist formulation, had *absolutely nothing to do with bringing harm to others*. On the contrary, authentic Buddhist awakening is characterized by a combination of wisdom and compassion—identifying oneself with others and seeking to eliminate suffering in all its forms. Thus, the question must be asked, even though it cannot be answered in this book—How is the Zen school to be restored and reconnected to its Buddhist roots? Until this question is satisfactorily answered *and acted upon*, Zen's claim to be an authentic expression of the Buddha Dharma must remain in doubt.

Epilogue

With the addition of chapter 12, "Was It Buddhism?" I hope to have at least begun to address the question first raised in the preface, i.e., "What went wrong?" That is to say, the reader can now see that Zen and institutional Buddhism's support for the warfare waged by Japanese militarists in the name of the emperor was not a momentary aberration of that tradition but had ample historical and doctrinal precedent, reaching as far back as India, let alone China. Nevertheless, I would be the first to admit that this second edition, like the first, still retains one glaring deficiency—it fails to address the question of how Japanese institutional Buddhism, most especially Zen, can be restored to its rightful place as an authentic expression of the Buddha Dharma.

There are clearly Buddhist leaders, especially in Japan, who believe (or hope) that by having admitted and apologized for their sect's past support of Japanese militarism, they can now safely put this issue behind them and move on. From their viewpoint, researchers like me are fixated on past wrongs in what appears to some as an ongoing attempt to denigrate the Zen tradition, if not institutional Japanese Buddhism as a whole.

In point of fact, as a Buddhist priest in the Sōtō Zen tradition myself, this has been far from an easy book to write, for I have been forced to reveal a "dark side" of Buddhist history even while retaining faith in my adopted religion. Given this, there is no one who would like more than me, on the basis of these statements of repentance in recent years, to declare "case closed" to this tragic past. What prevents me from doing so?

Somewhat surprisingly, part of the answer comes from one of the very few Rinzai Zen masters who, over the years, have seriously attempted to convince their fellow priests to address their war complicity. I refer to Kōno

Taitsū, former president of Hanazono University, first introduced in chapter 6. Even though he has referred to the Rinzai sect's support of militarism as "the most serious stain on Zen in the past 1,000 years," he stated, in response to my earnest entreaty to publicly disavow the "unity of Zen and the sword" that underlay that support, that he would not do so. Why? Because "the Japanese people have a special relationship with the sword that foreigners cannot understand." While I may not be able to understand the Japanese people's alleged affinity for the sword, I cannot help but ask if that affinity transcends Taitsū's own allegiance to the violence-foreswearing Buddha Dharma?

If even a Zen master of Taitsū's undoubted integrity is unwilling to divorce Zen from its past intimacy with the warrior class and the sword, how much hope is there that other Buddhist leaders are willing to do so? In fact, when they are examined carefully, it is clear that the statements of repentance issued to date view Zen and institutional Buddhism's support of Japanese militarism as but a temporary lapse from Buddhism's true principles of peace, albeit a lapse, as noted in the Sōtō Zen sect's statement, that dates back to the Meiji Restoration of 1868. None of those leaders making these statements have been willing to entertain, let alone admit, the possibility that the roots of their support lay in the very fabric of Buddhism's traditional role as "protector" of the nation and its rulers.

However, as David Brazier noted in his insightful book *The New Buddhism* (2001), far from a momentary lapse,

> the original message [of Buddhism] was buried under a series of compromises—some chosen, some coerced—with oppressive political systems in India, China, Japan and elsewhere. In all of these countries, Buddhism has, at one time or another, been used as an instrument of state policy for subduing rather than liberating the population . . . .
>
> In Japan, it was not possible for the sangha to maintain its independence and a series of military governments regulated and subordinated the practice of religion to national requirements. (pp. 66, 63)

If these statements are true, as chapter 12 suggests they are, then it is clear why institutional (Zen) Buddhism's support for Japanese militarism must not be ignored or relegated to past history. That is to say, until and unless the longstanding subjugation of the Buddha Dharma to the state is recognized as a fundamental distortion if not betrayal of the Buddha Dharma, there is no guarantee that this phenomenon will not once again raise its destructive head in Japan if not in other Asian countries, including, in due course, the West. As fanciful as this assertion may strike some, one only needs to look at the nationalistic and war-justifying pronouncements of some leaders of the Sri Lankan Sangha in recent years to know that Buddhism's support for war, including civil war, is far from past history.

Needless to say, the reforms required for Zen, or Buddhism as a whole, to cleanse itself of its ongoing support for state-sponsored violence are far too complex to be introduced in this book. Yet, if Buddhism (or any other faith) is to move beyond slogans and truly become a religion of peace, this must be done. This is the challenge I leave to my readers.

Notes

Preface

1. James, *The Varieties of Religious Experience*, p. 48.

Chapter One

1. See Kitagawa, *Religion in Japanese History*, p. 164.
2. Bellah, *Tokugawa Religion*, p. 51.
3. Anesaki, *History of Japanese Religion*, p. 260.
4. Two representative figures within the Rinzai Zen tradition are Bankei Yōtaku (1622–93) and Hakuin Ekaku (1685–1768). Hakuin is credited with having developed the practice of meditating on a series of *kōans*, with the goal of attaining enlightenment. Within the Sōtō Zen tradition, Manzan Dōhaku (1636–1714) and Menzan Zuihō (1683–1769) are the two most notable figures. Manzan's primary goal was the elimination of dishonesty relating to temple succession, while Manzan was a noted scholar. For a detailed history of the Zen tradition during the Tokugawa period, see Dumoulin, *Zen Buddhism: A History; Volume 2: Japan*, pp. 270–399.
5. Kitagawa, *Religion in Japanese History*, p. 166.

6. Quoted in Anesaki, *History of Japanese Religion*, p. 331.
7. Ketelaar, *Of Heretics and Martyrs in Meiji Japan*, p. 9.
8. Ibid., p. 7.
9. Ibid., p. 65.
10. Ibid., p. 13.
11. Quoted in Anesaki, *History of Japanese Religion*, p. 335.
12. See Ketelaar, *Of Heretics and Martyrs in Meiji Japan*, p. 105.
13. Ibid., p. 130.
14. Shibata, *Haibutsu Kishaku*, p. 195.
15. Kitagawa, *Religion in Japanese History*, p. 213.
16. Hardacre, *Shintō and the State, 1868–1988*, p. 6.
17. Quoted in Matsunami, *The Constitution of Japan*, p. 136.

Chapter Two

1. Kitagawa, *Religion in Japanese History*, p. 213.
2. Quoted in Ketelaar, *Of Heretics and Martyrs in Meiji Japan*, p. 132.
3. See Thelle, *Buddhism and Christianity in Japan*, pp. 195–96.
4. The term "New Buddhism" as used here refers to a wide variety of individuals and organizations, both lay and clerical,

working for the reform of Meiji-era Japanese Buddhism. Because this was a movement, not an organization, there were often conflicting, even opposing, views as to what changes should be made. In addition, there was a much more narrowly focused group of reformers, composed mainly of middle-class, unaffiliated Buddhists in their twenties and thirties, who established the Bukkyō Seito Dōshi Kai (Pure Buddhist Fellowship) in February 1899. In July of the following year they began a journal entitled Shin Bukkyō (New Buddhism) as a vehicle to express their views, featuring articles critical of both institutional Buddhism and state support of, and interference with, religion. On three occasions the journal's articles were so radical (in the government's view) that the journal's sale was prohibited. Although this group neither publicly opposed the Russo-Japanese War nor embraced socialism, it came under increasing government pressure and by 1915 had effectively collapsed, leaving little behind in terms of permanent impact on the subsequent development of Japanese Buddhism. For further information, see Yoshida Kyūichi, Nihon Kindai Bukkyōshi Kenkyū, pp. 355–433.

5. Anesaki, History Of Japanese Religion, p. 337.

6. See Ketelaar, Of Heretics and Martyrs in Meiji Japan, p. 126.

7. Sharf, "The Zen of Japanese Nationalism" in History of Religions 33/1 (1993), p. 18.

8. See Ketelaar, Of Heretics and Martyrs in Meiji Japan, p. 163.

9. Sharf, "The Zen of Japanese Nationalism" in History of Religions 33/1 (1993), p. 19.

10. See Yokoyama, "Two Addresses by Shaku Sōen" in The Eastern Buddhist (New Series) 26/2 (1993), p. 131.

11. Thelle, Buddhism and Christianity in

Japan, p. 219.

12. Ibid., p. 220.

13. Yatsubuchi, Shūkyō Taikai Hōdō, pp. 35–40, 44–45.

14. Anesaki, Bukkyō Seiten Shiron, p. 17.

15. See Ketelaar, Of Heretics and Martyrs in Meiji Japan, p. 171.

16. Ōhara, Bankoku Shūkyō Taikai Enzetsushū, pp. 5–6.

17. See Ketelaar, Of Heretics and Martyrs in Meiji Japan, p. 170.

18. As quoted in Ketelaar, Of Heretics and Martyrs in Meiji Japan, p. 168.

19. See Daitō, Otera no Kane wa Naranakatta, p. 58. The Meiji government recognized the importance of Japanese Buddhism's role on the continent as early as 1871. It was in this year that Eto Shimpei, the Meiji government's vice-minister of education and later minister of justice and councilor of state, wrote a memorandum on this topic to Prince Iwakura Tomomi. Noting the Chinese people's belief in Buddhism, Eto advocated sending Japanese Buddhist priests to China because over time such priests would become intimately acquainted with that country and thus be able to provide the government with valuable information.

20. Quoted in the 8 October 1877 issue of the Meikyō Shinshi (No. 534).

21. See Yoshida, Nihon Kindai Bukkyō Shakaishi Kenkyū, p. 44.

22. Quoted in Thelle, Buddhism and Christianity in Japan, p. 198.

23. Ibid., p. 198.

24. See Kitagawa, Religion in Japanese History, p. 230.

25. Quoted in the 11 March 1889 issue of Daidō Shimpō (No. 1).

26. For a detailed description of the clashes that occurred between Buddhists and Christians, see Yoshida, Nihon Kindai Bukkyōshi Kenkyū, pp. 166–201.

27. Ienaga, The Pacific War, 1931–1945, p. 6.

28. Inoue Enryō, Chūkō Katsu Ron, pp.

61–66.

29. Ibid., pp. 66–70.
30. Ibid., p. 71.
31. See Kitagawa, *Religion in Japanese History*, p. 231.
32. Quoted in the 31 July 1894 issue of the *[Honganjiha] Honzan Rokuji.*
33. Quoted in the 15 April 1895 issue of the *Jōdō Kyōhō* (No. 213).
34. Quoted by Kirita Kiyohide in his article, "Seinen Suzuki Teitarō Daisetsu no Shakaikan" (Young D. T. Suzuki's Views on Society) in *Zengaku Kenkyū* 72 (January 1994), p. 21. One concrete example of early military interest in Zen was the establishment of the Yuima Kai in 1881. Headed by Imperial Army General Torio Tokuan, this lay organization had a strong military focus and was headquartered at Shōkokuji, the head temple of a Rinzai Zen branch by the same name. As early as 1890 Gen. Torio had written the following in the Japan *Daily Mail:* "Though at first site Occidental civilization presents an attractive appearance, adapted as it is to the gratification of selfish desires, yet, since its basis is the hypothesis that men's wishes constitute natural laws, it must ultimately end in disappointment and demoralization. . . . Occidental nations have become what they are after passing through conflicts and vicissitudes of the most serious kind. . . . Perpetual disturbance is their doom. Peaceful equality can never be attained until built up among the ruins of annihilated Western States and the ashes of extinct Western peoples." Myōshinji, the single largest Rinzai Zen branch, volunteered sixteen of its priests as military chaplains in December 1894 (as did the Tendai and Shingon sects).
35. See Thelle, *Buddhism and Christianity in Japan*, p. 171.
36. Ibid., pp. 173–74.
37. D. T. Suzuki, *Shin Shūkyō–ron* in Vol.

23, *Suzuki Daisetsu Zenshū*, p. 134.
38. Ibid., pp. 136–37.
39. Kirita, "D. T. Suzuki and the State" in *Rude Awakenings*, p. 54.
40. Ibid., p. 54.
41. Ibid., pp. 53–54.
42. Ibid., p. 66.
43. Ibid., p. 72.
44. Suzuki was not the first to make use of these words written by Ssu-ma Ch'ien (145?–90? B.C.E.), China's greatest classical historian. The original text, contained in his *Shiji* (Records of the Historian), read as follows: "A man has only one death. That death may be as weighty as Mount Tai, or it may be as light as a goose feather. It all depends upon the way he uses it." Suzuki himself most likely borrowed these words from the "Imperial Rescript to Soldiers and Sailors" (*Gunjin Chokuyu*) promulgated under the name of Emperor Meiji in 1882. This emphasis on the nobility of death in the service of the state dominated the thinking of the imperial army until its ultimate defeat in 1945.
45. D. T. Suzuki, *Shin Shūkyō Ron* in Vol. 23, *Suzuki Daisetsu Zenshū*, pp. 139–40.
46. Shaku, *Sermons of a Buddhist Abbot*, p. 203.
47. Ibid., p. 203.
48. Ibid., pp. 199–203.
49. Ibid., pp. 211–14.
50. Imakita Kōsen was no stranger to government service, either, for in the 1870s he had been employed as a Doctrinal Instructor by the Ministry of Doctrine. There has been longstanding debate within Zen circles as to whether the *satori* experience of Zen is the equivalent of Buddha Shakyamuni's own experience of awakening, or enlightenment. For Sōen, however, there was nothing to debate: "To say the Buddha had a *satori* experience sounds as if we were talking about a Zen monk, but I think it is permissible to say that a monk's

attaining *satori* corresponds to the Buddha's awakening effortlessly" (As quoted in Yokoyama, "Two Addresses by Shaku Sōen" in *The Eastern Buddhist (New Series)* 26/2 (1993), p. 141).

51. Quoted in the 7 August 1904 issue of *Heimin Shimbun* (No. 39).
52. Inoue Enryō, *Enryō Kōwa-shū*, pp. 299–302.
53. See Anesaki, *History of Japanese Religion*, pp. 391–92.
54. "Bukkyō Nippon no Shihyō o Kataru Zadankai" (A Discussion on the Aims of Japanese Buddhism) in *Daihōrin* (March 1937), pp. 91–93.
55. Quoted in Daitō Satoshi, *Otera no Kane wa Naranakatta*, pp. 131–32.
56. Sawaki, *Sawaki Kōdō Kikigaki*, p. 6.
57. Ibid., p. 6.
58. Sawaki, "Zenkai Hongi o Kataru" (On the True Meaning of the Zen Precepts) (Part 9) in the January 1942 issue of *Daihōrin*, p. 107.
59. Akizuki, *Nantembō Zenwa*, p. 51.
60. Sharf, "The Zen of Japanese Nationalism" in *History of Religions* 33/1 (1993), pp. 11–12.
61. Akizuki, *Nantembō Zenwa*, p. 244.
62. This episode is recounted in Michel Mohr's article "Monastic Tradition and Lay Practice from the Perspective of Nantembō" in *Zen Buddhism Today* 12 (March 1996), p. 81.
63. Akizuki, *Nantembō Zenwa*, p. 244.
64. Iida, *Sanzen Manroku*, p. 264.
65. Akizuki, *Nantembō Zenwa*, pp. 244–45.
66. As quoted in Sharf, "The Zen of Japanese Nationalism" in *History of Religions* 33/1 (1993), p. 12.
67. Akizuki, *Nantembō Zenwa*, p. 51.

ōsha, p. 110.
3. Ibid., pp. 112–13.
4. Ibid., p. 115.
5. Quoted in Kashiwagi, *Taigyaku Jiken to Uchiyama Gudō*, p. 29.
6. Ibid., p. 197.
7. Quoted in Yokoyama, "Two Addresses by Shaku Sōen" in *The Eastern Buddhist (New Series)* 26/2 (1993), p. 136.
8. Quoted in Kashiwagi, *Taigyaku Jiken to Uchiyama Gudō*, pp. 198–201.
9. Kashiwagi, "Junkyōsha Uchiyama Gudō no Shōgai" in No. 9, *Nishisagami Shomin Shiroku* (1984), p. 11.
10. Hane, *Reflections on the Way to the Gallows*, p. 57.
11. There is a clear discrepancy in numbers between Kanno's court testimony, in which she clearly said "only the *four* of us," and her diary entry which mentions a total of *five*, herself included. One explanation put forward is that she was trying to protect her lover, Kōtoku, in her court testimony. Kōtoku's actual role in the plot is very ambiguous, and it is possible that while he may have had some knowledge of its existence, he was not directly involved.
12. Inagaki, *Henkaku o Motometa Bukkyōsha*, p. 128.
13. *Sōtō Shūhō*, No. 694 (July 1993), p. 16.
14. *Sōtō Shūhō*, No. 696 (September 1993), pp. 12–16.
15. Notehelfer, *Kōtoku Shūsui (Portrait of a Japanese Radical)*, p. 185.
16. Hane, *Reflections on the Way to the Gallows*, p. 56.
17. Yoshida, *Nihon Kindai Bukkyōshi Kenkyū*, p. 476.
18. Ibid., p. 478.

Chapter Three

1. Notehelfer, *Kōtoku Shūsui (Portrait of a Japanese Radical)*, p. 186.
2. Inagaki, *Henkaku o Motometa Bukky-*

Chapter Four

1. *Sōtō Shūhō*, No. 340 (15 February 1911).
2. *Sōtō Shūhō*, No. 340 (15 February 1911).
3. Quoted in Yoshida, *Nihon Kindai*

Bukkyōshi Kenkyū, p. 510.
4. See Ketelaar, *Of Heretics and Martyrs in Meiji Japan*, p. 134.
5. Contained in the 29 January 1911 issue of *Chūgai Nippō*, No. 3259.
6. Contained in the 15 October 1910 issue of the *[Honganjiha] Honzan Rokuji*.
7. Akiyama, *Sonnō Aikoku Ron*, p. 1.
8. Ibid., p. 2.
9. Ibid., pp. 49–52.
10. Ibid., pp. 144–49.
11. Thelle, *Buddhism and Christianity in Japan*, p. 252.
12. Ibid., p. 252.

CHAPTER FIVE

1. Beasley, *The Modern History Of Japan*, pp. 172–73.
2. Borton, *Japan's Modern Century*, pp. 272–73.
3. Nukariya, *Religion of the Samurai: A Study of Zen Philosophy and Discipline in China and Japan*, pp. xiii–xvi.
4. Ibid., pp. 50–51.
5. This editorial appeared on 15 September 1912 in the *Tokyo Asahi Shimbun*.
6. Nukariya, *Religion of the Samurai: A Study of Zen Philosophy and Discipline in China and Japan*, pp. 50–51.
7. Quoted in Yokoyama, "Two Addresses by Shaku Sōen" in *The Eastern Buddhist (New Series)* 26/2 (1993), p. 144.
8. Ibid., pp. 145–46.
9. Ibid., pp. 145–48.
10. See Sharf, "The Zen of Japanese Nationalism" in *History of Religions* 33/1 (1993), p. 10.
11. The Nishi Honganji branch of the Shin sect, together with members of the aristocratic Ōtani family who have traditionally headed that branch, were major stockholders in the South Manchuria Railway Company.
12. Murakami, *Japanese Religion in the Modern Century*, p. 54.

13. Quoted in Holtom, *Modern Japan and Shinto Nationalism*, p. 144.
14. Anesaki, *History of Japanese Religion*, pp. 393–94.
15. Arai, "A Buddhist View of World Peace" in the December 1925 issue of *Japan Evangelist*, pp. 395–400.
16. Shimizu, *Risshō Ankoku no Taigi to Nippon Seishin*, p. 46.
17. Yoshida, *Nihon Kindai Bukkyō Shakaishi Kenkyū*, p. 231.
18. See Hishiki, *Jōdo Shinshū no Sensō Sekinin*, pp. 49–50.
19. D. T. Suzuki, *Essays in Zen Buddhism (Third Series)*, p. 331.
20. See Hishiki, *Jōdo Shinshū no Sensō Sekinin*, p. 56.

CHAPTER SIX

1. Inagaki, *Henkaku o Motometa Bukkyōsha*, p. 68.
2. Inagaki, *Butsuda o Seoite Gaitō e*, pp. 3–6.
3. Ibid., pp. 6–7.
4. Senō, *Nikki 4*, p. 6.
5. Inagaki, *Butsuda o Seoite Gaitō e*, p. 139.
6. Ibid., p. 147.
7. See June 1933 issue of *Shinkō Bukkyō*.
8. Some readers may wonder why I have failed to include a small number of Nichiren–related splinter groups in my discussion of antiwar Buddhist movements. The reason for this is that the conflict between these groups and the government was characterized by mutual religious intolerance, not these groups' opposition to either Japanese colonialism or militarism. The best known (in postwar years) of these groups is Sōka Gakkai, founded in 1930 by Makiguchi Tsunesaburo (1871–1944) and his disciple, Toda Jōsei (1900–1958). Makiguchi's conflict with the government began in 1939 when he opposed legislation forcing the amalgamation of

smaller religious bodies with their parent organizations or with one another. In 1943 both Makiguchi and Toda were imprisoned because they refused to worship and enshrine replicas of the sacred tablets of the Ise Grand Shrine dedicated to the Shinto Sun goddess, Amaterasu Ōmikami. Like Nichiren, the thirteenth-century founder of their faith, Makiguchi, Toda, and their small band of followers vehemently rejected all other faiths, including other sects of Buddhism, as well as Shinto and Christianity. Although Makiguchi died in prison in 1944 and is held up by present-day Sōka Gakkai members as an "anti-war martyr," the group he founded continues to be characterized by its strident denunciations of other religious groups.

9. Ienaga, *The Pacific War, 1931–45*, pp. 214–15.
10. Ibid., p. 215.
11. Nozaki, *Jion no Hibiki*, p. 74.
12. Quoted in Daitō, *Otera no Kane wa Naranakatta*, p. 139.
13. Ibid, p. 139.
14. Quoted in Kōno Taitsū, *"Zuisho ni Shu to naru"* (Make Yourself Master of Every Place) *Komazawa Daigaku Zen Kenkyūjo Nempō* 7 (March 1996), pp. 10–11. Taitsū mentions that Tsuzuki ran his company in the postwar era in accord with the teachings of Ittō-en, a Zen-influenced spiritual movement founded by Nishida Tenkō (1872–1968) in the early 1900s. Ittō-en was an outgrowth of Meiji Buddhist reform efforts, teaching that one should work with a spirit of gratitude in order to repay one's benefactors. Although this movement had pacifist leanings, it nevertheless cooperated with Japanese colonialism and militarism on the Asian continent.
15. Ibid., p. 11. The maxim: "In every place make yourself master" appears twice

in the *Record of Linji (J. Rinzai-roku)*. In his speech at Komazawa University, Kōno Taitsū noted that this maxim "can also mean that there will be times when we must refuse to do something, even at the risk of our own lives."
16. Quoted in Ishihara, "Bukkyō Nippon no Shihyō o Kataru Zadankai" (A Discussion on the Aims of Buddhist Japan) in the March 1937 issue of *Daihōrin*, pp. 93–96.
17. Quoted in Daitō, *Otera no Kane wa Naranakatta*, p. 142.
18. Ketelaar, *of Heretics and Martyrs in Meiji Japan*, p. 215.

CHAPTER SEVEN

1. The Japanese term for "polity" is *kokutai*, literally "state body." The 'state' was not an abstract entity but, on the contrary, was regarded as a simple living organism of which every Japanese was an integral part. Just as the body has a 'head,' so the peerless Japanese state has its emperor from whom all Japanese had descended. As the father of the state, the emperor's edicts were to be obeyed unconditionally. Every Japanese's ultimate duty was to maintain, preserve, and expand this living body no matter what the cost to themselves. In so doing they gained a form of 'eternal life.'
2. Quoted in Ōkura Seishin Bunka Kenkyūjo, *Gokoku Bukkyō*, pp. 135–144.
3. Ibid., p. 158.
4. Ibid., pp. 159–60.
5. Ibid., p. 185.
6. Ibid., p. 188.
7. Ibid., pp. 208–09.
8. Ibid., p. 33.
9. Ibid., p. 37.
10. Ibid., p. 37.
11. Ibid., p. 38.
12. Ibid., p. 50.

13. Ibid., p. 50.
14. Ibid., pp. 50–51.
15. Ibid., pp. 129–30.
16. Ibid., pp. 130–31.
17. Ibid., p. 131.
18. Ibid., p. 132.
19. See Nakano, *Senjika no Bukkyō*, p. 195.
20. Ibid., p. 196.
21. Ibid., p. 238.
22. Daitō, *Otera no Kane wa Naranakatta*, p. 110.
23. Hayashiya and Shimakage, *Bukkyō no Sensō Kan*, p. 1.
24. Ibid., p. 2.
25. Ibid., p. 4.
26. Ibid., p. 7.
27. Ibid., pp. 18–19.
28. Ibid., p. 23.
29. Ibid., p. 27.
30. Ibid., p. 28.
31. Ibid., p. 37.
32. Ibid., p. 37.
33. Ibid., p. 45.
34. Ibid., p. 46.
35. Ibid., p. 47.
36. Ibid., p. 48.
37. Ibid., p. 72.
38. Ibid., p. 72.
39. Ibid., p. 72.
40. Ibid., p. 75.
41. Ibid., p. 76.
42. Ibid., p. 75.
43. Ibid., p. 93.
44. Ibid., p. 99.
45. Ibid., p. 99.
46. Ibid., p. 100.
47. Ibid., p. 105.
48. Furukawa, *Yakushin Nihon to Shin Daijō Bukkyō*, p. 2.
49. Ibid., p. 2.
50. Ibid., p. 2.
51. Ibid., p. 51.
52. Ibid., pp. 51–52. Japan had withdrawn from the League of Nations in March 1933 because of a League resolution criticizing Japan's control of Manchuria.
53. Ibid., p. 108.
54. Ibid., pp. 110–11.
55. Hata, "Kokumin Seishin Sōdōin to Bukkyō" (The General Spiritual Mobilization of the People and Buddhism) in the July 1938 issue of *Daihōrin*, pp. 16–18.
56. Tendaishū Kyōgakubu, *Fukyō Shiryō*, p. 1.

CHAPTER EIGHT

1. Sharf, "The Zen of Japanese Nationalism" in *History of Religions* 33/1 (1993), p. 6.
2. Nitobe, *Bushido: The Soul of Japan*, pp. xii–xiii.
3. Ibid., p. 11.
4. Ibid., pp. 11–12.
5. Ibid., p. 172.
6. Ibid., pp. 176–88.
7. Ibid., p. 183.
8. Ibid., pp. 192–93.
9. Nukariya, *Religion of the Samurai*, p. 50.
10. Shaku Sōen, *Kaijin Kaima*, p. 47.
11. Ibid., p. 65.
12. Ibid., p. 67.
13. Fueoka, *Zen no Tebiki*, p. 150.
14. Ibid., p. 151. The shouted word *"Katsu"* is meaningless. It has been used in the Rinzai Zen tradition to express a state of mind that has transcended dualism, cut through false notions of self and other, and manifested enlightenment.
15. Ibid., p. 152.
16. Ibid., p. 149.
17. Iida, *Sanzen Manroku*, pp. 262–63.
18. Ishihara, "Bukkyō Nippon no Shihyō o Kataru Zadankai" (A Discussion on the Aims of Buddhist Japan) in the March 1937 issue of *Daihōrin*, p. 86.
19. Ibid., pp. 117–18
20. Ibid., p. 117.
21. Furukawa, *Yakushin Nihon to Shin Daijō Bukkyō*, p. 155.
22. Ibid., pp. 156–61.
23. D. T. Suzuki, "The Zen Sect of Bud-

dhism," in the 1906 issue of *The Journal of the Pali Text Society*, p. 34.

24. D. T. Suzuki, *Zen and Japanese Culture*, p. 30.
25. Ibid., p. 61.
26. Ibid., p. 61.
27. Ibid., p. 62.
28. Ibid., p. 63.
29. Ibid., p. 62.
30. Ibid., p. 63.
31. Ibid., p. 70.
32. Ibid., pp. 71–72.
33. Ibid., p. 85.
34. Ibid., p. 89.
35. D. T. Suzuki, *Shin Shukyō Ron*, in vol. 23, *Suzuki Daisetsu Zenshū*, pp. 139–40.
36. Shaku, *Sermon of a Buddhist Abbot*, p. 201.
37. D. T. Suzuki, *Zen and Japanese Culture*, p. 145.
38. Handa, *Bushidō no Shinzui*, p. 1.
39. Ibid., p. 2.
40. Tōjō Hideki, *Senjin Kun*, pp. 12–17.
41. Ibid., pp. 18–19. In 1941 the Sōtō Zen sect made the *Senjinkun* part of their official collection of "Model Sermons," attaching a section to it entitled "Zen and the Military Spirit." Further, in their book *Soldiers of the Sun—The Rise and Fall of the Japanese Imperial Army*, Meirion and Susie Harries noted a Buddhist, especially Zen, influence on Tōjō Hideki and most of the officer corps. They found this Buddhist influence expressed, among other things, in Tōjō's statement that he felt "carefree" once the decision had been made to go to war with the United States. This attitude, they asserted, derived from Zen's emphasis on "giving up of thought," also noting that "It may help to explain the extraordinarily casual attitude of some generals to the practicalities of their campaigns." (p. 336)
42. D. T. Suzuki, "Zen to Bushido" in *Bushidō no Shinzui*, p. 75.
43. Ibid., p. 64. Suzuki's *Zen and Japanese Culture* first appeared in German in 1941, while the German edition of his *Introduction to Zen Buddhism* first appeared in 1939. Dr. Karl Haushofer, one of Hitler's chief advisers behind the scenes, wrote: "The Meiji Restoration could be carried through only with the inherited values of the Japanese feudal period, the unselfish, austere, pure, and really self-sacrificing simplicity which, despite Confucius, put the fatherland and state before the family and the family before the individual, and which was convinced that in the very moment of final sacrifice, it went through the gate to real life. The metaphysical forces which elsewhere were absorbed by doctrines of salvation were here at the disposal of the state, representing a national community of love." Haushofer's comments are included in Tolischus, *Tokyo Record*, pp. 158–59. Suzuki's *Zen and Japanese Culture* also influenced Italian facism through the introduction and high praise it received at the hands of Giuseppe Tucci, then one of Italy's greatest Buddhologists and an unabashed supporter of fascism. (Tucci's comments are included in an article entitled "Giuseppe Tucci, or Buddhology in the Age of Fascism" by Gustavo Benavides in Donald S. Lopez, Jr., *Curators of the Buddha—The Study of Buddhism under Colonialism*, pp. 161–196.)
44. Quoted in Ichikawa, *Fudōchi Shimmyō Roku/Taia Ki*, p. 165. Although the exact date is unknown, sometime before August 1941, Lieutenant General Yamashita Motoyuki, head of the Japanese military mission to the Axis, reported that Hitler had told him how interested he had been in Japan since his youth, including careful study of Japan's war tactics during the Russo-Japanese War. Yamashita went on to say: "Hitler emphasized that in the

coming age, the interests of Japan and Germany would be identical, because the two have a common spiritual foundation. And he hinted that he would leave instructions to the German people to bind themselves eternally to the Japanese spirit." As for Ambassador Kurusu, he went on to become a confidant of Rudolf Hess, Hitler's deputy führer. Following Hess's subsequent flight to England, Kurusu said: "There was something of an Oriental fighter in Hess. He was envious of Japan, whose people are fired with service to the state under the Japanese spirit. He used to tell me: "We too are battling to destroy individualism. We are struggling for a new Germany based on the new idea of totalitarianism. In Japan, this way of thinking comes naturally to the people!" Quoted in Tolischus, *Tokyo Record,* pp. 158–59.

45. Seki, *Bushidō no Kōyō,* p. 21.
46. Ibid., p. 22.
47. Ibid., p. 22.
48. Ibid., p. 30.
49. Ibid., pp. 64–65.
50. Yabuki, *Nippon Seishin to Nippon Bukkyō,* p. 4.
51. Holtom, *Modern Japan and Shinto Nationalism,* p. 149.
52. Humphreys, *The Way of the Heavenly Sword,* pp. 12–16.
53. Peattie, *Ishiwara Kanji, and Japan's Confrontation with the West,* p. 5. The emphasis on "an extreme code of sacrifice in the attack" in both the French and Japanese armies was more than mere coincidence. When the Meiji government first established a modern War Department in the 1870s, it was the French military system that furnished inspiration and guidance. Although the Prussian model influenced the subsequent formation of the imperial army in the 1880s, the French stress on morale, *esprit de corps,* and aggressive

combat was retained, especially in Japan's military academies. The incorporation of Bushidō into the Imperial military represented, in this sense, the imposition of indigenous content upon a Western model.
54. Sugimoto, *Taigi,* pp. 23–25. The title *Taigi* may also be translated as "Noble Cause," "Justice," or "Righteousness."
55. Ibid., pp. 36–39.
56. Kitagawa, *Religion in Japanese History,* p. 187.
57. Sugimoto, *Taigi,* p. 62.
58. Ibid., p. 53.
59. Ibid., p. 139.
60. Ibid., p. 19.
61. Ibid., p. 140.
62. Ibid., p. 101.
63. Ibid., p. 99.
64. Ibid., p. 143.
65. Ibid., p. 152.
66. Ibid., pp. 153–54.
67. Ibid., p. 156.
68. Ibid., pp. 160–61.
69. Ibid., p. 164.
70. Ibid., p. 167.
71. D. T. Suzuki, *Zen and Japanese Culture,* pp. 111–127.
72. Ibid., p. 111.
73. Sugimoto, *Taigi,* p. 192.
74. Ibid., p. 219.
75. Ibid., p. 178.
76. Ibid., p. 179.
77. Ibid., p. 195.
78. Ibid., p. 182.
79. Ibid., pp. 182–83.
80. Ibid., p. 254.
81. Ibid., pp. 255–56.
82. Ibid., pp. 256–57. Ekijū's description of someone "be[ing] reborn seven times over" is a reference to Kusunoki Masashige (1294–1336), a loyalist military leader during the period of the Northern and Southern Courts (1332–90). Having been defeated in battle and facing death, Masashige vowed to be "reborn seven times over in order to

annihilate the emperor's enemies."

83. Takizawa, "The Zen of Clothing and Food" (Ishoku Zen) in the September 1943 issue of *Sanshō* (No. 191), p. 741.
84. Ōyama, *Sugimoto Gorō Chūsa no Sonnō to Zen*, p. iii.
85. Ibid., p. vii.
86. Quoted in Ichikawa, *Nihon Fashizumu ka no Shūkyō*, p. 71.
87. Ienaga, *The Pacific War, 1931–1945*, pp. 195–96.

CHAPTER NINE

1. See reference in Ishihara, "Bukkyō Nippon no Shihyō o Kataru Zadankai" (A Discussion on the Aims of Buddhist Japan) in the March 1937 issue of *Daihōrin*, p. 116.
2. Sugimoto, *Taigi*, p. 198.
3. Ibid., p. 198.
4. Quoted in the December 1942 issue of *Sanshō*, pp. 409–10.
5. Ibid., p. 407.
6. Quoted in the 1 January 1941 issue of *Sōtō Shūhō* (No. 39), p. 1.
7. Yamada Reirin, *Zengaku Yawa*, p. 25.
8. Ibid., p. 26.
9. Ibid., pp. 53–54.
10. Ibid., p. 183.
11. Ibid., p. 190.
12. Ibid., p. 85.
13. Ibid., p. 81.
14. Kurebayashi, "The [China] Incident and Buddhism" (Jihen to Bukkyō) in the October 1937 issue of *Sanshō* (No. 121), p. 375.
15. Ibid., p. 375.
16. Ibid., pp. 376–77.
17. Ibid., p. 377.
18. Ibid., p. 378.
19. Ienaga, *The Pacific War, 1931–1945*, p. 167.
20. Hitane, "The Current Incident and the Vow and Practice of a Bodhisattva" (Konji no Jihen to Bosatsu no Gangyō) in the October 1937 issue of *Zenshū*

(No. 510), p. 19.
21. Ibid., p. 19.
22. Fukuba, "What is Japanese, What is Chinese" (Shinateki to Nihonteki) in the November 5, 1939, issue of *Zengaku Kenkyū* (No. 32), p.102.
23. Ibid, p. 99.
24. Ibid, p. 98.
25. Ibid, p. 98–99.
26. Ibid, pp. 99–100.
27. Ibid, p. 102.
28. Kapleau, *The Three Pillars of Zen*, pp. 273–74.
29. Maezumi and Glassman, *The Hazy Moon of Enlightenment*, p. 194.
30. Harada, *Sanzen no Kaitei*, p. 112.
31. Ibid., pp. 116–17.
32. Ibid., pp. 117–18.
33. Quoted in Ichikawa, *Nihon Fashizumu ka no Shūkyō*, p. 163.
34. Ibid., p. 197. In adding a Chinese-style verse to his comments, Daiun followed a time-honored Zen custom. Traditional collections of koan, such as the *Mumonkan* (Gateless Barrier) and *Hekiganroku* (Blue Cliff Record), typically have verses of appreciation and explanation attached to each of the koan contained in the collection.
35. Ibid., p. 252.
36. Ibid., p. 283.
37. Two of Masunaga's best-known works in English are: (1) *The Sōtō Approach to Zen* (Tokyo, 1948) and (2) *A Primer of Sōtō Zen: A Translation of Dōgen's Shōbōgenzō Zuimonki* (Honolulu: East-West Center, 1971).
38. As quoted in Ichikawa, *Nihon Fashizumu ka no Shūkyō*, p. 295.
39. The bodhisattva's six perfections of morality are: (1) making both material and spiritual donations to others, (2) leading a moral life, (3) being patient, (4) being vigorous in one's religious practice, (5) practicing meditation, and (6) acquiring wisdom.
40. Nakamura, *Ways of Thinking of Eastern*

Peoples: India—China—Tibet—Japan, p. 583.

41. Imai, "Wagashū Kodai no Gunji Kankei no Kitō to Ekōbun" (Prayers and "Merit Transfer Verses" relating to Military Activities in Ancient Times in Our [Rinzai] Sect) in the January 1938 issue of *Zenshū* (No. 513), p. 18.

42. Quoted in the combined November–December 1944 issue of *Sōtō Shūhō* (No. 122), p. 1. In Japan the belief in the efficacy of sutra copying on the outcomes of battles can be traced back at least as far as Taira no Masakado (d. 940), and his unsuccessful rebellion of 939–40 against the central government. Masakado is recorded as having vowed to copy the Golden Light Sutra in order to ensure the victory of his rebel forces. See Rabinovitch, *Shōmonki—The Story of Masakado's Rebellion*, pp. 138–39, n. 300.

43. Quoted in the 15 April 1942 issue of *Sōtō Shūhō* (No. 70), p. 6.

44. Imai, "Wagashū Kodai no Gunji Kankei no Kitō to Ekōbun" (Prayers and "Merit Transfer Verses" relating to Military Activities in Ancient Times in Our [Rinzai] Sect) in the January 1938 issue of *Zenshū* (No. 513), p. 17.

45. Ibid., pp. 21–22.

46. Quoted in the flyer, "Kōa Kannon ni tsuite," prepared by the Kōa Kannon Hōsan Kai, p. 2. The Kōa Kannon temple exists yet today and serves as the final resting place for the ashes (and graves) of generals Matsui Iwane, Tōjō Hideki and the five other Class A war criminals executed by the Allies. It is, however, by no means the only temple dedicated to Avalokiteshvara that maintains a military connection. The Tokkō (Special Attack) Kannon is located at the Fudō temple in Tokyo's Setagaya ward. Even now, on the eighteenth of every month, a ceremony is held to console the spirits of those kamikaze pilots who hurled themselves against the Allied fleet.

47. Contained in the 1 September issue of the *Sōtō Shūhō* (No. 55), p. 3. By comparison, it should be noted that the Nishi Honganji branch of the Shin sect donated a total of twenty-two warplanes to the imperial cause.

48. Unnamed reporter, "Sangyō Senshi no Shinjin Rensei" (The Training of the Body and Mind of Industrial Warriors) in the January 1942 issue of *Daihōrin*, p. 137.

49. Quoted in the 1 February 1944 issue of *Sōtō Shūhō* (No. 113), p. 1.

50. Ibid., p. 1.

CHAPTER TEN

1. D. T. Suzuki, *Nihonteki Reisei* in Vol. 8, *Suzuki Daisetsu Zenshū*, pp. 6–7.

2. D. T. Suzuki, "Zenkai Sasshin" (Renewal of the Zen World) in Vol. 28, *Suzuki Daisetsu Zenshū*, p. 411.

3. Ibid., p. 412.

4. Ibid., p. 413. Compare this quotation with what Suzuki wrote only two years earlier, in 1944, in *Nihonteki Reisei* (Japanese Spirituality): "When the bright and pure mind [of a Japanese] no longer works on the surface of consciousness but begins to move submerged in its deepest parts, when it is moving unconsciously, without discrimination, without discursive thought, then Japanese spirituality can be recognized." (*Suzuki Daisetsu Zenshū*, Vol.8, p. 29.)

5. Ibid., p. 415.

6. Ibid., p. 417.

7. D. T. Suzuki, *Nihonteki Reisei* in Vol. 8, *Suzuki Daisetsu Zenshū*, pp. 7.

8. Ibid., p. 7.

9. D. T. Suzuki, *Nihon no Reiseika*, p. 34.

10. Ibid., p. 1.

11. Ibid., pp. 5–6.

12. Ibid., p. 7.

13. Quoted in Abe, *A Zen Life: D. T. Suzuki Remembered*, p. 24.
14. D. T. Suzuki, "Daijō Bukkyō no Sekaiteki Shimei—Wakaki Hitobito ni Yosu" (The World Mission of Mahayana Buddhism—Given to Young People) in Vol. 28, *Suzuki Daisetsu Zenshū*, p. 343.
15. Recorded by Hidaka Daishirō in "Nogi Taishō to Suzuki Daisetsu Sensei no Inshō Oyobi Omoide" (Impressions and Remembrances of General Nogi and D. T. Suzuki) contained in Hisamatsu, *Suzuki Daisetsu*, p. 286. I find even further support for my conclusion in a postwar magazine article written by Suzuki in 1946 entitled "Special Attack Forces." *(Tokkō Tai).* Here Suzuki blamed the Japanese people's "lack of a scientific and technical nature" for the country's defeat. He went on to say: "As for the recent war, the Japanese people revealed from the beginning that as far as their scientific nature is concerned, they were vastly inferior to the peoples of Europe and America. This lack of insight and decisiveness is shown by their complete failure to plan for war; their failure to investigate how much military, economic, and spiritual power the enemy possessed; and their inability to watch for an opportunity to end the war when it became clear that defeat was inevitable. Furthermore, it can be said that Japan was certain to be defeated from the very beginning inasmuch as this country was unable to give the least freshness to the creative power of machinery; or control, organize, master, and efficiently use, scientific technology." (p. 401) This is, of course, the same Suzuki who during the war years urged Zen-inspired warrior-soldiers to "rush forward to one's ideal," ignoring everything else including questions of right and wrong.

16. Quoted in Nihon Shūkyō-sha Heiwa Kyōgikai, *Shūkyō-sha no Sensō Sekinin; Zange, Kokuhaku, Shiryō-shū*, p. 34.
17. Ibid., p. 39.
18. January 1993 issue of *Sōtō Shūhō*, p. 26.
19. Ibid., pp. 28–31. To its credit, the Sōtō sect's administrative headquarters, spearheaded by its Human Rights Division, continues the drive to distance itself from the emperor and the state. This is seen, most notably, in administrative directives issued in 1994 to discourage the inclusion in ritual prayers of references either to the emperor or the term "heroic spirits" *(eirei)* when referring to the nation's war dead. In addition, the sect's Human Rights Division has also sought to end sectarian practices that support either sexual discrimination or discrimination against Japan's former outcaste group *(burakumin).*
20. Quoted in Nihon Shūkyōsha Heiwa Kyōgikai, *Shūkyōsha no Sensō Sekinin; Zange, Kokuhaku, Shiryō Shū*, p. 54.
21. Yanagida Seizan, *Mirai kara no Zen*, pp. 56–7.
22. Interview in 16 February 1995 issue of *Chūgai Nippō*, p. 8.
23. Quoted in Ichikawa Hakugen, *Nihon Fashizumu ka no Shūkyō*, p. 311.
24. Yamada Mumon, *A Flower In The Heart*, p. 11.
25. Ibid., p. 28.
26. Ibid., p. 31.
27. The leaflet was entitled "Thoughts on State Maintenance of Yasukuni Shrine" (Yasukuni Jinja Kokka Goji o Omou), as quoted in Maruyama, *Nihonjin no Kokoro o Dame ni Shita Meisō, Akusō, Gusō*, p. 49. Mumon's attempt to find something good about the war is by no means unique among postwar Japanese leaders, especially conservative politicians and some historians. Typically those who seek to affirm Japan's wartime actions point to the liberation

of the nations of Southeast Asia, especially Indonesia, from the yoke of
Western colonialism. They consistently
fail, however, to address Japan's own
colonial control of Korea, Taiwan, and
Manchuria.

28. Yamada, *A Flower In The Heart*, p. 7.
29. Asahina Sōgen, *Kakugo wa Yoi ka*, pp. 151–52.
30. Ibid., p. 155.
31. Ibid., p. 157.
32. Ibid., pp 150–64.
33. Quoted in Ichikawa, *Nihon Fashizu-muka no Shūkyō*, p. 194.
34. Asahina, *Kakugo wa Yoi ka*, p. 168.
35. Ibid., p. 171.
36. Ibid., p. 171.
37. Ibid., p. 183.
38. Ibid., p. 189.
39. Ichikawa, *Fashizumuka no Shūkyō*, pp. 22–23.
40. Ibid., p. 35.
41. Ibid., p. 15.
42. Ibid., p. 16. Yamaguchi Ojiya was a rightest youth who stabbed to death the popular leader of the Socialist Party of Japan, Asanuma Inejiro, at an outdoor rally in Tokyo in October 1960. Mishima Yukio (1925–1970) was a famous novelist well-known in Japan for his right-wing views, which included restoring the emperor to his prewar status. In pursuit of his political goals, Mishima formed his own private army, the Shield Society (Tate no Kai), which trained together with the postwar Japanese military, the Self-Defense Forces. In November 1970 Mishima made a dramatic call for an uprising among members of the Self-Defense Forces. When this failed, he committed ritual suicide at the Self-Defense Force Head-quarters in Tokyo.
43. Ibid., p. 16.
44. Ibid., p. 15.
45. Quoted in *ZCLA Journal (Yasutani Roshi Memorial Issue)*, Summer / Fall,

1973, p. 46.
46. Ichikawa, *Fashizumuka no Shūkyō*, p. 87.
47. *Sōtōshū Kyōgi*. For a survey of the immediate postwar reactions of other Buddhist sects, see Ichikawa, *Fashizumu ka no Shūkyō*, pp. 305–11.
48. Ichikawa Hakugen, *Zen to Gendai Shisō*, p. 177.
49. Ibid., p. 111–12.
50. September 1942 issue of *Daihōrin*, p. 132.
51. Ibid., p. 139.
52. Ibid, p. 135.
53. See Ichikawa Hakugen, *Bukkyōsha no Sensō Sekinin*, pp. 150–54.
54. Ibid., p. 152.
55. Quoted in Paul Swanson's "Zen is Not Buddhism," in *Numen* 40 (1993), p. 123.
56. Hakamaya Noriaki, *Hihan Bukkyō*, pp. 297–98.
57. Ibid., p. 297.
58. Ibid., pp. 297–98. See pp. 275–304 for a more complete treatment of this thesis.
59. The short treatise entitled *Awakening of Faith in the Mahayana* is the primary vehicle through which the doctrines of original enlightenment and *tatha-gatagarbha* have been introduced into East Asian Buddhism. Although Chinese Buddhist tradition attributes this treatise to the Indian author Asvaghosha, who lived in the first or second century C.E., most scholars today regard it as an original Chinese composition. For further information on these two terms see either the "Introduction" to Yoshito S. Hakeda's translation, *The Awakening of Faith*, pp. 3–19, or Paul L. Swanson's article, "Zen Is Not Buddhism," in *Numen* 40 (1993) pp. 13–14.
60. D. T. Suzuki, *Zen and Japanese Culture*, p. 127.
61. Hakamaya, *Hihan Bukkyō*, pp. 293–94. For an in-depth look at the "Critical Buddhism" movement, see Jamie Hubbard and Paul Swanson, eds. *Pruning*

the Bodhi-tree—Storm over Critical Buddhism. Honolulu: University of Hawaii Press, 1997.

62. The closest to anything like an official Rinzai examination of its wartime conduct is to be found in a 1984 officially sponsored history of the Myōshinji branch entitled *Myōshinji: Roppyaku Gojūnen no Ayumi* (Myōshinji: Over the Course of Six Hundred and Fifty Years). In the only direct reference to the branch's wartime collaboration, the book's author, Kimura Jōyū, first noted the April 1945 donation of the fighter aircraft *Hanazono Myōshinji*. He then went on to say, ". . . [this donation] cannot help but be said to be a reflection of the times," p. 225. Should this be interpreted as a mere oversight, it is noteworthy that in an address given on April 26, 1995, the current president of Hanazono University, Kōno Taitsū (b. 1930), had the temerity to suggest to the Myōshinji branch hierarchy that, in conjunction with the fiftieth anniversary of the war's end, Myōshinji officially issue a statement repenting its war complicity. As he admitted, however, his proposal went over "like a lead balloon" *(nuka ni kugi)*. For a full discussion of this incident, see *Sensō, Sengo Sekinin to Sabetsu* (Discrimination and Responsibility for the War and its Aftermath), pp. 1–16, edited by Hanazono Daigaku Jinken Kyōiku Kenkyūshitsu.

63. Heisig and Maraldo, *Rude Awakenings*, p. 10.

64. Ibid., p. 11.

65. Ibid., p. 10.

66. Ibid., p. 10. For a description of the February 26th Incident and the events surrounding it, see, for example, Beasley's *The Modern History of Japan*, pp. 236–57.

67. Quoted in Endō Makoto, *Ima no Otera ni Bukkyō wa Nai*, p. 157.

68. Heisig & Maraldo, *Rude Awakenings*, p. 15.

CHAPTER ELEVEN

1. "Marching to the Company Tune" in the June 1977 issue of *Focus Japan*, p. 36.

2. See DeVos, "Apprenticeship and Paternalism" in *Modern Japanese Organization and Decision–Making*, pp. 221–23.

3. Sawaki, "Zenrin no Seikatsu to Kiritsu" in the June 1944 issue of *Daihōrin*, pp. 23–25.

4. "Marching to the Company Tune" in the June 1977 issue of *Focus Japan*, p. 36.

5. Quoted in Maruyama Teruo, *Nihonjin no Kokoro o Dame ni Shita Meisō, Akusō, Gusō*, p. 194.

6. Sakai Tokugen, "Onoda-san to Shōji no Mondai" (The Question of Life and Death and Mr. Onoda) in the May 1974 issue of *Daihōrin*, pp. 23–24.

7. Katsuhira, Takuan *Ishi no Satori*, p. 100. Sōtetsu's critique notwithstanding, there has been no lessening of the Rinzai Zen sect's interest in promoting "corporate Zen" over the intervening years. For example, shortly after the collapse of Japan's so-called "bubble economy" in 1992, the Zen Studies Institute at Hanazono University colloborated with the Rinzai sect's Tenryūji branch to produce a video tape in both Japanese and English entitled "Introduction to Zazen." The promotional material accompanying this tape began with the following headline: "Zazen, the Generative Power for Overcoming Economic Recession." It went on to add: "Zen, the wisdom fostered by Japanese culture, can be said to be the key to overcoming the current economic slump, the worst since the end of the war. . . . Zazen is now the focus of businessmen's attention."

8. Ibid., p. 40.

9. See Sugawara Gidō, *Shinde Motomoto!*, p. 182. Gidō also mentions on p. 178 that postwar temple visitors sometimes ask if his temple was established during the

Pacific War. This is because his temple's name included the word "hōkoku" which refers to "repaying the debt of gratitude one owes the state," a popular wartime slogan. Gidō, however, informs such visitors that his temple was founded and named by a feudal lord of the Ashikaga family during the Kamakura period (1185–1333). This fact again points to the medieval origins of the unity of Zen and the state, suggesting that its modern manifestation should be considered less an aberration than an extension of its premodern character.

10. Ibid., p. 189.

11. The phrase "Greater East Asian War" (Dai Tōa Sensō), was the official wartime term for the Pacific War. Due to the militarist connotations of the term, it has generally been shunned in postwar Japan. In fact, during the Allied Occupation (1945–52) its use was officially forbidden. Given this, it can be said that Gidō's use of the term here represents, at least to some degree, an endorsement of Japan's wartime actions.

12. Sugawara, *Shinde Motomoto!*, p. 182.

13. Ibid., p. 187.

14. Ibid., p. 188.

15. Ibid., p. 183.

16. Quoted in Hosokawa and Sayama, "The Chozen-ji Line (Omori Sogen Rotaishi)" in the *Journal of the Institute of Zen Studies* 3 (1988), p. 2.

17. Ōmori, *Ken to Zen*, p. 1.

18. Ibid., p. 69.

19. Ibid., pp. 7–8.

20. Ibid., pp. 206–207.

21. Hosokawa and Sayama, "The Chozen-ji Line (Omori Sogen Rotaishi)" in the *Journal of the Institute of Zen Studies* 3 (1988), p. 3.

22. Bergamini, *Japan's Imperial Conspiracy* Vol. 1, p. 340.

23. Norman, "The Genyōsha: A Study in the Origins of Japanese Imperialism" in Livingston, *The Japan Reader* I, pp. 366–67.

24. Hosokawa and Sayama, "The Chozen-ji Line (Omori Sogen Rotaishi)" in the *Journal of the Institute of Zen Studies* 3 (1988), p. 3.

25. Ibid., p. 2.

26. Ibid., p. 2.

27. Ibid., p. 3.

28. Ibid., p. 3.

29. The question of the exact number of participants in Zen-influenced corporate training programs is difficult to answer with any degree of specificity. When the author was in training himself at Sōtō Zen–affiliated Jōkuin temple in Saitama Prefecture in the mid-1970s, he helped support some three to four such programs per month, each one of which typically lasted three to four days and involved ten to fifty or more employees. More recently, in an interview on October 3, 1996, Saitō Meidō, a priest administrator at the Rinzai Zen–affiliated head temple of Myōshinji, informed the author that a total of five hundred and fifty company employees had participated in its corporate-training programs during the first nine months of 1996. Meidō went on to add, however, that this represented a significant drop in numbers in comparison with the past, something he attributed to Japan's economic slump.

30. Noted by Sharf, "Zen and the Way of the New Religions" in the *Japanese Journal of Religious Studies*, 22/3–4 (1995), p. 422.

CHAPTER TWELVE

1. Ananda K. Coomaraswamy, *Buddha and the Gospel of Buddhism*, pp. 52–53.
2. Kōgen Mizuno, *The Beginnings of Buddhism*, p. 174.
3. Ibid., p. 175.
4. A. L. Basham, *The Wonder That Was India*, p. 96.
5. All quotes adapted from Irving Babbitt, trans., *The Dhammapada*.
6. For a full discussion of this issue see Thera Nanavasa, ed., *Digha-nikaya*, I.
7. Richard H. Robinson, *The Buddhist Religion: A Historical Introduction*, p. 33.
8. Mizuno, *The Beginnings of Buddhism*, p. 185.
9. For a more complete discussion see Walpola Rahula, *What the Buddha Taught*, pp. 81–89.
10. Basham, *The Wonder That Was India*, p. 54.
11. J. S. Strong, *The Legend of King Ashoka*, p. 131.
12. Vishwanath Prasad Varma, *Early Buddhism and Its Origins*, p. 432.
13. T. W. Rhys Davids, *Buddhism*, p. 222.
14. Strong, *The Legend of King Ashoka*, p. 23.
15. Basham, *The Wonder That Was India*, p. 56.
16. Strong, *The Legend of King Ashoka*, p. 87.
17. See Basham, *The Wonder That Was India*, p. 83; and Rhys Davids, *Buddhism*, pp. 18–19.
18. Basham, *The Wonder That Was India*.
19. Strong, *The Legend of King Ashoka*, p. 61.
20. Kenneth Ch'en, *Buddhism in China*, p. 78.
21. Strong, *The Legend of King Ashoka*, pp. 131–32.
22. Ch'en, *Buddhism in China*, p. 197.
23. Holmes Welch, *Buddhism under Mao*, p. 297.
24. Strong, *The Legend of King Ashoka*, pp. 115–16.
25. For a more complete discussion of his life, see Kenneth Ch'en, *The Chinese Transformation of Buddhism*, p. 113.
26. Quoted in Ch'en, *Buddhism in China*, p. 221.
27. Ibid., pp. 223–24.
28. Ibid., p. 232.
29. Quoted in Yūhō Yokoi with Daizen Victoria, *Zen Master Dōgen: An Introduction with Selected Writings*, p. 163.
30. Ibid., p. 162.
31. Heinrich Dumoulin, *Zen Buddhism: A History*, vol. 1, *India and China*, p. 114.
32. For a more complete account of this incident, see Hu Shih, "Chūgoku ni okeru Zen Bukkyō—Sono Rekishi to Hōhō [Zen Buddhism in China: Its History and Methodology]," in *Zen ni tsuite no Taiwa*, pp. 51–55.
33. Quoted in Arthur Koestler, *The Lotus and the Robot*, p. 271.
34. Paul Demiéville, "Le Bouddhisme et la guerre," *Choix d'études Bouddhiques (1929–1970)*, p. 296.
35. Quoted in Ch'en, *Buddhism in China*, p. 357.
36. Dumoulin, *Zen Buddhism*, vol. 1, p. 244.
37. Yanagida, "Chūgoku Zenshū-shi," in *Kōza Zen*, vol. 3, pp. 96–97.
38. For further discussion see Dumoulin, *Zen Buddhism*, vol. 1, pp. 166–70.

39. Ch'en, *Buddhism in China*, p. 399.
40. Quoted in Kazumitsu Kato, *Lin-chi and the Record of His Sayings*, p. 104.
41. Quoted in Mizuno, *The Beginnings of Buddhism*, p. 180.
42. Dumoulin, *Zen Buddhism*, p. 216.
43. Quoted in Iriya Yoshitaka et al., trans., *Hekigan-roku*, vol. 1, p. 182.
44. Quoted in Welch, *Buddhism under Mao*, p. 277.
45. Ibid., pp. 278–79.
46. Contained in the *New Zealand Herald*, 31 May 1996, p. 8.
47. Quoted in Welch, *Buddhism under Mao*, p. 283.
48. Anesaki Masaharu, *History of Japanese Religion*, p. 12.
49. S. Keel, "Buddhism and Political Power in Korean History," *Journal of the International Association of Buddhist Studies* 1, no. 1 (1978), pp. 16–17.
50. Ch'en, *Buddhism in China*, p. 201.
51. Committee for the Celebration of the 70th Anniversary of the Introduction of Buddhism to America, ed., *The Teaching of Buddha*, p. 231.
52. Anesaki, *History of Japanese Religion*, p. 231.
53. Welch, *Buddhism under Mao*, p. 281.
54. "Zen Master Dōgen's Social Consciousness," *Journal of Asian Culture* 1, no. 1 (Spring 1977), p. 18, translated by the author.
55. William Bodiford, *Sōtō Zen in Medieval Japan*, p. 216.
56. Translated in Hajime Nakamura, *Ways of Thinking of Eastern Peoples: India-China-Tibet-Japan*, p. 684.
57. Heinrich Dumoulin, *Zen Buddhism: A History*, vol. 2, *Japan*, p. 153.

58. George Sansom, *A History of Japan to 1334*, p. 431.
59. Hee-jin Kim, *Dōgen Kigen: Mystical Realist*, p. 13.
60. Quoted in D. T. Suzuki, *Essentials of Zen Buddhism*, p. 458.
61. From Takuan's *Fudōchi Shinmyō-roku* as quoted in Ichikawa Hakugen, *Fudōchi Shinmyō-roku/Taia-ki*, pp. 57–58.
62. Ibid., p. 58.
63. Ibid., p. 101.
64. Ibid., p. 89–90.
65. See discussion of sectarian adherence in Royall Tyler, trans., *Selected Writings of Suzuki Shōsan*, pp. 1–3.
66. Quoted in ibid., p. 115.
67. Quoted in ibid.
68. Quoted in Jack Seward and Howard Van Zandt, *Japan: The Hungry Guest*, pp. 89–90.
69. Quoted in Charles A. Moore, ed., *The Japanese Mind*, p. 233.
70. Tsunetomo [Jōchō] Yamamoto, *Hagakure*, p. 164.
71. Ibid., p. 146.
72. Quoted in Philip B. Yampolsky, trans., *The Zen Master Hakuin: Selected Writings*, p. 69.
73. Ibid., p. 72.
74. Tomonaga study introduced in William Bodiford, "Zen and the Art of Religious Prejudice," *Japanese Journal of Religious Studies* 23, nos. 1–2 (1996), p. 11. "Ten Fates Preached by the Buddha" quote found on p. 15.
75. Tsugunari Kubo and Akira Yuyama, *The Lotus Sutra*, p. 339.
76. Bodiford, "Zen and the Art of Religious Prejudice," p. 13.

77. Quoted in Charles Eliot, *Japanese Buddhism*, p. 305.

78. Makoto Hayashi, "The Historical Position of Early Modern Religion as Seen through a Critical Examination of R. Bellah's 'Religious Evolution,'" *Acta Asiatica* 75 (1998), p. 31.

79. Quoted in Garma C. C. Chang, ed., *A Treasury of Mahāyāna Sūtras*, pp. 456–57.

80. Quoted in Paul William, *Mahayana Buddhism*, p. 161.

81. Demiéville, "Le Bouddhisme et la guerre," p. 267.

82. Quoted in Moore, *The Japanese Mind*, p. 153.

83. Ibid., p. 153.

84. Yamamoto, *Hagakure*, p. 95.

85. Ibid.

86. Ibid.

87. Ibid.

Concise Glossary of
Buddhist Terminology

Amida Buddha The Buddha of Infinite Light and/or Life. The central figure of worship in the Pure Land school that teaches that anyone invoking his name (*nembutsu*) with a sincere heart will achieve entrance to his Pure Land.

Bodhidharma (Daruma) An Indian Buddhist priest who, according to Zen tradition, arrived in China in 520 C.E. where he emphasized the importance of meditation practice (zazen) in the realization of enlightenment. He is regarded as the founder of Ch'an (Zen) Buddhism in China.

bodhisattva (*bosatsu*) In Mahayana Buddhism, someone who vows to save all beings and compassionately works in both spiritual and secular ways to end their suffering.

Buddha A title designating someone who has awakened to the true nature of reality. Often used to designate the historical founder of Buddhism, Gautama Siddhartha, respectfully referred to as Buddha Shakyamuni following his enlightenment.

Buddha nature (*busshō*) The generally accepted view in Mahayana Buddhism that all beings innately possess the seeds of Buddhahood and therefore have the potential to realize enlightenment.

Buddha Shakyamuni See Buddha.

Ch'an school (of Buddhism) See Zen.

daigo **(great enlightenment)** Typically used in the Zen tradition to designate someone who has realized full and perfect enlightenment.

dependent co-arising (*engi*) A central doctrine of Buddhism teaching that all phenomena are produced by causation. For this reason, all phenomena lack an essential self-nature and are impermanent.

Dharma Literally, something that always maintains a certain character, thereby becoming a standard of things. Sometimes translated as "Law" or "Truth," it refers in Buddhism to the universal norms or laws that govern existence. It is also used to designate Buddha Shakyamuni's teachings.

Diamond Sutra (*Kongō-kyō*) Highly esteemed in the Zen tradition as one of its basic texts, it sets forth the doctrines of emptiness (*kū*) and wisdom (*chie*).

Dōgen (1200–53) Thirteenth-century founder of the Sōtō Zen sect in Japan, and author of the ninety-five-fascicle masterwork *Shōbōgenzō* (Treasury of the Essence of the True Dharma).

Eiheiji monastery Founded by Zen Master Dōgen in 1243 in Fukui prefecture, it is today one of the two major training monasteries of the Sōtō Zen sect. See also Sōjiji monastery.

emptiness (Skt. *shunyata; J. kū*) In Mahayana Buddhism, the doctrine that all of existence is dependent upon causation and therefore changing at every moment. In theory, it does not deny the existence of the phenomenal world, but rather the impossibility of any form of *static* existence within that world.

enlightenment Awakening to the true nature of existence.

Hinayana school (of Buddhism) See Theravada school.

hongaku shisō **(original or inherent enlightenment)** See original enlightenment.

issatsu tashō **(killing one in order that many may live)** In Mahayana Buddhism, the contentious view as taught in the *Upaya-kaushalya Sutra* that it is sometimes necessary for a bodhisattva to kill one or more sentient beings in order to save a far greater number of sentient beings from suffering.

jōriki See samadhi power.

karma Typically understood as deeds produced by the body, mind, or mouth that result in either positive or negative effects in the future, including future lives.

koan In the Zen school, koan are paradoxical exchanges attributed to leading Chinese Ch'an (Zen) patriarchs and their disciples. In the Rinzai Zen sect, novices use these exchanges as objects of meditation in order to fathom their meaning and realize enlightenment.

Law (of the Buddha) See Dharma.

Lotus Sutra One of the most important sutras in Mahayana Buddhism, it teaches that there is ultimately only one school of Buddhism with even followers of the Lesser Vehicle, i.e., the Hinayana school, being able to attain perfect enlightenment. Further, the Buddha is said to have achieved perfect enlightenment many eons ago.

Mahayana school (of Buddhism) One of the two most fundamental schools of Buddhism, it literally means "Great Vehicle." Based on the Sanskrit canon, the Mahayana school is today found in the countries of East Asia including China, Korea, and Japan, but also Vietnam. As its name suggests, it is a very inclusive form of Buddhism that incorporates a broad range of philosophical speculation as well as a wide variety of religious practices. In general, its religious ideal is that of the bodhisattva.

meditation See zazen.

merit (*kudoku*)   The belief that religious practice or pious acts such as reciting sutras generates a form of spiritual power that can be transferred to benefit named recipients.

Mu (**Zen koan**)   The reference is to the famous Zen koan "Chao-chou's Dog," case 1 in the Chinese koan collection *Wu-Men Kuan* (The Gateless Barrier). One day, a monk asked Chao-chou, a leading Ch'an master, "Does a dog have Buddha nature or not?" Chao-chou replied, "Mu." Although *mu* can be translated as "nothingness," Chao-chou was admonishing his monk questioner to transcend dualistic thoughts such as "have" and "not have," and instead, to intuitively experience reality as it is.

mu (**nothingness**)   Although this word is negative in character and can be translated as "nothingness," it refers to a state of mind that has transcended discursive thought, including the distinction between self and other.

muga (**no-self**)   The belief that there is no permanent, unchanging self or soul.

mukei (**formlessness**)   The belief that there is a transcendent realm of formlessness behind the temporal world of form and based on the ultimate emptiness of the phenomenal world, even though ultimately these two realms are identical to each other.

munen (**no-thought**)   A state of mind that has transcended discursive thought and is totally concentrated in the present.

mushin (**no-mind**)   In the Zen school, a state of mind totally absorbed in the present, acting intuitively, and attainable through the practice of zazen.

musō (**no-reflection**)   In the Zen school, a state of mind that does not look back but acts intuitively.

Nichiren sect   Founded by Nichiren (1222–82 C.E.), it takes the Lotus Sutra as its basic scripture. The chief religious practice of this school is the recitation of the mantra *Namu-myōhō-renge-kyō* (Adoration to the Lotus Sutra). The Nichiren sect, though composed of numerous competing subsects, has traditionally viewed itself as the only true sect of Buddhism in Japan if not the world, with all other sects regarded as false and heretical.

Nirvana   Literally meaning "extinction," it originally referred to the state of enlightenment attained by Buddha Shakyamuni. However, in the Mahayana school it denotes both nonproduction and nondestruction and is equated with wisdom and *dharma-kaya*, i.e., the absolute nature of the Buddha mind. It is characterized by eternity, happiness, substantiality, and pureness.

Nirvana Sutra   The abbreviated title of the *Mahayana Mahaparinirvana-sutra*, which advocates the doctrine that the *dharma-kaya*, i.e., the absolute nature of the Buddha mind, is everlasting, and that all human beings possess the Buddha nature.

no-self   See *muga*.

no-thought   See *munen*.

on (**debt of gratitude**)   A form of moral or spiritual indebtedness owed to those persons from whom favors are received, traditionally identified as one's parents, the ruler, all sentient beings, and either heaven and earth or the Three Treasures of Buddhism, i.e., the Buddha, Dharma, and Sangha.

original enlightenment   See *hongaku shisō*.

Pali canon   Together with Sanskrit, one of the two classical languages of India in which the Buddhist sutras were written. It is associated with the Theravada school of Buddhism primarily found in Sri Lanka, Burma, Thailand, Laos, and Cambodia.

Perfection of Wisdom Sutras   A group of Mahayana sutras focused on the doctrine of emptiness (*kū*).

Prajnaparamita Hridaya Sutra (Hannya-haramitta-shin-gyō)   Often translated in English as "Heart Sutra," this is a one-page summary of the Wisdom Sutras in the Mahayana school.

Pure Land (Jōdo) sect   Established in Japan by Hōnen in 1175, this sect emphasizes the need for faith in the vow of Amida Buddha to lead all those who call on his name to the Pure Land. Hōnen called for the unceasing repetition of the *nembutsu*, i.e., the mantra, *Namu-amida-butsu* (Adoration to Amida Buddha).

True Pure Land (Jōdo-shin) sect   Founded by Shinran, a disciple of Hōnen, at the beginning of the thirteenth century, it is typically referred to by its abbreviated title, Shin sect. Shinran taught that one recited the *Nembutsu* not to gain salvation in the Pure Land, but to express gratitude to Amida Buddha, believing that salvation comes solely through Amida's grace. As a consequence, Shinran abandoned the traditional Buddhist monastic precepts and advocated clerical marriage, eating meat, and following a lay life in most respects.

Rinzai Zen sect   Originally established in China as one of five Chinese Ch'an (Zen) sects, it was introduced to Japan by Eisai in 1191 C.E. This sect of Zen, now divided into numerous subsects or branches, emphasizes the use of koan as objects of meditation. It traditionally flourished in Japan due to the patronage of the samurai class.

samadhi **power** (*jōriki*)   The mental or spiritual power believed to derive from the concentrated state of mind (*samadhi*) acquired through specific Buddhist religious practices, most especially the practice of zazen.

Sangha   The community of Buddhist male and female clerics, often understood to include Buddhist male and female laypersons as well.

Sanskrit   Together with Pali, one of the two classical languages of India in which the Buddhist sutras were written. It is associated with the Mahayana school of Buddhism primarily found in such East Asian countries as China, Korea, Japan, and Vietnam.

satori (**enlightenment**)   While *satori* is identified with the enlightenment of Buddha Shakyamuni, the Rinzai Zen sect in particular recognizes varying degrees of enlightenment, beginning with shallower realizations that lead to great or full enlightenment (*daigo*). See Rinzai Zen sect.

selflessness   See *muga*.

Shin sect   See True Pure Land sect.

Shingon sect   A form of esoteric Buddhism that was first transmitted to China and then introduced to Japan by Kūkai in the early eighth century. Esoteric rituals form one of the major elements of this sect, and involve the use of both secret words (Skt. *mantras*; J. *shingon*) and diagrammatic pictures representing the cosmic nature of Buddhas, bodhisattvas, and other divine beings (Skt. *mandala*; J. *mandara*).

Sōjiji monastery   Founded by Zen Master Keizan in the fourteenth century, this temple is now located near Yokohama and is one of the two major training monasteries of the Sōtō Zen sect.

Sōtō Zen sect   Originally established in China as one of five Chinese Ch'an (Zen) schools, it was introduced to Japan by Dōgen in the first half of the thirteenth century. Dōgen took the view that zazen was itself the manifestation of enlightenment, and therefore he advocated the practice of themeless meditation, i.e., "just sitting" (*shikan taza*).

sutra   The purported teachings of Buddha Shakyamuni, originally written in one of two classical Indian Buddhist languages, Pali or Sanskrit.

Tathagata (fully enlightened being)   Literally meaning one who has "thus come," it is one of the epithets of the Buddha.

tathagatagarbha (nyoraizō)   The Buddha nature inherent in all sentient beings.

Tendai sect   Originally established in China as one of thirteen Buddhist schools, it was introduced into Japan by Saichō in the early ninth century. Because of its broad, inclusive characteristics, including elements of esoteric Buddhism, it became the mother of the major Buddhist schools: Pure Land, Zen, and Nichiren, emerging from the Kamakura period (1185–1333).

Theravada school (of Buddhism)   One of the two most fundamental schools of Buddhism, it literally means the "Way of the Elders," although it has typically been referred to in the Mahayana school by its pejorative title, Hinayana, or "Lesser Vehicle." Based on the Pali canon, the Theravada school is more conservative in doctrine and stricter in its interpretation of the monastic precepts than the Mahayana school. Its religious ideal is the *arhat*, someone who is free from all defilements and has obtained perfect knowledge, among other things.

Three Treasures of Buddhism   The Buddha, Dharma, and Sangha.

wago **(harmony)**   Originally referring to the harmonious relationship existing between members of the Sangha, its meaning was broadened to include the ideal relationship that ought to exist between all members of society.

zazen **(meditation)**   The form of mental concentration practiced primarily in the Zen tradition in which one sits upright, legs crossed, typically with the buttocks elevated by a mat or cushion. During zazen, the ordinary reasoning process of the intellect is cut short and consciousness is heightened by refusing to grasp extraneous thoughts. Depending on the Zen sect in question, there may or may not be an object of meditation. See Rinzai and Sōtō Zen sects.

Zen school   Originally established in China as Ch'an (meditation), it is the school of Buddhism that focuses on meditation (zazen) as its primary religious practice. In contemporary Japan, it consists of three major sects: Rinzai, Sōtō, and the much smaller Ōbaku.

Works Cited

I. Works in Western Languages

Abe, Masao, ed. *A Zen Life: D. T. Suzuki Remembered*. New York: John Weatherhill, 1986.

Anesaki, Masaharu. *History of Japanese Religion*. Rutland, VT: Tuttle, 1963.

Antinoff, Steven. "The Problem of the Human Person and the Resolution of That Problem in the Religio-Philosophical Thought of the Zen Master Shin'ichi Hisamatsu." Ann Arbor, MI: UMI Dissertation Information Service, 1991.

Arai, Sekizen. "A Buddhist View of World Peace." *Japan Evangelist* (December 1925), pp. 395–400.

Babbitt, Irving, trans. *The Dhammapada*. New York: New Directions, 1965.

Basham, A. L. *The Wonder That Was India*. New York: Grove Press, 1959.

Beasley, W. G. *The Modern History of Japan*. 2nd ed. New York: Praeger, 1974.

Behr, Edward. *Hirohito: Behind the Myth*. New York: Vintage, 1989.

Bellah, Robert N. *Tokugawa Religion*. Boston: Beacon Press, 1957.

Bergamini, David. *Japan's Imperial Conspiracy*. New York: William Morrow, 1971.

Berrigan, Daniel, and Thich Nhat Hanh. *The Raft Is Not the Shore*. Boston: Beacon Press, 1975.

Blyth, R. H. *Zen and Zen Classics: Mumonkan*. Vol. 4. Tokyo: Hokuseido Press, 1966.

Boas, George. *The History of Ideas*. New York: Charles Scribner's Sons, 1969.

Bodiford, William. *Sōtō Zen in Medieval Japan*. Honolulu: University of Hawaii Press, 1993.

———. "Zen and the Art of Religious Prejudice." *Japanese Journal of Religious Studies* 23, nos. 1–2 (1996), pp. 1–27.

Borton, Hugh. *Japan's Modern Century*. 2nd ed. New York: Ronald Press, 1970.

Brazier, David. *The New Buddhism*. New York: Palgrave, 2001.

Byas, Hugh. *Government by Assassination*. London: Bradford and Dicken, 1943.

Chang, Garma C. C., ed. *A Treasury of Mahayana Sutras*. University Park: Pennsylvania State University Press, 1983.

Ch'en, Kenneth. *Buddhism in China*. Princeton, NJ: Princeton University Press, 1964.

———. *The Chinese Transformation of Buddhism*. Princeton, NJ: Princeton University Press, 1973.

Cleary, Thomas. *The Japanese Art of War*. Boston: Shambhala, 1991.

Committee for the Celebration of the 70th Anniversary of the Introduction of Buddhism to America, ed. *The Teaching of Buddha*. Tokyo: Buddhist Center, 1963.

Coomaraswamy, Ananda K. *Buddha and the Gospel of Buddhism*. New York: Harper Torchbooks, 1964.

Dale, Peter N. *The Myth of Japanese Uniqueness*. London: Routledge, 1988.

Davis, Winston. *Japanese Religion and Society*. Albany: State University of New York Press, 1992.

Demiéville, Paul. "Le Bouddhisme et la guerre." *Choix d'études Bouddhiques (1929–1970)*. Leiden: W.J. Brill, 1973, pp. 261–99.

DeVos, George A. "Apprenticeship and Paternalism." In *Modern Japanese Organization and Decision-Making*, edited by Ezra F. Vogel. Berkeley: University of California Press, 1975.

Dower, John W. *War without Mercy: Race and Power in the Pacific War*. New York: Pantheon Books, 1986.

Draeger, Donn F. *Modern Bujutsu and Budo*. New York: Weatherhill, 1974.

Dumoulin, Heinrich. *Zen Buddhism: A History*. Vol. 1, *India and China*. New York: Macmillan, 1988.

———. *Zen Buddhism: A History*. Vol. 2, *Japan*. New York: Macmillan, 1990.

Earl, David Magarey. *Emperor and Nation in Japan*. Seattle: University of Washington Press, 1964.

Eliot, Charles. *Japanese Buddhism*. London: Edward Arnold, 1935.

Faure, Bernard. *Chan Insights and Oversights*. Princeton, NJ: Princeton University Press, 1993.

Fisher, David H. *Historians' Fallacies*. New York: Harper Torchbooks, 1970.

Fo Kuang Shan Foundation for Buddhist Culture and Education, ed. *1990 Anthology of Fo Kuang Shan International Buddhist Conference*. Kao-hsiung, Taiwan: Fo Kuang Shan Press, 1992.

Fuji Flyer. Unofficial publication, Yokota U.S. Air Force Base, Tokyo, Japan, 18 August 1995.

Gluck, Carol. *Japan's Modern Myths*. Princeton, NJ: Princeton University Press, 1985.

Hakeda, Yoshito S. *The Awakening of Faith*. New York: Columbia University Press, 1967.

Hane, Mikiso. *Reflections on the Way to the Gallows*. New York: Pantheon, 1988.

Hardacre, Helen. *Shintō and the State, 1868–1988*. Princeton, NJ: Princeton University Press, 1989.

Harries, Meirion, and Susie Harries. *Soldiers of the Sun: The Rise and Fall of the Imperial Japanese Army*. New York: Random House, 1991.

Hayashi, Makoto. "The Historical Position of Early Modern Religion as Seen through a Critical Examination of R. Bellah's 'Religious Evolution.'" *Acta Asiatica* 75 (1998), pp. 17–31.

Heisig, James W., and John C. Maraldo, eds. *Rude Awakenings*. Honolulu: University of Hawaii Press, 1995.

Hitler, Adolf. *Table Talk*. Translated by Norman Cameron and R. H. Stevens. London: Weidenfeld and Nicolson, 1953.

Holtom, D. C. *Modern Japan and Shinto Nationalism*. New York: Paragon Books, 1963.

Hosokawa, Dogen, and Mike Sayama. "The Chozen-ji Line (Omori Sogen Rotaishi)." *Journal of the Institute of Zen Studies* 3 (1988), pp. 1–4.

Humphreys, Christmas. *Zen Buddhism*. London: Unwin, 1976.

Humphreys, Leonard A. *The Way of the Heavenly Sword*. Stanford, CA: Stanford University Press, 1995.

Ienaga Saburo. *The Pacific War, 1931–1945*. New York: Pantheon, 1968.

Ives, Christopher. *Zen Awakening and Society*. Honolulu: University of Hawaii Press, 1992.

Jaffe, Richard. "Buddhist Clerical Marriage in Japan: Origins and Responses to the 1872 *Nikujiki Saitai* Law." In *1990 Anthology of Fo Kuang Shan International Buddhist Conference*, edited by Fo Kuang Shan Foundation for Buddhist Culture and Education. Kao-hsiung, Taiwan: Fo Kuang Shan Press, 1992, pp. 470–81.

James, William. *The Varieties of Religious Experience*. New York: Mentor Books, 1958.

Kapleau, Philip. *The Three Pillars of Zen*. Tokyo: Weatherhill, 1965.

Kato, Kazumitsu. *Lin-chi and the Record of His Sayings*. Nisshin: Nagoya University of Foreign Studies, 1994.

Keel, S. "Buddhism and Political Power in Korean History." *Journal of the International Association of Buddhist Studies* 1, no. 1 (1978), pp. 9–24.

Ketelaar, James Edward. *Of Heretics and Martyrs in Meiji Japan*. Princeton, NJ: Princeton University Press, 1990.

Kim, Hee-jin. *Dōgen Kigen: Mystical Realist*. Tucson: University of Arizona Press, 1987.

King, Winston L. King. *Zen and the Way of the Sword*. Oxford: Oxford University Press, 1993.

Kirita, Kiyohide. "D. T. Suzuki and the State." In *Rude Awakenings*, edited by James W. Heisig and John C. Maraldo. Honolulu: University of Hawaii Press, 1995, pp. 52–74.

Kishimoto, Hideo, comp. and ed. *Japanese Religion in the Meiji Era*. Translated by John F. Howes. Tokyo, 1956.

Kitagawa, Joseph. *Religion in Japanese History*. New York: Columbia University, 1966.

Koestler, Arthur. *The Lotus and the Robot.* London: Hutchinson, 1960.

Kubo, Tsugunari, and Akira Yuyama, trans. *The Lotus Sutra.* Berkeley, CA: Numata Center for Buddhist Translation and Research, 1993.

Lancaster, Lewis, and Whalen Lai, eds. *Early Ch'an in China and Tibet.* Berkeley, CA: Berkeley Buddhist Studies Series, 1983.

Large, Stephen S. "For Self and Society: Senō Girō and Buddhist Socialism in the Post-War Japanese Peace Movement." In *The Japanese Trajectory: Modernization and Beyond,* edited by Gavan McCormack and Yoshio Sugimoto. Cambridge: Cambridge University Press, 1988, pp. 87–104.

Livingston, Jon et al., eds. *The Japan Reader I: Imperial Japan 1800–1945.* New York: Pantheon, 1973.

Loori, John Daido. *The Heart of Being: Moral and Ethical Teachings of Zen Buddhism.* Boston: Charles E. Tuttle, 1996.

Maezumi, Hakuyu Taizan, and Bernard Tetsugen Glassman. *The Hazy Moon of Enlightenment.* Los Angeles: Center Publications, 1977.

Marty, Martin E. "An Exuberant Adventure: The Academic Study and Teaching of Religion." *Academe* 82, no. 6 (1996), pp. 14–17.

Maruyama, Masao. *Modern Japanese Politics.* London: Oxford University Press, 1969.

Matsunami, N. *The Constitution of Japan.* Tokyo: Maruzen, 1930.

McBrien, Richard P. *Catholicism.* Minneapolis, MN: Winston Press, 1981.

McFarlane, Stewart. "Mushin, Morals, and Martial Arts: A Discussion of Keenan's Yogācāra Critique." *Japanese Journal of Religious Studies* 17, no. 4 (1990), pp. 397–432.

McRae, John. "American Scholars in Dialogue with our Mentors." In *1990 Anthology of Fo Kuang Shan International Buddhist Conference,* edited by Fo Kuang Shan Foundation for Buddhist Culture and Education. Kao-hsiung, Taiwan: Fo Kuang Shan Press, 1992, pp. 530–49.

Minami, Hiroshi. *Psychology of the Japanese People.* Occasional papers of research publications and translations. Honolulu: East-West Center, 1970.

Miyamoto, Musashi. *A Book of Five Rings.* Translated by Victor Harris. Woodstock, NY: Overlook Press, 1974.

Mizuno, Kōgen. *The Beginnings of Buddhism.* Translated by Richard L. Gage. Tokyo: Kōsei, 1980.

Mohr, Michel. "Monastic Tradition and Lay Practice from the Perspective of Nantenbō." *Zen Buddhism Today* 12 (Kyoto, March 1996), pp. 63–89.

Moore, Charles A., ed. *The Japanese Mind.* Honolulu: University Press of Hawaii, 1967.

Morreale, Don, ed. *Buddhist America.* Santa Fe: John Muir, 1988.

Morris, I. I. *Nationalism and the Right Wing in Japan.* London: Oxford University Press, 1960.

Murakami, Shigeyoshi. *Japanese Religion in the Modern Century.* Translated by H. Byron Earhart. Tokyo: University of Tokyo Press, 1980.

Najita, Tetsuo, and Irwin Scheiner, eds. *Japanese Thought in the Tokugawa Period.* Chicago: University of Chicago Press, 1978.

Nakamura, Hajime. *Ways of Thinking of Eastern Peoples: India-China-Tibet-Japan.* Honolulu: East-West Center, 1964.

Nanavasa, Thera, ed. *Digha-nikaya I.* Colombo, Sri Lanka: 1929.

New Zealand Herald, 31 May 1995.

Nhat Hanh, Thich. *The Miracle of Mindfulness!* Boston: Beacon Press, 1976.

Niebuhr, Reinhold. *Moral Man and Immoral Society.* New York: Charles Scribner's Sons, 1932.

Nitobe, Inazō. *Bushido.* Rutland, VT: Tuttle, 1969.

Norman, E. H. *Japan's Emergence as a Modern State.* New York: Institute of Pacific Relations, 1946.

Notehelfer, F. G. *Kōtoku Shūsui: Portrait of a Japanese Radical.* London: Cambridge University, 1971.

Nukariya, Kaiten. *Religion of the Samurai: A Study of Zen Philosophy and Discipline in China and Japan.* Luzac's Oriental Religions Series 4. London: Luzac, 1913.

Pauwels, Louis, and Jacques Bergier. *The Morning of the Magicians.* Translated by Rollo Myers. New York: Stein and Day, 1964.

Peattie, Mark R. *Ishiwara Kanji, and Japan's Confrontation with the West.* Princeton, NJ: Princeton University Press, 1975.

Phipps, William E. *Mark Twain's Religion.* Macon, GA: Mercer University Press, 2003.

Queen, Christopher S., and Sallie B. King, eds. *Engaged Buddhism.* Albany: State University of New York Press, 1996.

Rabinovitch, Judith N., ed. and trans. *Shōmonki: The Story of Masakado's Rebellion.* Tokyo: Monumenta Nipponica, 1986.

Rhys Davids, T. W. *Buddhism.* London: Society for the Promotion of the Christian Religion, 1925.

Robinson, Richard H. *The Buddhist Religion: A Historical Introduction.* Belmont, CA: Dickenson, 1970.

Rosenberg, Alfred. *Selected Writings.* Edited by Robert Pois. London: Jonathan Cape, 1970.

Saddhatissa, Hammalawa. *Buddhist Ethics.* London: Wisdom Publications, 1987.

Sansom, George. *A History of Japan to 1334.* Kent, England: Wm Dawson and Sons, 1978.

Saunders, Dale E. *Buddhism in Japan.* Westport, CT: Greenwood Press, 1964.

Schopenhauer, Arthur. *The World as Will and Idea.* Translated by R. B. Haldane and J. Kemp. London: Kegan Paul, Trench, Trubner, 1948.

Schumann, Hans Wolfgang. *Buddhism: An Outline of Its Teaching and Schools.* Translated by Georg Feuerstein. Wheaton, IL: Theosophical Publishing House, 1973.

Seward, Jack and Howard Van Zandt. *Japan: The Hungry Guest.* Rev. ed. Tokyo: Yohan, 1985.

Shaku, Soyen [Sōen]. *Zen for Americans*. Translated by Daisetz Teitaro Suzuki. La Salle, IL: Open Court, 1974.

Sharf, Robert H. "Whose Zen? Zen Nationalism Revisited." In *Rude Awakenings*, edited by James W. Heisig and John C. Maraldo. Honolulu: University of Hawaii Press, 1995, pp. 40–51.

———. "The Zen of Japanese Nationalism." *History of Religions* 33, no. 1 (1993), pp. 1–43.

———. "Zen and the Way of the New Religions." *Japanese Journal of Religious Studies* 22, nos. 3–4 (1995), pp. 417–58.

Shore, Jeff. "Japanese Zen and the West: Beginnings." In *1990 Anthology of Fo Kuang Shan International Buddhist Conference*, edited by Fo Kuang Shan Foundation for Buddhist Culture and Education. Kao-hsiung, Taiwan: Fo Kuang Shan Press, 1992, pp. 438–60.

Speer, Albert. *Inside the Third Reich: Memoirs*. Translated by Richard and Clara Winston. New York: Macmillan, 1970.

Storry, Richard. *The Double Patriots*. London: Chatto and Windus, 1957.

Strong, John S. *The Legend of King Ashoka*. Princeton, NJ: Princeton University Press, 1983.

Suzuki, Daisetz T. *Essays in Zen Buddhism*. 3rd ser. London: Luzac, 1934.

———. *Essentials of Zen Buddhism*. Princeton, NJ: Princeton University Press, 1962.

———. *Zen and Japanese Culture*. Princeton, NJ: Princeton University Press, 1959. Originally published in 1938 as *Zen and Its Influence on Japanese Culture*. Kyoto: Eastern Buddhist Society, Otani Buddhist University.

Swanson, Paul. "Zen Is Not Buddhism." *Numen* 40 (1993), pp. 115–49.

Thelle, Notto R. *Buddhism and Christianity in Japan*. Honolulu: University of Hawaii Press, 1987.

Tolischus, Otto D. *Tokyo Record*. London: Hamish Hamilton, 1943.

Tyler, Royall, trans. *Selected Writings of Suzuki Shōsan*. East Asia papers no. 13. Ithaca, NY: Cornell University, China-Japan Program, 1977.

Utley, Freda. *Japan's Feet of Clay*. London: Faber and Faber, 1936.

Varma, Vishwanath Prasad. *Early Buddhism and Its Origins*. New Delhi: Munshiram Manoharlal, 1973.

Victoria, Daizen (Brian). "Zen Master Dōgen's Social Consciousness." *Journal of Asian Culture* 1, no. 1 (Spring 1977), pp. 1–23.

———. *Zen at War*. 1st ed. New York: Weatherhill, 1997.

———. *Zen War Stories*. London: RoutledgeCurzon, 2003.

Walpola, Rahula. *What the Buddha Taught*. 2nd ed. New York: Grove Press, 1974.

Walshe, Maurice, trans. *Thus Have I Heard: The Long Discourses of the Buddha*. London: Wisdom Publications, 1987.

Welch, Holmes. *Buddhism under Mao*. Cambridge, MA: Harvard University Press, 1972.

Werblowsky, R. J. Zwi et al., eds. *Studies in Mysticism and Religion, Presented to Gershom G. Scholem*. Jerusalem: Magnes Press, 1967.

William, Paul. *Mahayana Buddhism*. London: Routledge, 1989.

Woodard, William P. *The Allied Occupation of Japan 1945–1952 and Japanese Religions*. Leiden: E.J. Brill, 1972.

Yamada, Mumon. *A Flower in the Heart*. Translated by Gyō Furuta. Tokyo: Kodansha International, 1964.

Yamamoto, Tsunetomo [Jōchō]. *Hagakure*. Translated by William Scott Wilson. Tokyo: Kodansha International, 1979.

Yampolsky, Philip B., trans. *The Zen Master Hakuin: Selected Writings*. New York: Columbia University Press, 1971.

Yasutani, Hakuun. "The Crisis in Human Affairs and the Liberation Found in Buddhism." *ZCLA Journal* 3, nos. 3–4 (1973), pp. 36–47.

Yokoi, Yūhō, with Daizen Victoria. *Zen Master Dōgen: An Introduction with Selected Writings*. New York: Weatherhill, 1976.

Yokoyama, Wayne S., trans. "Two Addresses by Shaku Sōen." *Eastern Buddhist* (New Series) 26, no. 2 (1993), pp. 131–48.

Yusa, Michiko. "Nishida and Totalitarianism: A Philosopher's Resistance." In *Rude Awakenings*, edited by James W. Heisig and John C. Maraldo. Honolulu: University of Hawaii Press, 1995, pp. 107–131.

II. Works in Japanese

Akiyama Goan, ed. *Sonnō Aikoku-ron*. Tokyo: Benkyōdō Shoten, 1912.

Akizuki Ryōmin, ed. *Nantenbō Zenwa*. Tokyo: Hirakawa Shuppan, 1985.

Anesaki Masaharu. *Bukkyō Seiten Shi-ron*. Tokyo: Keisō Shoin, 1899.

Asahina Sōgen. *Kakugo wa Yoi ka*. Tokyo: PHP Kenkyūjo, 1978.

Chūgai Nippō. 29 January 1911 (no. 3259).

———. 25 May–1 June 1944.

Chūō Bukkyō. March 1934. "Nihon Seishin to Bukkyō." *Ima no Otera ni Bukkyō wa nai* by Endō Makoto.

Daidō Shinpō. 11 March 1889 (no. 1).

Daihōrin. March 1937.

———. July 1938.

———. January 1942.

———. September 1942.

———. June 1994.

———. May 1974.

Daijō Zen. November 1939.

———. July 1944.

Daitō Satoshi. *Otera no Kane wa naranakatta*. Tokyo: Kyōiku Shiryō Shuppan-kai, 1994.

Endō Makoto. *Ima no Otera ni Bukkyō wa nai.* Tokyo: Nagasaki Shuppan, 1986.

Fueoka Seisen. *Zen no Tebiki.* Tokyo: Yūkōsha, 1927.

Fukuba Hōshū. "Shinateki to Nihonteki." November 5, 1939, issue of *Zengaku Kenkyū* 32, pp. 85–103.

Furukawa Taigo. *Yakushin-Nihon to Shin Daijō-Bukkyō.* Tokyo: Chūō Bukkyōsha, 1937.

Gyōshō. March 1971.

———. January 1972.

———. July 1972.

Hakamaya Noriaki. *Hihan Bukkyō.* Tokyo: Daizō Shuppan, 1990.

Hanazono Daigaku Jinken Kyōiku Kenkyū-shitsu, ed. *Sensō, Sengo-sekinin to Sabetsu.* Kyoto: Hōsei Shuppan, 1996.

Handa Shin, ed. *Bushidō no Shinzui.* Tokyo: Teikoku Shoseki Kyōkai, 1941.

Harada Sogaku. *Sanzen no Kaitei.* Tokyo: Kokusho Kankōkai, 1915.

Hata Eshō. "Kokumin Seishin Sōdōin to Bukkyō." July 1938 issue of *Daihōrin*, pp. 16–23.

Hayashiya Tomojirō, and Shimakage Chikai. *Bukkyō no Sensō-kan.* Tokyo: Daitō Shuppansha, 1937.

Heimin Shimbun. 7 August 1904 (no. 39).

Hisamatsu, Shin'ichi, ed. *Suzuki Daisetsu.* Tokyo: Iwanami Shoten, 1971.

Hishiki, Masaharu. *Jōdo Shinshū no Sensō Sekinin.* Iwanami booklet no. 303. Tokyo, 1993.

Hitane, Jōzan. "Konji no Jihen to Bosatsu no Gangyō." October 1937 issue of *Zenshū* 510, pp. 19–21.

[*Honganji-ha*] *Honzan Rokuji.* 31 July 1894.

———. 15 October 1910.

Hu Shih. "Chūgoku ni okeru Zen Bukkyō—Sono Rekishi to Hōhō." In *Zen ni tsuite no Taiwa*, translated by Kudō Sumiko. Tokyo: Chikuma Shobō, 1967.

Ichikawa Hakugen. *Bukkyōsha no Sensō-sekinin.* Tokyo: Shunjūsha, 1970.

———. *Fudōchi Shinmyō-roku/Taia-ki.* Tokyo: Kōdansha, 1982.

———. "Kokubō-kokka Shisō." In *Senji-ka no Bukkyō*, edited by Nakano Kyōtoku. Tokyo: Kokusho Kankōkai, 1977, pp. 35–68.

———. *Nihon Fashizumu ka no Shūkyō.* Tokyo: Enuesu Shuppankai, 1975.

———. "Sensō—Kagaku—Zen." September 1942 issue of *Daihōrin*, pp. 132–41.

———. "Shūkyō-sha no Sensō Sekinin o tou." *Nihon no Shūkyō* 1, no. 1 (1973), pp. 30–46.

———. *Zen to Gendai-shisō.* Tokyo: Tokuma Shoten, 1967.

Iida Tōin. *Sanzen Manroku.* Tokyo: Chūō Bukkyō-sha, 1934.

Imai Fukuzan. "Waga-shū Kodai no Gunji-kankei no Kitō to Ekōbun." January 1938 issue of *Zenshū* (no. 513), pp. 17–23.

Inagaki Masami. *Butsuda o seoite Gaitō e.* Tokyo: Iwanami Shinsho, 1974.

———. *Henkaku o motometa Bukkyō-sha.* Tokyo: Daizō Shinsho, 1975.

Inoue Enryō. *Chūkō Katsu-ron.* Tokyo: Tetsugaku Shoin 1893.

———. *Enryō Kōwa-shū.* Tokyo: Kōmeisha, 1904.

Inoue Nisshō. *Ichinin issatsu.* Tokyo: Nihon Shūhō-sha, 1953.

Inoue Zenjō, ed. *Suzuki Daisetsu Mikōkai Shokan.* Kyoto: Zen Bunka Kenkyūjo, 1989.

Iriya Yoshitaka et al., trans. *Hekigan-roku.* Vol. 1. Tokyo: Iwanami Shoten, 1992.

Ishihara Shunmyō, moderator. "Bukkyō Nippon no Shihyō o kataru Zadankai." March 1937 issue of *Daihōrin,* pp. 85–123.

Jōdo Kyōhō. 15 April 1895 (no. 213).

Kagaku Bunka 2, no. 3 (1942).

Kampō. Proceedings of the Twenty-seventh Session of the House of Representatives, pp. 388–89.

Kanaoka Shūyū. *Bukkyō no Fukken.* Tokyo: Kōsei Shuppansha, 1973.

Kashiwagi Ryūhō. "Junkyōsha Uchiyama Gudō: Uchiyama Gudō no Shōgai." In *Nishisagami Shomin Shiroku,* no. 9. Tokyo: Nishisagami shomin shirokukai, 1984.

———. *Taigyaku Jiken to Uchiyama Gudō.* Tokyo: J. C. A. Shuppan, 1979.

Katano Tatsurō. *Kongō-hōzan Rinnōji gohyaku-gojū-nen-shi.* Sendai: Kongō-hōzan Rinnōji, 1994.

Katō Totsudō. "Zengaku Ryūkō no Shuin oyobi Zenshū no Gensei." *Taiyō,* February 1895.

Kimura Jōyū. *Myōshinji (Roppyaku Gojū-nen no Ayumi).* Tokyo: Shogakkan, 1984.

Kirita Kiyohide. "Seinen Suzuki Teitarō Daisetsu no Shakai-kan." *Zengaku Kenkyū* 74 (1994), pp. 17–40.

Kōa Kannon Hōsan-kai, ed. *Kōa Kannon ni tsuite.* Flyer. Atami, 1996, pp. 1–4.

Komazawa Daigaku Zen Kenkyūjo Nenpō. March 1996 (no. 7).

Kono Taitsū. "Zuisho ni Shu to naru." *Komazawa Daigaku Zen Kenkyūjo Nenpō* 7 (March 1996), pp. 1–13.

Kurebayashi Kōdō. "Jihen to Bukkyō." October 1937 issue of *Sanshō* (no. 121), pp. 374–79.

Kuroda Shunyū, ed. *Kokka to Tennō.* Tokyo: Shunjūsha, 1987.

Maruyama Teruo. *Nihonjin no Kokoro o dame ni shita Meisō, Akusō, Gusō* Tokyo: Yamate Shobō, 1977.

Matsumoto Shirō. *Engi to Kū—Nyoraizō Shisō Hihan.* Tokyo: Daizō Shuppan, 1989.

Meikyō Shinshi. 8 October 1877 (no. 534).

Mitsugon Kyōhō. 25 January 1885 (no. 128).

———. 25 July 1894 (no. 116).

Miyamoto Shōson. *Meiji Bukkyō no Shichō.* Tokyo: Kōsei Shuppansha, 1975.

Morinaga Eizaburō. *Uchiyama Gudō.* Tokyo: Ronsōsha, 1984.

Nakano Kyōtoku, ed. *Senji-ka no Bukkyō.* Tokyo: Kokusho Kankōkai, 1977.

Nihon Shūkyō-sha Heiwa Kyōgikai, ed. *Shūkyō-sha no Sensō Sekinin; Zange, Kokuhaku, Shiryō-shū.* Tokyo: Shiraishi Shoten, 1994.

Nishida Kitarō. *Nishida Kitarō Zenshū.* Vol. 12, 3rd ed. Tokyo: Iwanami Shoten, 1979.

Nōnin. 8 August 1894 (no. 302).

————. 16–18 August 1894 (no. 309–11).

Nozaki Shinyō, ed. *Jion no Hibiki*. Tokyo: Keibunsha, 1983.

Ōhara Kakichi, trans. *Bankoku Shūkyō Taikai Enzetsu-shū*. Osaka: Kanekawa Shoten, 1893.

Okamura Ao. *Ketsumeidan jiken*. Tokyo: San-ichi Shobō, 1989.

Ōkura Seishin Bunka Kenkyūjo. *Gokoku Bukkyō*. Tokyo: Sanseidō, 1938.

Ōmori Sōgen. *Ken to Zen*. Tokyo: Shunjūsha, 1966.

Onuma Hiroaki. *Ketsumeidan jiken kōhan sokki-roku*. 3 vols. Tokyo: Ketsumeidan Jiken Kōhan Sokki-roku Kankō-kai, 1963.

————. *Ketsumeidan jiken-jōshinsho-gokuchū nikki*. Tokyo: Ketsumeidan Jiken Kōhan Sokki-roku Kankō-kai, 1971.

Ōyama Sumita. *Sugimoto Gorō Chūsa no Sonnō to Zen*. Tokyo: Heibonsha, 1938.

Sakai Tokugen. "Onoda-san to 'Shōji' no Mondai." May 1974 issue of *Daihōrin*, pp. 22–26.

"Sangyō Senshi no Shinjin Rensei." January 1942 issue of *Daihōrin*, pp. 136–37.

Sanshō, pub. by Eiheiji Sanshō-kai (Fuku-koku edition, 1977–78). October 1937 (no. 121).

————. December 1942 (no. 181).

————. April 1943 (no. 186).

————. September 1943 (no. 191).

Sawaki Kōdō. *Sawaki Kōdō Kikigaki*. Tokyo: Kōdansha, 1984.

————. "Zen-kai Hongi o kataru." Pt. 9 in the January 1942 issue of *Daihōrin*, pp. 98–112.

————. "Zenrin no Seikatsu to Kiritsu." June 1944 issue of *Daihōrin*, pp. 22–25.

Seki Seisetsu. *Bushidō no Kōyō*. Kyoto: Kendō Shoin, 1942.

Senoo Girō. *Senoo Girō Nikki 4*. Tokyo: Kokusho Kankōkai, 1974.

————. *Shakai Henkaku tojō no Shinkō Bukkyō*. 3rd ser. Tokyo: Shinkō Bukkyō Seinen Dōmei Shuppan, 1933.

Shaku Sōen. *Kaijin Kaiba*. Tokyo: Nisshinkaku, 1919.

Shibata Dōken. *Haibutsu Kishaku*. Tokyo: Kōronsha, 1978.

Shimizu Ryūzan. *Risshō Ankoku no Taigi to Nippon Seishin*. Kyoto: Heirakuji Shoten, 1934.

Shinkō Bukkyō. June 1933.

Shōbōrin. 12 February 1911 (no. 283).

Sōtō Shūhō. 15 February 1911 (no. 340).

————. 1 January 1941 (no. 39).

————. 1 September 1941 (no. 55).

————. 15 April 1942 (no. 70).

————. 1 November 1943 (no. 107).

————. 1 February 1944 (no. 113).

————. November–December 1944 (combined issue, no. 122).

————. January 1993 (no. 688).

————. July 1993 (no. 694).

————. September 1993 (no. 696).

Sōtō-shū Kaigai Kaikyō Dendō-shi Hensan Iinkai, ed. *Sōtō-shū Kaigai Kaikyō Dendō-shi*. Tokyo: Sōtō-shū Shūmu-chō, 1980.

Sugawara Gidō. *Shinde motomoto*. Tokyo: Nisshin Hōdō, 1974.

Sugimoto Gorō. *Taigi*. Tokyo: Heibonsha, 1938.

Suzuki Daisetsu/Daisetz. "Daijō Bukkyō no Sekaiteki Shimei—Wakaki Hitobito ni yosu." In vol. 29, *Suzuki Daisetsu Zenshū*. Tokyo: Iwanami Shoten, 1970, pp. 338–53.

————. *Isshinjitsu no Sekai*. Tokyo: Kondō Shoten, 1941.

————. "Jijoden." In vol. 30, *Suzuki Daisetsu Zenshū*. Tokyo: Iwanami Shoten, 1970, pp. 563–622.

————. "Nihonjin no Shōji-kan." In. vol. 28, *Suzuki Daisetsu Zenshū*. Tokyo: Iwanami Shoten, 1970, pp. 317–25.

————. *Nihonteki Reisei*. In vol. 8, *Suzuki Daisetsu Zenshū*. Tokyo: Iwanami Shoten, 1968, pp. 3–223.

————. *Nihon no Reiseika*. Kyoto: Hōzōkan, 1947.

————. *Reiseiteki Nihon no Kensetsu*. In vol. 9, *Suzuki Daisetsu Zenshū*. Tokyo: Iwanami Shoten, 1968, pp. 1–258.

————. *Shin Shūkyō-ron*. In vol. 23, *Suzuki Daisetsu Zenshū*. Tokyo: Iwanami Shoten, 1969, pp. 1–147.

————. "Tokkō-tai." In vol. 28, *Suzuki Daisetsu Zenshū*. Tokyo: Iwanami Shoten, 1970, pp. 398–403.

————. *Tōyōteki Ichi*. In vol. 7, *Suzuki Daisetsu Zenshū*. Tokyo: Iwanami Shoten, 1968, pp. 305–442.

————. *Zen Hyaku-dai*. Tokyo: Daitō Shuppansha, 1943.

————. "Zenkai Sasshin." In vol. 28, *Suzuki Daisetsu Zenshū*. Tokyo: Iwanami Shoten, 1970, pp. 410–17.

————. "Zen to Bushidō." *Bushidō no Shinzui*, edited by Handa Shin. Tokyo: Teikoku Shoseki Kyōkai, 1941, pp. 64–78.

Taiyō. February 1895.

Takisawa Makoto. *Gondō Seikyō*. Tokyo: Pelikan-sha, 1996.

Takizawa Kanyū. "Ishoku Zen." September 1943 issue of *Sanshō* (no. 191), pp. 740–42.

Tamaki Benkichi. *Kaisō Yamamoto Gempō*. Tokyo: Shunjū-sha, 1980.

Tendai-shū Kyōgaku-bu. *Fukyō Shiryō*. Kyoto: Kinseidō, 1942.

Tōa no Hikari 7, no. 3 (March 1912).

Tōjō Hideki. *Senjin-kun*. Tokyo: Japanese Imperial Army, 1941.

Tōkyō Asahi Shimbun. 15 September 1912.

Yabuki Keiki. *Nippon Seishin to Nippon Bukkyō*. Tokyo: Seiundō, 1934.

Yamada Kyōdō. *Mugai-san no Fūkei*. Sendai: Hōbundō, 1991.

Yamada Mumon. "Yasukuni Jinja Kokka-goji o omou." In *Nihonjin no Kokoro o dame ni shita Meisō, Gusō, Akusō* by Maruyama Teruo.

Yamada Reirin. *Zengaku Yawa*. Tokyo: Daiichi Shobō, 1942.

Yanagida Seizan. *Mirai kara no Zen*. Kyoto: Jinbun Shoin, 1990.

———. "Chūgoku Zenshū-shi." In vol. 3, *Kōza Zen*, edited by Nishitani Keiji. Tokyo: Chikuma Shobō, 1967, pp. 7–108.

Yasutani Hakuun. *Dōgen Zenji to Shūshōgi*. Tokyo: Fuji Shobō, 1943.

Yatsubuchi Banryū. *Shūkyō-taikai Hōdō*. Kyoto: Kōkyō Shoin, 1894.

Yoshida Kyūichi. *Nihon Kindai Bukkyō Shakai-shi Kenkyū*. Tokyo: Yoshikawa Kōbunkan, 1964.

———. *Nihon Kindai Bukkyō-shi Kenkyū*. Tokyo: Yoshikawa Kōbunkan, 1959.

———. *Nihon no Kindai Shakai to Bukkyō*. Tokyo: Hyōronsha, 1970.

Zen no Seikatsu. February 1943.

Zengaku Kenkyū 32. Hanazono University. 5 November 1939.

——— 72. January 1994.

Zenshū. October 1937 (no. 510).

———. January 1938 (no. 513).

Index

Note: Italicized letters following note numbers should be used to distinguish between different notes with identical numbers on the same page. For example, the "*a*" in "235n4*a*" signifies that the first note 4 (note 4 from chapter 1) on page 235 is the note being referenced.

Enō [Hui-neng]); *Hsin-hsin Ming*, 204; iconoclasm of, 203–6; Kuei-shan Ling-yu, 208; Liang Su, 205; Lin-chi (Rinzai) school, 205; Lin-chi I-hsüan, 207–8; Seng-ts'an, 204; Shen-hui, 203–4; Southern school of, 203–4; *Special Transmission of the Great Master from Ts'ao-ch'i,* 203; Yang-ch'i line (Lin-chi school), 205

Charter Oath, 4–5

Ch'en, Kenneth, 200, 206

China: anti-West alliance and, 64–65; Japanese Buddhism in, 40–41, 63–64, 166; Japanese expansionism and, 17, 21, 60, 62, 92, 105, 150, 156, 190; Japanese war with (1937–1945), 19, 74, 86–88, 90–93, 101, 116, 133; Russo-Japanese War and, 29–30; Zen in, 104, 123, 134–35. *See also* Sino-Japanese War

China Incidents, 116, 142

Christianity, 13, 15, 152, 223; government control of, 53–54, 221; missionary work of, 10, 21, 64; sentiment against, 3, 6, 10–11, 16, 17–18, 30, 52, 171

Churchill, Winston, 112

communism, 72, 107, 134, 209–10

compassion, war as, xiv, 86–91, 108–10, 113, 119–20, 133; bodhisattvas and, 37, 142; Buddha and, 29–30, 80

Conference of the Three Religions: (Sankyō Kaidō), 53–54

Confucianism, 10, 59, 199–203, 205; critique of early Buddhism in China, 199; Zen monks and, 216

corporate Zen: soldier Zen and, 186, 190–91; training programs of, 182–87, 248n7, 249n29

"Crimes Against the Throne" (Article 73 of the criminal code), 45

Critical Buddhism (*Hihan Bukkyō*; Haka- maya Noriaki), 175

daigo, 37. *See also* enlightenment

Daigu, 218

Daihōrin magazine, 33, 35, 77, 93, 102–3, 170, 185

daijihishin (compassion), 119. *See also* compassion, war as

Daijuji temple, 224

Daikyū Shōnen (Ch. Ta-hsui Cheng-nien), 216

Dainichi. *See* Mahavairocana (*Dainichi*; Sun Buddha)

Daitō Satoshi, 85

Daiun. *See* Harada Daiun Sōgaku

Daiun Gikō, 75–77

Dean, Thomas, xvi

Demiéville, Paul, 204, 227

democracy, 46, 148, 182

Denchōrō, 224

dependent co-arising doctrine, 172, 176, 178

DeVos, George A., 183

Dhammapada, 194

Dharma (aka Buddha Dharma), 41, 83–84, 102, 104, 173, 198, 205; authentic, 233; betrayal of, 228; Fudō Myō-ō and, 217; protection of, 226; war and, x, 92, 119, 137, 147

Dharma Raja (Dharma King), 199. *See also* Law of the Sovereign (*Raja Dharma*)

Diamond Sutra, 41

Dōbun Shoin, 190

Doctrinal Instructors (Kyōdōshoku), 7–9, 144

Dōgen, Sasaki, 38–39, 48, 133, 176, 187

Dōgen (Sōtō Zen sect founder), 120, 131, 135–36, 170, 214–15; critique of Confucianism, 202–3; *Gokoku-shōbōgi*, 214; *Shōbōgenzō*, 214; state and, 212–15

Dokutan, Toyoda, 50

Dumoulin, Heinrich, 203, 215

economy: anti-militarism and, 67–70, 72; corporate Zen and, 186, 248n7, 249n29; imperialism and, 99, 105, 134, 150

Eiheiji Betsuin temple, xiii

Inoue Enryō, 17–19, 29–30, 52–53
Inoue Tetsujirō, 12, 52
Ishiga Osamu, 73
Ishihara Shummyō, 102–3
Ishikawa Rikizan, xvi
Ishin Sūden, 221
Islam, xii. *See also* Muslim
issatsu tashō (killing one in order that
    many may live), 87, 167
Itō Hirobumi, 63
Iwakura Tomomi, 9–10, 236n19

James, William, xiv
Japan: anti-West alliance and, 64–65; in
    China, 17, 21, 60, 62, 92, 105, 150, 156,
    190; defeat of, 147–81; divinity of, 5,
    19, 92, 118, 228; expansionism of, 17,
    21, 50, 65, 180; Great Depression in,
    69; in Korea, 17, 21, 57, 60, 156, 190; in
    Taiwan, 21, 69, 190; the West and, 105,
    151, 179
Japanese Spirituality (*Nihonteki Reisei*;
    Suzuki), 147, 149
Japan External Trade Organization
    (JETRO), 182
Jataka stories, 197
Jen-wang-ching (Sutra on Benevolent
    Kings), 226
Jiki Shin Dōjō, 189
Jimon branch (Tendai sect), 157
jisshō (self nature), 88
Jōdo (Pure Land) sect, 8, 20, 63, 73, 81
Jōin, Saeki, 79–80
Jōsenji temple, 43
Jōzan, Hitane, 134
Jufukuji temple, 214
junshi (ritual suicide upon the death of
    one's lord), 58
just war: Buddhist view of, 28, 93, 119, 133,
    174; Russo-Japanese War as, 29–30;
    Sino-Japanese War as, 133, 167; World
    War II as, 90, 92, 134, 142, 158, 161–62,
    167; Zen view of, ix, xiv, 113, 152–53,
    170–71

Kaiten, Nukariya, 58–60, 98
Kaizōji monastery, 40
Kamakura period (1185–1333), 3, 99, 187;
    political situation at beginning of,
    212–13
kamikaze pilots, 129, 139, 160, 245n46
Kanno Sugako, 45–46, 48, 238n11
Kapilavastu, 193
Kapleau, Philip, xiv, 135
Kashiwagi Ryūhō, 45, 47
Katō Totsudō, 21
Katsuhira Sōtetsu, 186–87
Katsura Tarō, 48
Keel, S., 211
Keikichi. *See* Uchiyama Gudō
Kemmyō, Takagi, 38–39, 48, 51
Kendō (Way of the Sword): double office
    of sword in, 108–9, 167, 171; sword as
    life giving in, 110, 112–13, 137, 157, 167;
    sword as symbol in, 100, 119, 188; Zen
    and, xv, 116, 124–25, 129, 149, 177–78,
    181, 190–91
Kenninji temple, 214
kenshō, 22. *See also* enlightenment
ken Zen ichinyo (sword and Zen are one),
    188
Ketelaar, James, 5, 7
killing: Bushido and, 112; as compassion,
    xiv, 37, 87–89, 167; imperial-way Bud-
    dhism and, 86; precept forbidding, 29,
    36, 86, 92; Sawaki on, 35; Zen and, 110
Kim, Hee-jin, 216
Kimmei, Emperor, 132
Kirita Kiyohide, 23–25
Kitabatake Chikafusa, 227–28
Kitagawa, Joseph, 4, 10, 119
Kōa Kannon temple, 142, 245n46
koans, 28–29, 36, 188, 235n4a, 244n34
Kobayashi Enshō, xvi
Kodama Gentarō (General), 36–37
Kōdō. *See* Kurebayashi Kōdō; Sawaki
    Kōdō
kōdō (imperial way), 19, 53. *See also*
    imperial system

kōdō Bukkyō. *See* imperial-way Buddhism (*kōdō Bukkyō*)
Koga Seiji, 152
Kokan Shiren, 135
Kokuryūkai (Black Dragon Society), 189
Konchiji temple, 224
Kondō Genkō, 74
Konoe Fumimaro, 62, 90, 190
Konō Taitsū, 75–76, 248n62, 232–33
Korea: Japanese expansionism in, 17, 21, 57, 60, 69, 156, 190; Russo-Japanese War and, 29–30; Sino-Japanese and, 19, 163
Kōshō-gokokuji, 214
Kōtoku Shūsui, 42–43, 45–46
Koyama Kishō, 74
Kozuki Yoshio, 127
Kubota Jiun, x
Kurebayashi Kōdō, 133–34
Kurusu Saburō, 112, 242–43n44
Kutadanta Sutta, 195
Kuwakado Shidō, 51

Law of the Buddha (*Buddha Dharma*), 41, 52, 79, 175, 178, 199
Law of the Sovereign (*Raja Dharma*), 51–52, 79, 85, 175, 178, 181, 198, 201. *See also* Law of the Buddha (*Buddha Dharma*)
Lieutenant Colonel Sugimoto Gorō's Reverence for the Emperor and Zen (*Sugimoto Gorō Chūsa no Sonnō to Zen*; Ōyama Sumita), 127
Lotus Sutra, 35, 41, 80, 84, 222

MacArthur, Douglas, 165
Maezumi Hakuyu Taizan, xiv, 136
Mahavairocana (*Dainichi*; Sun Buddha), 212
Mahavamsa, 198
Makiguchi Tsunesaburō, 239–40n8c
makoto (truth), 187
Manchuria, 63–64, 128–29; Japan in, 60, 71, 92, 101, 116, 190, 241n52

Manchurian Incident (1931), 101, 116, 134, 150
Manzan Dōhaku, 235n4a
Mark Twain's Religion (Phipps), xii
Masunaga Reihō, 138–39, 160
Matsui Iwane, 142, 245n46
Matsumoto Shirō, x, 174–79
Matsuura Fumio, 72
Mazaki Jinzaburō, 190
meditation, 32, 130, 168. *See also* zazen
Meido, Saitō, 249n29
Meiji, Emperor, 4, 7, 58, 83, 111
Meiji period (1868–1912): anti-Christianity in, 3, 6, 13, 16–18, 171; anti-socialism in, 53–54, 171; Buddhism in, xv, 3–13, 53–54, 172, 236n19, 233. *See also* High Treason Incident (*Taigyaku Jiken*); New Buddhism (Shin Bukkyō)
Meiji Restoration, 4–6, 9, 16, 105, 161, 213, 242n43
Menzan, Zuihō, 235n4a
Middle Way doctrine, 173
militarism, xiii, xv; Buddhist resistance to, 66–78, 166–67, 239–40n8c; Buddhist support of, 154, 157, 170–71, 174; of civilians, 66, 98, 102, 138, 143–44, 164; nationalism and, 70, 168, 180; Shintoism and, 147, 150; socialism and, 69; Suzuki on, 147–52; Zen and, 154, 174–76, 190
military: postwar, 187–97; priests in, 6, 29, 63, 65, 237n34; training of, 16, 91, 99–100, 114–16, 124, 130, 183–84, 187. *See also* Bushido (Way of the Warrior)
Mineo Setsudō, 38–39, 48
Ministry of Doctrine (Kyōbushō), 7–9
Mishima Yukio, 168, 247n42
Miyagi Jitsumyō. 40
Miyashita Takichi, 45–46
Mokurai, Shimaji, 9, 11, 13, 18, 41–42, 50
Momotarō, 112
Mongolia, 128–29

sacrifice: Bushido and, 58, 98, 104, 116, 243n53; for emperor, 58–61, 118, 120, 122; of Japanese people, 150–51; of kamikaze pilots, 129, 139, 160, 245n46; Meiji Restoration and, 242n43; in Zen, 108–9, 111, 120

Saeki Jōin, 79–80

Saichō, 81

Saitō Meidō, 249n29

Sakai Tokugen, 185–86

Sakazume Kōjū, 40

Sakura Sōgorō, 40

samadhi (meditative) power (*jōriki*), 126, 186, 215, 219, 230

samurai: Bushido and, 98, 105, 108, 112; ideal of, 58–59, 107–8; spirit of, 114–15, 187; Zen teaching and, 100, 108, 215–21, 228–30

Sanbō-kyōdan (Three Treasures Association), x

Sangha, 41, 81, 173, 233; Sri Lankan, 234; state and, 195–96, 201–2

Sasaki Dōgen, 38–39, 48, 133, 176, 187

satori, 148–49, 237–38n50. *See also* enlightenment

Sawaki Kōdō, 35–36, 175–76, 183–85

Sect Shinto (Kyōha Shintō), 10

Seikō, Hirata, 179–81

seikyō bunri (separation of government and religion), 9

seikyō itchi (unity of religion and politics), 30

Seiran, Ōuchi, 18, 52

Seisen, Fueoka, 99–101, 126

Seisetsu, Seki, 112–13, 160, 179–80, 188

seishin (human spirit), 114

Seiunji monastery, 74

Seizan, Yanagida, xvi, 158–60, 166

Seki Seisetsu, 112–13, 160, 179–80, 188

Sekizen, Arai, 62

Self-Defense Forces, 184, 187–88, 190, 247n42

selflessness, 70, 170, 175, 178, 187–88; corporate Zen and, 184–85; loyalty to the emperor and, xiv, 117–18, 131, 172; in war, 103–4, 120, 123–24, 132, 139

self-sacrifice. *See* sacrifice

Senō Girō, 66, 69–73

Senshō, Murakami, 52

sensō Zen (war Zen), 136–37

Separation Edicts (Shimbutsu Hanzen Rei), 5–6

seppuku (ritual disembowelment), 187

Setsudō, Mineo, 38–39, 48

Seventeen Article Constitution, 80, 172

Shaku Sōen, 43, 162, 237–38n50; on militarism, 25–29, 57, 59–60, 96, 98–99, 109–10; as New Buddhist, 14, 17, 114

Shaku Unshō, 20

Sharf, Robert, 14, 95

Shibata Dōken, 10

Shidō, Kuwakado, 51

Shiio Benkyō, 81–84

Shimaji Mokurai, 9, 11, 13, 18, 41–42, 50

Shimakage Chikai, 86–91

Shimizu Ryūzan, 64

Shin (True Pure Land) sect, 3; anti-militarism in, 73–74; High Treason Incident and, 38, 51–53; missionary work of, 16–17, 63–64; nationalism of, 9, 18, 71, 85–86; repentance for war by, 152–53; war philosophy of, 31, 35. *See also* Higashi (East) Honganji branch (Shin sect); Nishi (West) Honganji branch (Shin sect)

Shin Bukkyō (journal), 235–36n4*b*

Shingon sect, 64, 81, 214, 237n34

Shinkō Bukkyō Seinen Dōmei (Youth League for Revitalizing Buddhism), 66–73

Shinran, 153

Shinto, 150, 162, 224; Buddhism and, 8, 9, 170, 227; government control of, 5, 7, 53–54; Japan's defeat in World War II and, 147–48; spirit of Japan and, 59, 137; as state religion, 5, 8, 10–12, 30, 171, 174, 180; Zen and, 169

shisōsen (thought war), 144

Shōgan, Takenaka, 74–75
Shogunate (military government): in Kamakura period, 213–15; in Tokugawa period, 218, 221, 223
Shore, Jeffrey, xvi
Shōtoku Taishi (Prince), 30, 80–81, 172; introduction of Buddhism to Japan and, 210–12; Seventeen Article Constitution and, 211
Shōwa period (1926–1989), 80, 84, 166
Sino-Japanese War, 17, 19–21, 37, 53, 163; imperial-way Buddhism and, 97–98; as just war, 133–34, 167
social activism: Buddhism and, 43, 49–54; of Uchiyama Gudō, 39–43, 46, 179; of Youth League, 66, 70, 72
socialism, 41–43, 53–54, 69, 171–72
Socialist Party, 42
Sōen. *See* Shaku Sōen
Sogen (Ch. Tsu-yūan/Ziyuan), 100, 125, 163, 215–16
Sōgen. *See* Asahina Sōgen; Ōmori Sōgen
Sōjiji monastery, 62, 140
Sōka Gakkai, 239–40n8c
soku ("just as it is"), 174
soldier Zen (*gunjin Zen*), 124, 147, 165–66, 219; corporate Zen and, 186, 190–91, 219
Sonyū, Ōtani, 51–52, 60–62
Sōtetsu, Katsuhira, 186–87
Sōtō Zen sect, 214–15; aircraft donation, 142–43; acceptance of, 213; Division of Human Rights in, 223; establishment in Japan, 214; Harada Daiun Sōgaku and, 135–36; High Treason Incident and, 38–50, 107; militarism and, 74–77, 174–76; missionary work of, 63, 154–56; religious services of, 140–41, 242n41; repentance for war by, x, 153–57, 246n19; social discrimination in, 222; state and, 169; on Sugimoto Gorō, 126–27; Ten Fates Preached by the Buddha (*Bussetsu Jūrai*) and, 222; war support of, 95, 131–34, 142–44, 204

Special Attack Forces, 129, 139, 160, 245n46
Spirit of Japan (*Yamato damashii*): Buddhism and, 64, 83, 133, 137, 181; Bushido and, 37, 112; war victories and, 59–60, 114–16
spirituality, 131, 148–49, 245n4
Spiritualizing of Japan, The (*Nihon no Reiseika*; Suzuki), 150
spiritual training: for military, 91, 114–16, 124, 187; for society, 130, 143–44
Ssu-ma Ch'ien, 237n44
state, the: Buddhist resistance to, 67–78; Buddhist support of, xiv, 114, 131, 147–48, 155, 163, 170–74; corporate Japan and, 185; High Treason Incident and, 38–49, 53–54; religious control by, 3–11; sacrifice for, xiv, 60–61, 82; socialism and, 42–43, 53–54; Sōtō Zen support of, 155, 169. *See also* imperial-state Zen (*kōkoku Zen*); imperial system; imperial-way Buddhism (*kōdō Bukkyō*)
"Statement of Repentance" (*sanshabun*), 153–54
State Shinto (Kokka Shintō), 10–12, 174, 180. *See also* Shinto
Sugawara Gidō, 187–88
Sugimoto Gorō, 116–30, 164, 169
suicide: of kamikaze pilots, 129, 139, 160, 245n46; ritual, 58, 159, 187
sutras, 35, 41, 80, 84, 119, 125, 163, 245n42; merit and, 139–40
Suvarnaprabhasa [Golden Light] *Sutra*, 200
Suzuki, D. T. (Daisetz), 30, 58, 124, 185, 190; on *Hagakure*, 107, 219–20, 229–30; on Mahayana Buddhism, 14; on militarism, xiv, 22–25, 36, 64–65, 105–12, 167, 246n15; on *munen* (no-thought), 123, 177–78; on *samadhi* power, 126; on war responsibility, 147–52; on Zen and the sword, 110, 129, 157, 177–78, 208

About the Author

Brian Daizen Victoria is a fully ordained Sōtō Zen priest, having trained at Daihonzan Eiheiji in Fukui prefecture and received Dharma transmission from Asada Daisen, late abbot of Jōkūin temple in Saitama prefecture. He holds an M.A. in Buddhist Studies from Sōtō Zen sect-affiliated Komazawa University in Tokyo, and a Ph.D. from the Department of Religious Studies at Temple University.

In addition to his most recent book, *Zen War Stories* (2003), Victoria's major writings include an autobiographical work in Japanese entitled *Gaijin de ari, Zen bozu de ari* (*As a Foreigner, As a Zen Priest*), published in 1971; *Zen Master Dōgen*, coauthored with Professor Yokoi Yūhō of Aichi-gakuin University (1976); and a translation of *The Zen Life* by Sato Koji (1972).

Victoria currently serves as the director of Antioch College's Buddhist Studies in Japan Program.